The Oral Histories of
Lts. Sandy Daniels, Tina-Marie D'Ercole, Maureen P. Foley, Chrystal A. Lewis, Barbette Henry Lowndes, and Pamela Wacek Svendsen, USN, U.S. Naval Academy Class of 1980

Interviewed by
Susan B. Sweeney, 1984–87

U.S. Naval Institute • Annapolis, Maryland

Preface

On 28 May 1980, 55 female midshipmen graduated from the U.S. Naval Academy for the first time in history. I entered 41 days later, on Induction Day for the Class of 1984. As that first class had done, I took my vow: "I, Jan Elizabeth Chinn, do solemnly swear that I will support and defend the constitution of the United States against all enemies, foreign and domestic; that I will bear true faith and allegiance to the same; that I take this obligation freely without mental reservation or purpose of evasion; and that I will well and faithfully discharge the duties of the office upon which I am about to enter, so help me God."

Those of us who entered the Academy in the wake of the first class benefited greatly from their struggles. We also likely suffered from their mistakes, whether perceived or actual, based on truth or fiction, since these legends persisted in the memories of the brigade upper-class midshipmen who remained after the first class had graduated. Generations of women who followed them have played a role in shaping the environment at the Academy today, but I doubt any of our experiences compare with those who went first.

Their varying perspectives, backgrounds, and experiences share some important similarities, most notably the fact that they were not prepared for or aware of the quite hostile environment they were entering in 1976. Nor could they have prepared themselves to be ostracized by peers, seniors, and in some cases faculty members, as most came from loving and supportive families and friends who had accurately heralded them in high school as leaders, scholars, athletes, or all three.

Recorded between 1984 and 1987, these interviews document the early Navy career perspectives of Sandy Daniels, Tina-Marie D'Ercole, Maureen P. Foley, Chrystal A. Lewis, Barbette Henry Lowndes, and Pamela Wacek Svendsen. Among these remarkable women, I have known of Sandy Daniels since about 2007, after she was selected for flag rank and I saw her at the Pentagon. We eventually served together in 2012 at OPNAV in N2N6, and if I ever knew she was from the Academy, much less a member of the Class of 1980, I don't recall it. Reading her interview explains why: it isn't something she wears on her shoulder—as either a chip or a badge of courage. This attitude is typical of the women's stories presented here. They are uniformly proud of their accomplishments, but they do not broadcast them. They wanted to serve their country, and they have done that with dignity and honor.

I, like some of them, selected a miniature class ring, one with a diamond surrounded by my birthstones. Some of my classmates were also concerned that their rings might be confused with those worn by fiancées or spouses rather than graduates. But having made it through the gauntlet, with an atmosphere characterized by trials and tests both physical and mental, an environment somewhere between those of *Lord of the Flies* and *Lord of the Rings*, with a bit of the reverse time travel of *Outlander*, I wanted a symbol that I would be willing to wear. And today I wear it as neither a chip nor a badge, but to represent a part of me in which I take great pride. And I also happen to like it!

In some ways the Class of 1980 women were like firefighters, as they ran seemingly fearlessly into a situation most would not have wanted to tackle: not knowing exactly what might happen but believing it had to be done, and they had to be the ones to do it. Unlike firefighters, they did not experience risk to life on a daily basis at the Academy, and they were not heralded as heroes. They were oddities who entered the fleet after graduation—where daily risk to life is very real. My perspective on those years differs from theirs because I never felt restricted or held back in my chosen community of cryptology. I was judged entirely on my ability to contribute to the mission success, and I was able to fully engage the enemy from any of our shore-based facilities around the globe. That said, I did covet assignments aboard tactical platforms, which were all classified as combatants and restricted by law from women. Within four years of graduation, however, I was authorized to become a special evaluator aboard EP-3 aircraft. I had requested this opportunity 18 months earlier, via my chain of command, which was very supportive. Ultimately, the Defense Advisory Committee on Women in the Services (DACOWITS) helped to make it possible, and I was on mission flying over the Persian Gulf the first night of Operation Desert Storm.

Yet there is at least something about each of these six oral histories that I connect with completely. What they express in common is a willingness and determination to go where no woman had gone before. Entering the Academy as strong and confident young women, they were clearly shaken to the core by the experience, which challenged their sense of self and nearly ripped them up from their roots. They chose a path that most have avoided. By succeeding, they not only faithfully discharged the duties of the office upon which they entered, they also grew into stronger, more resilient leaders who would succeed in fields outside the Navy. At the time their stories were recorded, all six were young lieutenants. They are as candid and forceful in their denunciations of poor treatment as they are in their expressions of pride in being members of the first Naval Academy class to include women. Their hard-won accomplishment served them well, and has also served us well as a Navy and a Nation.

Vice Admiral Jan Tighe, U.S. Navy (Ret.)

April 2016

The U.S. Naval Institute Oral History Program

Legacy Series

Publisher's Note

Researchers and authors have been drawing on the Naval Institute's Oral History Program since 1969, the year it was established by Dr. John T. Mason Jr. He and his successor, author and historian Paul Stillwell, sought to capture, preserve, and disseminate a permanent record of the stories of significant figures in naval history. Under the leadership of Vice Adm. Peter H. Daly, U.S. Navy (Ret.), CEO of the Institute, the program has expanded, with increasing numbers of historians conducting more interviews.

The program also possesses valuable, previously unprocessed interviews that were conducted during the period 1969 through 2004. The Legacy Series now makes available the transcripts of a select number of these in nearly their original form. Without extensive editing or annotation, works included in this new series are indexed and published so that researchers and other interested readers may easily access them. The reader is reminded, as with all oral history interviews, that this is a record of the spoken word.

The Naval Institute wishes to acknowledge the many donors who make this program possible, in particular the generous support of the Tawani Foundation of Chicago and Jack C. Taylor of St. Louis.

Brief Biographies

Chrystal Lewis Campbell, who grew up on Marine Corps bases and air stations, served eight years in the Navy. Her duties included jet transition training, weapons delivery, and carrier qualification, Fleet Composite Squadron Five (VC-5) at NAS Cubi Point, and flight instructor, specializing in the "out of control" or Spin Recovery program. She flew the A-4E Skyhawk in support of U.S. fleet training and Western Pacific foreign navy training. VC-5 deployed all over East Asia including Japan, Korea, Indonesia, Guam, Thailand, and the Philippines. After leaving naval service, as a line pilot for Delta Air Lines Campbell accumulated more than 10,000 flight hours.

The early career assignments of naval aviator **Rear Adm. Sandy Daniels, USNR (Ret.)**, included the Naval Research Laboratory, Space Science Division, and Naval Space Surveillance Center. After transitioning to the Reserve component in 1991, she served in the Navy Reserve Space Program and as director of the Navy Space and Network Warfare Program before being selected for flag rank. Among her responsibilities in that capacity were those of director, Warfare Integration on the Chief of Naval Operations' staff (N6F); senior advisor for Space to the Deputy Chief of Naval Operations for Information Dominance (OPNAV N2/N6); reserve deputy Commander, U.S. Pacific Fleet; and Patrol and Reconnaissance Group/Patrol and Reconnaissance Group Pacific. With a master's in science, technology, and public policy with a space policy emphasis, she also worked in industry as a contractor. Rear Admiral Daniels retired from the Navy in October 2015.

Comm. Tina-Marie D'Ercole, USN (Ret.). served for 20 years. retiring in 2000. Her assignments included technical representative in the Space Program Office, Aerospace Engineering duty officer (as the first non-aviator space systems engineer in that community), deputy program manager at NAVAIR, plant representative at Teledyne Ryan Aeronautical Corporation for the unmanned aerial vehicle program. and military deputy to the director of the Joint Research and Development Center of the Naval Command, Control and Ocean Surveillance Systems command. She holds master's degrees in electrical engineering (with a space systems concentration) and national resource strategy.

Capt. Barbette H. Lowndes, USN (Ret.). served 27 years of active duty in the Navy followed by eight years as a civil servant. At the time of her retirement from the military she was a captain in the Supply Corps. After graduating from the Naval Academy with a bachelor's in oceanography. she earned master's degrees in business management and national security and strategic studies. as well as graduating from the Senior Executive Institute at the University of North Carolina Kenan-Flagler Business School. Now serving on the board of trustees for the USNA Alumni Association, she was formerly president of the San Diego chapter.

Following her graduation and commissioning, **Maureen Foley Nunez** served as a plane captain branch officer. a communications officer. and finally an instructor in leadership at the U.S. Naval Academy. In 1984 she earned a master's degree in administrative science from Johns Hopkins University. and since that time she has worked in financial management and organizational leadership in positions of increasing responsibility.

Dr. Pamela Wacek Svendsen owns and directs the Wellness Center at Navarre, Florida, where she practices family medicine. She served on active duty in the Navy for seven years before raising children and then graduating from medical school and completing a residency. She has practiced since 1998 in Mississippi and Florida. The clinic incorporates conventional and alternative medical treatments in patient care.

Deed of Gift

The U.S. Naval Institute is hereby authorized to make available in any format it chooses, from bound-book hard copy to electronic/digital Internet access and as part of videorecordings, the audio recordings, transcripts, and videorecordings of the oral-history interview series conducted concerning the life and career of the undersigned. Disposition, repositories, and access shall be at the discretion of the Naval Institute. The undersigned shall be offered the opportunity to review the transcribed oral history prior to its finalization, and to make any corrections thereto that the undersigned deems necessary.

The undersigned does hereby release and assign to the U.S. Naval Institute the rights and title to these interviews, with the exception that the undersigned and heirs retain the right to use the material for personal, noncommercial purposes. The copyright in the oral, transcribed, and videorecorded versions shall be held by the U.S. Naval Institute. All recordings, transcriptions, and videorecordings of the interviews shall remain the property of the U.S. Naval Institute.

Signed and sealed this ___11th___ day of ___December___ 2015.

Signed name _____

Printed name ___Sandy L. Daniels___

Deed of Gift

This Deed of Gift supersedes and replaces the document signed in May 1988. The U.S. Naval Institute is hereby authorized to make available in any format it chooses, from bound-book hard copy to electronic/digital Internet access and as part of videorecordings, the audio recordings, transcripts, and videorecordings of the oral-history interview series conducted concerning the life and career of the undersigned. Disposition, repositories, and access shall be at the discretion of the Naval Institute.

The undersigned does hereby release and assign to the U.S. Naval Institute the rights and title to these interviews, with the exception that the undersigned and heirs retain the right to use the material for personal, noncommercial purposes. The copyright in the oral, transcribed, and videorecorded versions shall be held by the U.S. Naval Institute. All recordings, transcriptions, and videorecordings of the interviews shall remain the property of the U.S. Naval Institute.

Signed and sealed this _1st_ day of _December_ 2015.

Signed name _Tina-Marie D'Ercole_

Printed name _Tina-Marie D'Ercole_

Authorization

The U.S. Naval Institute is hereby authorized to make available to individuals, libraries, and other repositories of its choosing the transcript of an oral history interview concerning the life and career of the undersigned. The interview was conducted on 1 November 1985 in collaboration with Susan B. Sweeney for the Naval Institute.

The undersigned does hereby release and assign to the U.S. Naval Institute all right, title, restriction, and interest in the interview. The copyright in both the oral and transcribed versions shall be the sole property of the U.S. Naval Institute. The tape recording of the interview is and will remain the property of the U.S. Naval Institute.

Signed and sealed this ___28___ day of ___January___ 1999.

Chrystal L. Campbell
Chrystal L. Campbell

Authorization

The U.S. Naval Institute is hereby authorized to make available to individuals, libraries and other repositories of its choosing the transcripts of an oral history interview concerning the life and career of the undersigned. The interview was recorded on 17 November 1985 in collaboration with Susan B. Sweeney for the U.S. Naval Institute.

The undersigned does hereby release and assign to the U.S. Naval Institute all right, title, restriction, and interest in the interview. The copyright in both the oral and transcribed version shall be the sole property of the U.S. Naval Institute. The tape recording of the interview is and will remain the property of the U.S. Naval Institute.

Signed and sealed this ___15th___ day of _October_ 1986.

Barbette H Lowndes
Barbette Henry Lowndes
Lieutenant, U.S. Navy

Authorization

The U.S. Naval Institute is hereby authorized to make available to individuals, libraries, and other repositories of its choosing the transcript of an oral history interview concerning the life and career of the undersigned. The interview was conducted on 15 November 1984 in collaboration with Susan B. Sweeney for the Naval Institute.

The undersigned does hereby release and assign to the U.S. Naval Institute all right, title, restriction, and interest in the interview. The copyright in both the oral and transcribed version shall be the sole property of the U.S. Naval Institute. The tape recording of the interview is and will remain the property of the U.S. Naval Institute.

Signed and sealed this __23rd__ day of __May__ 1985.

Maureen P. Foley
Lieutenant, U.S. Navy

Authorization

The U.S. Naval Institute is hereby authorized to make available to individuals, libraries and other repositories of its choosing the transcripts of an oral history interview concerning the life and career of the undersigned. The interview was recorded on 8 November 1984 in collaboration with Susan B. Sweeney for the U.S. Naval Institute.

The undersigned does hereby release and assign to the U.S. Naval Institute all right, title, restriction, and interest in the interview. The copyright in both the oral and transcribed version shall be the sole property of the U.S. Naval Institute. The tape recording of the interview is and will remain the property of the U.S. Naval Institute.

Signed and sealed this ____10th____ day of December 1986.

Pamela Wacek Svendsen
Pamela Wacek Svendsen
Lieutenant, U.S. Navy

Interview with Lieutenant Sandy Daniels, U.S. Navy

Place: Upper Marlboro, Maryland

Date: 21 December 1987

Sue Sweeney: Thanks for giving me your time in the pre-Christmas rush.

Lieutenant Daniels: Oh, that's all right.

Sue Sweeney: If you could start out by telling me a little bit about your family and your background.

Lieutenant Daniels: Sure. Well, my father was enlisted in the Air Force. Intelligence was his background. My mother's German——his most permanent German souvenir, I guess you could say. We grew up moving. I was born in Germany. We moved back and forth from Germany to the U.S. during my childhood——Germany to Omaha, where my brother was born. I have one younger brother. Ended pretty much back on the East Coast. Fort Belvoir was his last duty station, and they live in the area, for now at least. He's working for the government, in customs.

Sue Sweeney: How big an influence was he on your going into the military?

Lieutenant Daniels: Not too much. It was largely practical. I was looking for scholarships to pay for school, because they couldn't afford to pay for all of my schooling. So it was sort of a practical deal.

Sue Sweeney: Did you have other academies or schools in mind?

Lieutenant Daniels: None of the other academies. I was looking for Air Force and Navy ROTC. And Air Force refused me because they didn't like my blood. My hematocrit was too low—ratio of red blood cells to total blood volume. Despite a doctor's note saying it was okay, they rejected me. And so, of the other academies, Navy was the only one that had flying at the time. ROTC didn't even work out, actually. I was a finalist, but the selection process for women is a nationwide percentage, as opposed to state by state, because there are so few slots. We always thought it was sort of ironic that I got into the Academy but didn't make ROTC. But I was an alternate for the Academy also.

Sue Sweeney: What civilian schools were you looking into?

Lieutenant Daniels: I was being practical there too, since I had to pay all the application fees, so I chose schools that had ROTC, in case that came through. I was looking at the University of Virginia [UVA], Rensselaer, and Rochester, I guess. And Duke; I looked at Duke, but I don't think Duke looked back at me, but the other ones said fine. I was going to go to the University of Virginia, because they were a school I could afford, being a state school, and had what I wanted. In fact, I had already paid my little $250 application fee when, two weeks before Induction Day, they called me, "Oh, by the way, the other guy doesn't want to go. Would you like to go?" Kind of last minute.

Sue Sweeney: How much did you know about the Academy before you came?

Lieutenant Daniels: Not a heck of a lot. I just knew what I read in the catalog. I never knew anybody who went to one. I thought—the catalog was, sort of, very idealistic. So I think I kind of went in thinking everybody was supposed to be godlike or something. I think I hoped that some of that discipline and talent would rub off on me. I was brought back down to reality there right away.

Sue Sweeney: Did you visit before you entered?

Lieutenant Daniels: No, I'd never seen it before Induction Day. I just showed up.

Sue Sweeney: What was your first impression?

Lieutenant Daniels: Well, I was looking around for all these godlike people I expected to be there. I thought all the women were going to be incredibly intelligent and incredibly athletic—you see, I was never that athletic—and the same with everybody. I just thought, oh, my God, these are extraordinary people, and I just sort of slid in under the door. I'm going to last a whole two weeks here. That and the newspaper people. I always thought that was bizarre, because, of course, it was the first year of women, so all these people are running around interviewing and asking you all sorts of dumb questions. You were too nervous to even worry about them. "Well, what do you think?" "Well, I don't know. I don't have anything to say right now. I'm just here." It was just a bizarre, confusing day. There's a lot that goes on that day.

Sue Sweeney: How long before the "godlike thing" was dispelled?

Lieutenant Daniels: Within a few weeks, really. Just looking around and finding more out about people, my own classmates as well as the upper class. I found out that they weren't incredibly wonderful all the time. They were people.

Sue Sweeney: That must have given you a big boost of confidence.

Lieutenant Daniels: Well, it was, you know, reality. It was just dealing with reality.

Sue Sweeney: You mentioned that the media was present right off. How much were they in the way?

Lieutenant Daniels: Not for me so much. See I never—I've always been sort of an average-looking person, not the sort the photographers went after. I was never rude, but I must have sent signals that said I never really liked that sort of thing, so I think people probably just left me alone. I don't know. That varied with different people. I didn't get my picture taken. In fact, I don't think my picture appeared in much of anything.

Sue Sweeney: Through the whole four years you weren't bothered?

Lieutenant Daniels: Not personally. Like I said, I'm not the photogenic type. It works out to my advantage, especially at that time. Many of my classmates were.

Sue Sweeney: Being from a military family, you didn't have a hometown paper following you.

Lieutenant Daniels: No, I never really had that either, never had a particular paper because no locality was really my hometown. I think as far as the media goes, I have a tendency to be distrustful of them, because I saw a lot of it get misused here with the women as well as—I mean it happens all the time anybody gets interviewed. But sometimes people would come in to interview several of the women—newspapers and magazines—and they'd come in with preconceived notions one way or the other, either favorable or not favorable. And everything would go that way. And then if you'd talk to the women afterwards: "I didn't say that." Or, "This was with another paragraph, in another context," you know.

And, of course, the guys the next day: "Oh, did you see what your classmate said in the paper?" And you don't have a telephone line to these women; you don't know what went on, you know. They thought we had some secret communication method or something between us, even though we were all spread out. I always thought that was pretty silly.

Sue Sweeney: One of your classmates mentioned the difficulty communicating among the women because you were so spread out. You found that to be the case, as well?

Lieutenant Daniels: Yes. I never really knew that many women that closely, except my roommate—we keep in touch—and people you did your sports or activities with. Or maybe had in a class with them and hit it off. But I always thought it was most amusing because the guys there just assumed that we all really adored each other, and that we all were really close. In reality we didn't have a chance to get to know each other that well. And also, you may not adore every other woman just because she's a common person in your group. Even though you would be supportive of her in whatever way you could, the assumption on their part was sort of silly. They thought we had some sort of little gossip line going, you know. And we hardly ever saw each other. It was really pretty funny.

Sue Sweeney: Do you know them better now that you've graduated?

Lieutenant Daniels: No, I don't think so, really, because I haven't come across too many. Not that many of the women went aviation. And if you're in one career path, you don't often run across other people—except maybe in D.C. You may run into a few more people there. But the people I stayed friends with, I stayed in touch with, were the people I got to know there. I haven't really had a chance to get to know anybody new too well. We haven't crossed paths for the most part.

Sue Sweeney: How did your parents feel about you going to the Academy?

Lieutenant Daniels: Well, they loved it because it was a full scholarship, you know. They're practical people, too. So, of course they were quite proud, as parents always are about this sort of thing. But I don't think they knew—I mean my dad probably knew of it, but my mother didn't know much about it until she would go there a couple times to visit or something. They thought it was great.

Sue Sweeney: They brought you here on your first day?

Lieutenant Daniels: Yes. Since they were close by here, they could visit once in a while. My mother always would bring food, being the wonderful German cook that she is.

Sue Sweeney: Care packages.

Lieutenant Daniels: Lots of care packages.

Sue Sweeney: What else do you remember about I Day?

Lieutenant Daniels: Oh, I always found it sort of funny, you know, some of the things that happened during the day. You go through there and you stand in the big gym and you get shifted around in half a dozen lines, picking up different uniforms. And you get your little card with your name and alpha code and room. People talk at you, but I don't think you absorb half of what's going on, really. And they section you off here, and section you off there. I think you're just sort of overwhelmed. You remember sort of vaguely the whole thing. You get marched around here and there. But the upperclassmen, at that point, were fairly nice. And then they wait until the swearing-in ceremony when all of us are in these ugly little white outfits, you know, standing out there and Mom and Dad are out in the audience: "Oh look at this!"

And we're all standing up swearing in, and then it's time. This is it—separation until Christmas, or whenever. I never thought of that as a real big deal, because being away from home really didn't bother me too much. You always have phones and the mail, so it's not that big a deal. But I think that for some people who maybe hadn't moved so much and always, perhaps, grew up in the same small town, it was a little harder for them. They weren't used to leaving people behind. There was a lot of emotion—different levels for different people, depending on what they were used to.

But the thing I remember is after we split up from the swearing in, we were all trying to go—we had been told we were supposed to run down the middle of the hall and all that other jazz, you know, square corners and this business.

But we were pretty confused—and the Hall [Bancroft] has all these wings in it and no one knew their way around. We knew that the room numbers were coded so that the wing was perhaps the first number, and then the floor, and all that stuff. It would tell you kind of where your room was, but even so, we were clueless. We'd get in the hallway, and we're all wandering around and looking around, and of course we're supposed to keep eyes in the boat and all that. And, of course, the upper class had now planted themselves at strategic corners and staircases, so they could proceed to scream at us for not running, and—I mean some people, you know, would just burst into tears right there. The upper class were just loving it. They were eating it up.

This was our introduction into discipline. I remember going toward one staircase and there were five people standing in line there waiting to get yelled at by this guy at this corner. And I thought, "I'm turning around and going another way!" All I remember is just everybody running through these halls trying to find their rooms. We had no clue where we were going. And finally sort of finding this room and there were two other people in it. "Hi, my name is . . ." and sort of introducing ourselves.

Sue Sweeney: You didn't meet your roommates until after you were sworn in?

Lieutenant Daniels: Yes. I had two roommates to start with and one of them quit during plebe year. She decided that the military really wasn't for her and she had done it to please her father. So, you know, it's a very hard thing to admit to. Sometimes it's almost harder to quit than it is to stay. But after that my other roommate and I stayed roommates the whole four years.

Sue Sweeney: Who was she?

Lieutenant Daniels: Pat O'Neill. She just got married.

Sue Sweeney: Was there any sense from the first day that women were singled out for harassment?

Lieutenant Daniels: Well, we knew it was the first year and that this was sort of a male bastion. I expected a certain amount of hostility, and I don't know if we got too much the first day. And the upper class in our company—at least the ones for the summer I remember, were really trying hard to make sure they treated us equally. I think they were so nervous about it that in our company the tendency was to overcompensate, which was no big deal. I mean looking back, it was much better for us, you know, to have had it some smidgen tougher because at least our own classmates, then, would not have a problem with thinking that we got by easy. So that worked out rather well. And they really—they tried.

But they were so funny sometimes, you know. It was embarrassing. We had the clothes-folding session, where you have to have everything folded a certain way in the locker. And of course these guys are folding guys' underwear, and they're kind of embarrassed doing this in front of us. They didn't have any women's underwear to demonstrate with, and they weren't about to ask for a loaner. "You guys just make it look even and the same, okay?" is what they told us. And they just—you could see that they had certain things that they were trying to deal with too, so it was pretty funny. I think during the school year when the other guys got back—you had the whole group, and of course they were all together—then you got a little more sense of the hostility. Because you'd actually have some people come up to you and say, "Women don't belong here and we're going to get your ass out of here."

"Oh, thank you very much and Merry Christmas to you, too," you think to yourself. You can't say any of that, of course. You just nod your head and shut up. But a lot of guys, for them it was just as much a learning experience. I mean there were some that were just hostile. And there were other groups that didn't have a problem with it. To many it was a grand discovery that women could actually be normal people, and friends. Because they had limited their view of women, and the few they had dealt with in their lives, I guess. They just had never looked at us as people.

The biggest problem with the approach the Academy took with inducting the women was that they made such a fuss about it, and started from the basis that we were so different from guys—like we were another species or something—rather than start from the approach that we're all people therefore we have a lot in common. And then perhaps some socialization has caused, maybe, these differences and you might want to work with this, that, and the other. But it always seemed like they were starting from, "There is this other species here that we're dealing with. They are really weird."

Sue Sweeney: Have you kept up with the Academy enough to know if this has gotten better?

Lieutenant Daniels: Not too much purposely. However, I dropped in on a sailing party last year—early this year. I forget when. I've been wanting to go back and do a little coaching, because I enjoyed sailing. But between the traveling that I do here and taking classes sometimes, I just really haven't had the time. And I kind of regret it, too, because in talking to people at the party, apparently the hostility toward the women is still there. I mean, we figured that it would be a lot better after the first generation of men came along that were sort of "raised," so to speak, by upper-class women, and then all of it would go away. But it looks like it hasn't worked that way. Apparently, it's still not popular to date women mids. On the sailing team, specifically, what I was being told was that a lot of the women were—a lot of the men were trying to keep women off the big boats, sailing the big boats. And so they were having a hard time breaking in, because there was a lot of hostility. That kind of surprised me. I thought, "Gee, that's pretty sad if it's still like that."

Sue Sweeney: Are some of your female classmates starting to be stationed at the Academy?

Lieutenant Daniels: I don't personally know of anybody in my class who actually is. Although I would think that this would be around the time. But I guess it's simply that there are just so few women. And in the fleet, the emphasis is so much on warfare specialties and on the ships and planes that women can't go to, it's hard to duplicate the guys' career paths. There're not that many role models, you know. Fleet support and that sort of thing—especially there—still isn't viewed with, you know—"That's not a real manly kind of thing to be out there doing." The manly thing is to be out there flying the Tomcats and being on carriers, and whatever—destroyers and subs. And all these things are still not open to women. So I think that's really more of the problem. I mean it's gotten better to some extent. And certainly the guys going in to the Academy nowadays are a little more used to it.

But what I notice is, I think a lot of it seems to be peer pressure, especially at that age when everybody is trying to fit in. And so a lot of guys who could be perfectly nice to you one on one, if they got in with a group of peers, they kind of go with the crowd. They wouldn't——you know, there would obviously be some mature and courageous guys, but for the most part, you just saw them sort of give in to peer pressure. But they're individuals——you don't want to lump them too much, as much as you don't want to be lumped either.

Sue Sweeney: Before you arrived, did the Academy offer any guidance on what to expect?

Lieutenant Daniels: No, I don't remember ever getting anything like that. "Gee, expect a real hostile atmosphere here." No, I'd remember that.

Sue Sweeney: But you were aware the upperclassmen had gotten some type of training about dealing with the women?

Lieutenant Daniels: They got some training, yes. In fact, the thing that amused me the most was at one point during the summer—I forget, it was like a month into the plebe summer, I think—they got all the women together to go march over to look at a couple of films. And, of course we get into this room—we'd all been spread out, and we're all dying to know, "What's it like in your company?"—all that stuff. So we're just chattering away in this room. And they had a couple of these psychologists, sociologists, whatever they were, and some of the—a few of the upper class who had sort of brought us over there. The purpose was to show us hygiene films, okay.

Watching the first one, I thought, "Where do you think they're getting us from?" These are old films, like from the '50s. They've got the first one, a mild-mannered hygiene film where these WACs from the '50s or whenever, they're out there with their red lipstick, and the red nail polish, and these weird uniforms they don't even have any more, and talking about hygiene. How to, after you shower, be sure to dry between your toes or you'll get a fungus. And how to put your makeup on. Of course we're laughing our heads off, because during plebe summer showering was running in and running out. Your roommate ran in and ran out. You had to be doing your little chow call and all the other garbage.

And makeup—makeup is something maybe for Sunday, when you had the luxury of extra time. You didn't have time for that stuff in the summer. So we thought this was an absolute scream. And of course all these sociologists, or whatever, were shushing us up. They think this is real serious. And we're thinking, "We know about basic hygiene. What crowd do you think we were drawn from here?"

The next film was the absolute real killer, because it starts talking about menstruation. And this film is so old and we sat there—I remember the line, "Well, now girls, don't worry about the rumors you've heard about tampons. You can still be a virgin and use them," you know. We died! We absolutely were on the floor because we hadn't even heard the rumor. We didn't even come from the generation that worried about that sort of thing. We were on the floor.

They couldn't even finish showing the film. We thought, "What is this stuff?" We were absolutely rolling. And I kept thinking, "This is what they showed the men? This is how they were telling them that we're like, you know, worrying about drying in between our toes—and doing our nails every 30 seconds?" I mean, come on. This is a great way to really welcome us in here. But we thought it was a scream. We just couldn't believe it. And we knew that they'd [the men] had this same indoctrination. We knew they had told the guys, for example, that women cry, we're allowed to cry in society, so therefore you can keep talking to a woman, she's still actually functioning.

Whereas a male usually—if you get him to that point, you've really broken him because he will hold back all the time. But I still asked my squad leader one time at the table during the summer what was the thing he feared the most, and that was women crying. Because these guys felt like they had a hard time handling that, I guess, because they were used to being comforting and all that sort of business.

Sue Sweeney: From your viewpoint, would you say they reacted appropriately to the women?

Lieutenant Daniels: I don't know. You see my roommates and I—well, my one roommate did cry. And in our company, they must have just kept yelling at her or something or doing whatever they were doing, which is what they were supposed to do. And my other roommate and I, we never—we refused to ever cry in front of them. We'd be upset, of course. In fact, I used to have a real problem because I'd get angry—my way of dealing with it usually would be not so much to cry, but I'd get really pissed off with them for yelling at me like that. And I used to have—I have a rather mobile face, so I used to roll my eyes when I was angry. I did it unconsciously. I had no clue I was doing it. And one day this guy's in my face, yelling at me for whatever. And I was getting really teed off, "Who is this guy? I'm tired of this garbage." I just rolled my eyes unconsciously.

He yelled at me for doing that. "How dare you get pissed off at me, blah, blah, blah." I didn't know I did it, you know. And then he said it again, yelling at me some more now because I got angry again. I started to roll my eyes, and I could feel it at the top of my head, and I thought, "Uh, oh, I did it again." And I got called in for showing my anger—disrespect—like that. But we never cried, but everybody's different, so everybody handles things differently.

Sue Sweeney: You said that when the women got together they compared companies. Did you feel lucky in your placement?

Lieutenant Daniels: I don't know about that. I mean within each company, some guys are pretty nice, some guys hated it but they did their duty, and other guys who were total jerks and stayed jerks. So, I think, every company had some equivalent of that. The only thing that was good with ours, they were—they tried very hard to be as fair as they could. Now that was pretty much during the summer. You got more of the jerks, I think, during the school year.

They really tried hard to make sure they weren't letting us get by, or that they weren't, you know—they made sure they never flirted with us or did any of that sort of thing, so that there would be no special attention, or anything like that. But, as far as that goes, I think that that worked out. But, I think it always depends—it's always two ways. It always depends on who you're working with and how you behave. We wouldn't cry publicly and we wouldn't flirt either. So, you know, it always goes both ways.

Sue Sweeney: What do you remember of your squad leader?

Lieutenant Daniels: We had two different squad leaders. I remember one was a real mild-mannered kind of guy. He ended up in the Marines, I think. I can't remember his name. I'm not great at remembering names from the place, I think, because I sort of tried to eliminate certain memories. And I'm not very good at names in the first place. But, it was something like McDonald, something "Mc." And I remember one of them during the school year. And I think another one—I forget if he was the platoon leader or what—a little short guy who ended up becoming a SEAL. He loved to sort of razz people, and just go crazy. But he thought he was God's gift to women, too—a little short, blondish guy, you know. It was interesting watching that particular class because this was the—I think there's been some transition from the people who always bought sports cars—you know, "the manly thing to do"—to where you got to our class and people bought used cars and more normal cars, as well as sporty cars with their car loans.

I always remember some of the class of '77 guys who were always thinking they're like Mr. Studly, they'd wander around in these half cutoff T-shirts and go, like, work out during study hour. "Oh geez, lay off." It was pretty funny. The best thing there was, I think, learning about men, in really close-up fashion. Because you sort of learn about their side of dating, and their views of women and of themselves, and things like that. And so you could sort of see the games a little bit easier when you were going out—a different kind of experience. I don't know what it would be like in a normal college, if you'd really be separated or not. I guess it just depends on your own personality, and whether you live in a coed dorm or not. It was kind of an interesting perspective.

Sue Sweeney: How much of a revelation was it to you?

Lieutenant Daniels: Well, I'd never dated too much in high school, so it was all new to me. But I don't have really any other experience to compare it to. Perhaps the women who were already older when they got there, it may have been news to them, one way or the other. But I just sort of found them kind of amusing sometimes. The first year we weren't allowed to drink, but I always remember the second year, once you were allowed to drink, a lot of the guys would just sort of go hog-wild on it, go out in town. And, of course, their excuse was, "We're going to go out and pick up babes," but they'd drink so much beer that they couldn't have done anything with a babe if they'd found her. I think it was almost like their way of getting out of having to really do anything sometimes. So it was kind of amusing to watch. You know, you'd watch them deal with their own little fears too, as well as some guys that were just total jerks all the time. They thought that women were out there just to please them.

The other thing that always used to kill me was guys and their big thing with looks, you know. All the women have to look like some goddess or something, right, or else they won't bother with her. And I remember these two guys talking one day about, "Aw, there were only dogs at Dahlgren this past weekend," and I said, "Listen you bozos, why don't you two look in the mirror and see what you look like," you know. "If you get your equivalent, then you might just go out to pasture." Because these people, they thought they were all—just because they were at the Academy, just like sometimes aviators, or whatever can get to be—by virtue of that, somehow they deserved to be worshipped or something. So that would be sort of amusing. I think a lot of them do it. I've talked to other guys, as I've had my friends and stuff. And a lot of it is just guys talking to guys. They talk to each other about these kinds of things very differently than women talk to each other about this sort of thing.

It was very funny to compare how they boast about whatever they're doing, you know, whereas women really seem to get more down—at least between close friends—comparing notes, much more into the details.

Sue Sweeney: How difficult was it to date at the Academy?

Lieutenant Daniels: For the most part, if you went out at all—you really couldn't go out much—but it tended to be very much closet relationships, very secretive for the most part, because I think a lot of the guys were sort of embarrassed by it, especially with their other classmates. I mean there were some couples that were pretty well known, and you might find a few brave souls, but for the most part it was fairly secretive. And we certainly couldn't go running around holding hands anyway.

Sue Sweeney: Did the women resent having to keep relationships quiet?

Lieutenant Daniels: No, I think—at the time I remember—at least for me, and I can't speak for how it worked for anybody else—I think that other women who had dated before probably had a little more confidence, so I don't think they let certain things get [to] them as much. But I know that as far as me, it affected me by making me feel less attractive, or something that, you know, guys are embarrassed to be with me or something. So at that point you tend to take it—for me, I kind of take those kinds of things personally, anyway. So that was kind of a problem.

Sue Sweeney: How undeservedly insulting!

Lieutenant Daniels: Yeah. Well, it depends, too, though—I mean, it's up to you. If you're not feeling that self-confident, it sort of amazes you what you'll put up with at the time. You figure it all out later, I think, but you put up with a lot. I think, in the beginning, as you're learning in a relationship, and it has to do with the levels of self-confidence.

Sue Sweeney: How did you find the academics at the Academy?

Lieutenant Daniels: Well, I was one of the lowest-ranking women; I slept through most of my classes. I think I got into a mode where—I'd always done well academically before I got to the Academy, but I got there and found the emphasis was—it was very much an engineering-type of school and it was very much memorize and spit out, and I don't have a very good memory about certain things. And I got to the point where—and I think it was just because I really didn't like being there very much—that I fell asleep in almost all my classes. I never flunked anything, but I never did very well at a lot of things, either. And so I kind of rebelled by withdrawing and not trying very hard. And then the whole place—it ended up, I felt really stupid. I think the other problem that you have to realize—you may not realize right in the beginning—is that while you were used to being a top student in high school, all these people were top students in their high schools. And so the competition makes it a whole different ball game. So that gets to be a real eye-opener for everybody.

Sue Sweeney: What was your major?

Lieutenant Daniels: English. I was going to start out by majoring in chemistry. I had validated a lot of the English requirements, because I validated a semester of English, and all the language requirements because of my high school Spanish, which I can hardly speak any of now. It amazes me that I validated anything.

Sue Sweeney: Do any professors stick out in your mind?

Lieutenant Daniels: I stayed awake in most of my English classes. I did okay there. But I don't remember specific people very well. I remember one of those Navy courses we had—a guy who had the black uniform on and had a real bad dandruff problem. It used to drive me crazy. I used to want to go up and brush him off. Other than that, not really. You remember some profs, a couple—one guy was a—it was history. Sea power—we used to call it "Z Power" because everyone fell asleep in it. This old guy had been there when Carter had been there. He *knew* everybody in World War II and World War I. But anyway, we got one guy who fell asleep in class once. He went to the back of the class and was really tired and had everybody pile their coats on him. So here he was under this pile of coats sound asleep. And I guess finally the prof noticed these feet sticking out from the pile of coats and went over with a big ruler and slapped the desk, and the poor guy just jumped right up. Coats were flying everywhere, almost gave him a heart attack!

Another chemistry prof would always throw erasers at our black uniforms. His big thing was getting chalk on those that fell asleep. Other than that, not too much, as far as the profs. As I said, I kind of withdrew a lot, which was pretty foolish of me, looking back. All I did was spite myself. Live and learn.

Sue Sweeney: You graduated—that's no small accomplishment!

Lieutenant Daniels: Yeah, well, I suppose.

Sue Sweeney: Do any of the military officers stick out in your mind?

Lieutenant Daniels: Not really. I had one physics prof who was really a chemistry major and they had stuck him in teaching physics. He really worked hard at it. He was a nice guy. He would study the material and present it, but when you got to the hardest questions—because physics wasn't his thing—you'd have to wait another day until he went back and got the answer for you. I thought that was kind of sad, that they didn't pay a little more attention to when they assigned the military people, to make sure it was really their area of expertise. I think it made him feel bad—he really worked hard at it.

Sue Sweeney: What was your perception of the attitude from above toward the women?

Lieutenant Daniels: I think there were a few that were unhappy, but I don't remember any specific thing that makes me think that, you know, anything that embarrassed me in class or anything. For the most part they tried to stay fairly neutral, as far as I could tell. So I just—I don't remember that much about that.

I'm sure—I don't think all of them agreed with our being there, but they never really made a point of being too mean to us. To really let us know that they, in no uncertain terms, thought we shouldn't be there. It wasn't too bad. It was mostly just the other guys going through. One of the things we picked up on with our own classmates—a lot of women were afraid to go to flight school in our class. Because after four years of putting up with this garbage, they said, "Hey, the hell with this, I'm not going into another macho avenue. I'm going to go into regular line, get out of the Navy, and forget it." So it was surprising, but there were only five billets for pilots, five for NFOs [naval flight officers]—and generally, aviation is very competitive. Everybody wants to get in. I never thought I'd make it with my class rank. But only four women went pilot and one NFO.

In the beginning I remember we would all talk about what were you going to do, and everybody wanted to fly. That was sort of the big thing, just like with the guys—even though they might change their minds later. So that was surprising. But a lot of it was because some of the women said, "Hey, I'm not putting up with any more of this garbage. I've had it." And that surprised us—because I was afraid, I thought, "Oh, geez, that's just what I need," you know. Non-support in flight school. I was scared to death of flunking out anyway. And one of the women who was down in NFO school, Kathy Karlson—she was ahead, and I was going to move down with her in Pensacola for a little while—she came back for a break in between other things, and I asked her about it, and she said, "Really, they're not bad." The guys down there somehow grew up. And they were actually pretty supportive. They were helping her with the physical stuff. No one was laughing at her if she couldn't do something right away. She was athletic and really a hard-working person, too, but still—it turned out to be a lot nicer than we thought. So getting them out into the real world must have helped.

Sue Sweeney: Chrystal Lewis said she couldn't believe more of your classmates didn't go air because the men in naval air are the most liberal and most open-minded in the Navy. She was surprised more women couldn't see the big picture.

Lieutenant Daniels: Well, you see, I figured that I had suffered through four years and I was going to do exactly what I wanted to do, which was fly. There wasn't anything else in the Navy that I could see that I wanted that badly. The ships that we could get on were pretty limited, and I thought, "No this isn't my thing." I had always wanted to learn how to fly from day one. I wasn't going to change my mind now. Not after four years. It would be, "Well, if it's a little more, it's a little more. So what." But—I don't know about the most liberal, but the aviators do tend to be the less paperwork, more action-oriented people, and also, I think, the more wild group overall. I suppose you could look at it that way. A lot of the women just got tired of the negative environment and they wanted the shortest way out, and with aviation you wouldn't start your five-year obligation until after you got your wings, which could be a year. And then some time until you got into flight school—so a lot of them were looking at, "Get me out of here as soon as possible."

Sue Sweeney: How often—or how seriously—did you think of quitting the Academy?

Lieutenant Daniels: Well, I didn't really like it there very much, but I think I felt an obligation. I don't like to quit anything, in the first place. I think I felt two things. I didn't want to quit, because I didn't want to be a wimp. And I didn't want to—I felt like if too many of us quit, then they'd say, "Aw, the women can't hack it." I guess in a way, I sort of—you might think this is sort of foolish—but I thought I was also representing a number of other women. If I quit, if I couldn't do it, all these guys would say, "I remember the one woman I knew—she quit." I sort of felt obligated. But I think I needed to see for myself that I could do it, too. So probably that would be the most underlying reason, to see if I could do it for myself.

Sue Sweeney: Was it easier for you when subsequent classes with women came in?

Lieutenant Daniels: Well, as you get to be an upper class, it gets to be easier. I found, actually, in a lot of ways, the second year was my hardest to deal with. Because the first year, as a plebe, you know your role. How to be a plebe. It's very easy, in a way. You do what they tell you to do. And you try real hard, and all that good stuff. It's clearly defined. In the second year, now you're sort of part of the upper class. But then again, you're really not part of anything, because you don't feel like you really fit. So I found the second year the most depressing. You didn't have as clearly a defined role to play anymore. And I felt really kind of confused as to what I was supposed to be doing. So it was kind of the hardest. You were still resented. You were still low enough on the totem pole that what you said didn't make a hill of beans of difference. I found that the most depressing year, really.

Sue Sweeney: By the time you graduated, did you feel you were a part of your class?

Lieutenant Daniels: I personally never really did. But, see, that's sort of me as an individual. I think my tendency—one of the things that you learn any time you're under stress is that whatever your weaknesses are will become rather pronounced. So my weakness would be, basically, taking things personally and allowing myself to get depressed. And to feel, you know, kind of like a lowlife. And the other tendency was to, sort of, withdraw. I think I withdrew a lot and I probably missed out on a lot of socialization. I mean I pretty much stuck with sailing. That was my thing to do and sort of my escape from the place. But I've never been to a reunion, and I don't know that many people. I just guess I just cut myself off in a lot of ways.

And graduation week, for me, was very depressing. I thought it was very—yeah, I'm done. But when I looked back that week and thought, "Gee, I wasted four years of my life." My goal had originally been to go to UVA and major in biochemistry, go to med school, and become a space doctor. I had all these wonderful goals. Well, here I'd gone to the stinking Academy, majored in English—didn't do very well at that—so I felt like I'd failed. I mean, for what my dreams and goals had been, and the route that life had taken me here—or I'd allowed life to take me, was like a 180-degree out. And so here I was, I thought, "Shoot, this stinks." So I thought it was really pretty depressing. I almost didn't make it to my own graduation. It was a relief, in a way, and "Yeah, you made it through." But see, just sliding in, in the back of the class, wasn't my idea of really making it through too well, so I wasn't awfully proud of that.

Sue Sweeney: You're too hard on yourself! What were your summer programs like?

Lieutenant Daniels: Oh, let's see. Oh yeah, for me—I was lucky that way, I think. Because women weren't allowed on ships that first summer; third-class cruise—that's when you went and sort of played enlisted person on a ship, you know. So they had the YPs [yard patrol boats], and the women had to go on them because they weren't allowed on ships, they sent an equal number of men. Basically they visited Navy ports up and down the East Coast. The purpose was to learn different things about ships, and the sea, and all this good stuff.

And just luckily enough that year, they had obtained *Mistral*, which is a schooner, a Herreshoff-designed schooner, a really lovely craft. And they were going to have the first sail-training cruise—credit type of training cruise—in years. They hadn't had that big a boat, and the program was still in a growth period then. So I very accidentally—I'd heard about it—but I thought, I don't know how to sail. And I'd had a real hard time plebe summer, when they took us out a few times in the little knockabouts. I couldn't remember the terms. "Jibing, tacking, what the heck is that?" I was clueless. I didn't know anything about this stuff.

That spring, I was going to do some company knockabout sailing so I could learn. Several of us had gone down to the sailing center and I saw a guy who had been on the swimming team. I had swum a little bit in the fall, but in the winter when it got serious, I thought I wasn't going to be good enough. So I became a manager for a little bit. So I went over to the one guy I recognized from the team and said, "Hey, what're you doing here?" He was a part of this crew going out in this boat. And they were looking for women. They wanted to make sure that they were being fair, equal opportunity and all that stuff. So he said, "You should try. You know, they can't get any women from the sailing team to go."

The women on the sailing team at the time all sailed the dinghies and Lasers. There were some real good sailors in our class, too. But they were all looking at the loss of time on leave—this would be about a two-month cruise. *Mistral* was going to go across the Atlantic and back. The normal training cruise stuff only takes about four to five weeks. So I guess a lot of women wanted to spend more time at home and be with their family and friends. For me, going home, sitting around the house? Hey, I like sailing a lot better! This sounded more exciting and adventurous. Besides, I knew I'd regret not trying.

So I told them, "Yeah, I can cook" (even though I'd never really cooked much at all), and "Yeah, I can do first aid, I've done that stuff before." So they let me on. I was the token woman, except for, of course, the coach, Louise Burke, the coach on the boat. She's head of offshore sailing there now. She's a real neat lady. She became kind of a role model to me. So I got to go across the ocean while these other people were rolling around off the East Coast. Of course, while I was out there, I didn't think it was good all the time.

Sue Sweeney: How big a crew?

Lieutenant Daniels: There were about 14.

Sue Sweeney: Twelve men and you and Louise Burke?

Lieutenant Daniels: Yeah.

Sue Sweeney: Was it a great break from being at the Academy?

Lieutenant Daniels: Oh yeah. I mean you're out in the real world. You don't have to do the musters and all these other little annoyances. I mean it's the real world—you're there and everybody's going to do whatever they can do based on their abilities. Of course, you get a lot closer to people in that kind of situation. You become friends and learn a lot. So I enjoyed it. By the time I got back from this business, I was in love with sailing. I mean, this was it for me. I just found something I liked to do. That's kind of how I got started in it. It was really fun.

Sue Sweeney: Did the camaraderie you established on the boat go back to the Academy with you?

Lieutenant Daniels: Yes, the people you knew. And really, I mean, the people you started working with on an individual basis—I mean, if you earn people's respect on an individual basis it works out in the long term. Usually it's people you don't know who will make assumptions or something, I think, that you'll have a problem with. Or people who just will always stay hostile, period, even though—you'll meet somebody in flight school or something, and the one woman they knew before was a real, you know, nerd, but you're okay. It's like, very individual. Or else they don't like you. It's kind of like the two or three people that they've met. That's one of the other problems, that because there're so few women, the one or two that some of these guys ever get to meet is what they base their entire opinions on. Unless they have a wife or other people in their lives that help give them a little broader perspective.

Sue Sweeney: Did you sail during the year?

Lieutenant Daniels: Well, when I got back I—I tried to learn—everybody said you should try to learn on the little boats first. I tried to get on with dinghies, but that didn't work out so well. So I got on a big boat that was a sailing club boat—at the time we had a bit of a sailing club—so I could learn. And because I didn't have all of the strength that they're usually looking for—the usual way to start out on a boat is to be your basic winch-grinder, and there strength is everything. And while I could grind the winch—and I'm certainly not petite—I still wasn't as strong as some of the bigger guys. That usually wasn't the way I got on the boat.

I usually got on as a cook and learned. And I had a guy who was the skipper of the little sailboat we were on, the yawl, and I got a chance because it was a very casual atmosphere. Summer racing was pretty casual. So I got a chance to learn about different aspects of the boat. And I found I could drive the boat okay. And I learned about trimming sails and all that stuff, so finally I was developing skill. And then after that, for some reason, this club boat—the whole crew got put on one of the Class A's [category]— for a short part of the fall season. And we had a coach there—I became the main trimmer on it, and he really taught us how to trim sails. I learned a lot. He was really kind of tough on you all the time, which was good in the long run—I learned a lot about sail trimming, and I developed a fairly decent reputation for that from some people, I guess, on some of the other boats. Finally—it was the biggest honor—finally some guy in my company who was on one of the other yawls, asked for me to be on their boat as a main trimmer and navigator.

I thought, "Oh, now I don't have to start out as a cook anymore." That was good. And then I sailed with them on that boat in the spring and part of the summer. And then a friend of Louise's, a civilian woman, was doing a Bermuda one-two race.[1] She was working up for a single-handed transatlantic doing smaller races, and she did sail alone from Newport to Bermuda and then we double-handed back. And so I got to fly down there to Bermuda and then be her crew. And so we did that. In fact, it was so funny because it was getting up to be my first-class year, and because I was the only woman

---

[1] The first leg of the race is solo and the second leg has two people.

who'd been in big boats for very long at all, they were looking kind of, you know, if someone had the qualifications to be a woman skipper, to break the ice, to have it happen.

And there was one woman, Kay Hire, who was in '81. She ended up becoming a skipper the next year. She was also on the yawls, or "the great blue pigs," as we called them. The captain, who was kind of in charge of everything, had threatened me because I was going off to sail with this other woman instead of staying with my team boat for the rest of the summer. You know, "Well, we may not give you your boat," and all this stuff.

I said, "This was a great opportunity," and the people on my boat didn't resent me. They said, "Hey, yeah, go for it. You can learn a lot." I wasn't that critical one way or the other. We had two navigators and enough crew that everybody could handle it. So anyway, I did that. And I still got my boat when I got back. I learned a lot from that. We had a real good crew. It was a little hard at first, because I think I ended up with a lot of people who didn't know much about sailing. All the good sailors wanted to go with the guys who they felt were the real good guys. And I figure I was kind of middle of the pack.

I don't think I—I wasn't the best. I don't think I was the worst either. But it was a lot of fun. But some of the people in that—well, the guy who was the XO in that crew, we still keep in touch. He's a real nice guy. But he was pretty open-minded—like he flies jets, his wife flies helos, she's another Academy grad, I think even a classmate of his. They're even both out in the Med, both in different ships, but they see each other once in a while. Pretty neat. Yeah, we had a real good time. It was a real challenge for me. And I learned a lot.

Sue Sweeney: There was a lot of socializing to break the ice among the mids?

Lieutenant Daniels: Oh, well sure, I mean with sailing, that was the big thing, you know. The after-race parties and stuff. I always enjoyed sailing. You had your social life. You had people you became friends with and all that. So, you know, that was kind of my crowd. The people that I knew and have known the longest, they were the people pretty much that I sailed with. Aside from my roommate. Then again, it was kind of true. Most people had a particular sport that they stuck with, or a particular activity that they did all the time, as opposed to when people did more a variety of things—company and battalion rather than varsity. The other advantage to being on the varsity sailing team is you didn't have to march to football games. I never liked football. They always thought I was very un-American because I didn't like football at all.

Sue Sweeney: I thought you'd say you enjoyed getting out of parades, because they use the yawls as a backdrop.

Lieutenant Daniels: Oh, yeah, we did that during June Week and stuff. Also we didn't have to wear a uniform, just our little blue shirts and white pants. So for us, that was fine.

Sue Sweeney: Did sailing excuse you from the regular summer activities?

Lieutenant Daniels: Oh, no. We did all the regular stuff. Everybody had to check their boxes, so, you know. The sail credit one was the only summer I didn't do what the other people did, which suited me just fine. We still learned navigation. Still learned a lot about seamanship. The next summer is where they drag you around to show you a week here, in Quantico, and Pensacola, and all that. This is when they had money, of course. I think they reduced it somewhat now. That was really a blast, because that was really going around and finding out about the different communities. Quantico, I thought, was pretty funny because they'd cammie us up and we'd run around the woods like kids playing soldier. They spent a lot of money—they'd haul us around in these helos, drop us here. It was like we ate this up, you know—the jet ride and stuff. And so we always thought that was fun.

The first-class cruise—luckily I got on a ship. They finally opened it up for ships that year. In fact they made a big fuss about it. The funniest thing I always remember was, when we obligated, which is when you go to your first class at the start of second-class year, the women had no clue what we were going to do when we graduated. Because I really think that the people—the lawmakers said, "Okay, blah, blah, bless you all, you can now go to the Academy." Nobody even worried about it. I don't think they ever thought we'd graduate, because no one seemed to be concerned. Then all of a sudden now second-class year started rolling around, and our summer cruise was coming up.

And I think it finally started dawning on some upper people—I always remember having different times when DACOWITS [Defense Advisory Committee on Women in the Services] people would come visit us. And I remember an incident where I think before things were determined, a woman came out to talk to a group of us. And we brought up the fact that, "Hey, we've obligated and we don't know a hill of beans about how many billets of anything, or what's going to be open to us.[2] And that's kind of taking a big risk here. We can all become public-affairs officers someplace for all we know." And we didn't go through all this just to do that.

But, anyway, it finally dawned on them that they must figure out what to do with these women. So for first-class cruise, they got it changed around where they had a few ships, repair ships and whatnot that we could go to. So that was quite interesting. And I went out on a repair ship that was out of San Diego. We picked it up in Japan—it was on its way home from the WestPac group. So we actually got to be out on the ocean. That was really cool. We sailed from Japan to Hawaii to San Diego. The thing that was sort of ironic, though—they had several women on the ship and we talked to them—one was an engineer, one was a doctor, and one was a—I think she ran disbursing and a couple of other things. And they were all quite nice, very nice to talk to.

_____

[2] Female midshipmen did not yet know what career opportunities they could have, especially in the surface Navy.

And we were asking them, "What's it like from you guys' perspective," etc. Well, they found—because they had, of course, their contemporaries out on different ships. And the biggest difference that was made, was your CO's attitude on the ship. On this particular ship, the CO was a real good guy and he gave them real jobs, treated them like the rest of the wardroom, and they loved it. They enjoyed what they did; they liked their ship, you know. And that—because the CO sets the example. And if the CO decides that he doesn't think that women really know what they're doing, then the other males in the wardroom will often follow suit if they have that opinion in the first place. They feel like they can now get away with not worrying about them.

So on this ship the CO was very positive and very supportive. So then you just had to work with individuals, you know, as far as changing your mind, or earning your respect. And that, again, takes time, but you can work that out. But if you feel like you have the support there, at least it doesn't feel so hopeless. There're always going to be a few people who will never change their mind. For the most part, everybody seemed pretty decent on the ship. We enjoyed it. It was a pretty good crowd.

Sue Sweeney: Did you get a feeling from them how widespread it was?

Lieutenant Daniels: Oh, there were quite a number, because they had talked to friends of theirs who went out of SWO [surface warfare officer] school at the same time, went off to different ships, and on their ship, the CO was a jerk. He didn't like them at all. He didn't think they belonged. He gave them the old assistant's assistant type of job, or made

up jobs that were never there. So they never really got a chance to do something real, and

to really earn respect. And that attitude, I found that from some of my own classmates

who went on ships. That made the biggest difference in the universe, having a CO set the

pace, as far as are they going to be accepted or not.

Is he going to treat them like the other guys, you know, give them a regular job

and let them fall on their own face on their own time, or do whatever—treat them like

everybody else? Or is he going to kind of treat them like they're really incompetent

anyway? That was the biggest difference. Some of the same people from the same class

going off in different directions, and some were very unhappy, and some had found a

good spot. The other thing that was sort of ironic was before we were allowed on a ship,

apparently, they thought that they would send us to certain shore billets, and then,

perhaps, get us out on weapons demonstration, or something, right? Because of the way

the laws are written, dependents—you know, wives, and mothers, and sisters, whoever—

can go out and watch a weapons demonstration, but we couldn't in uniform.

So the Academy says, "Well, we're not sending them off there in civilian clothes

for this. No way. That's a slap in the face." And that was good of them to push that way.

That was really ironic. So they finally changed it. But the ironic thing for our ship, which

was a regular repair ship, pretty slow moving—we got into Hawaii, and there was a

dependents' cruise, which they have periodically where we're not really doing anything

in particular, just cruising home. So here they are picking up a lot of sons, and whatever, friends of the men on the ship. No women, no daughters were allowed. Here they are, these little kids, and they have movies for them and all these little activities planned.

They're allowed on the ship, and it just took us how many years to get ourselves on the ship. We're like adults who have some clue of what's going on. I mean, that seems pretty ironic to me.

Sue Sweeney: For your first-class cruise, were there enough billets or did you have to vie for the spaces?

Lieutenant Daniels: Well, I can't remember now. I can't remember. I think they provided a really good number of billets for us. Two of us were on this ship, plus some midshipmen, you know, one man and one female from some other school. I know they had some on the East Coast. The problem was a lot of them don't usually go places. We were very lucky with the ship we got, because it actually happened to be coming back on a cruise. But a lot of the ships aren't going anyplace. So you'd actually be in port the whole time you were there. In the beginning they had already—this change in rule came so late because the women were—they'd already handed out assignment preference sheets for us. And there were a lot of overseas assignments. These were all shore assignments initially.

And so everyone had selected, usually based on location, "Yeah, I want to go to Germany," or wherever. And we'd already gotten word on, "Now you're going to go here and you're going to go there," so a lot of the women at that point, didn't want to go to ships. They said, "Hey, I want to go to France—forget this ship stuff." So I think there were a number of women that were pissed about it and said, "Geez, we could have had more fun the other way." But that's the way it goes, I guess.

Sue Sweeney: Did you do Plebe Detail your first-class summer?

Lieutenant Daniels: No, I didn't do Plebe Detail.

Sue Sweeney: You didn't want to?

Lieutenant Daniels: No, I didn't want to. I thought, "I don't want to do that stuff." I couldn't quite picture it, so I did the cruise and I did sailing.

Sue Sweeney: Was first-class year the best for you?

Lieutenant Daniels: Well, in a lot of ways, certainly. Because you have some privileges and people aren't yelling at you so much anymore.

Sue Sweeney: Did you yell much as an upperclassman?

Lieutenant Daniels: Oh no. See I withdrew too much, too. The only thing I ever was was a squad leader, and everybody kind of becomes that. Your basic midshipman ensign rank there. And I just never got into it because I think I resented it so much, I just couldn't participate in it much at all.

Sue Sweeney: How were you on demerits?

Lieutenant Daniels: I would get demerits for being late for formation. I always wait till the last minute. For the most part, fairly minor stuff, but I'd have a few here and there. I never got caught at the big stuff.

Sue Sweeney: You did the big stuff—you just didn't get caught?

Lieutenant Daniels: Yeah. Sometimes. You know, nothing really god-awful.

Sue Sweeney: Going over the wall and things like that?

Lieutenant Daniels: Yeah, being UA [unauthorized absence] or something like that. Every once in a while I'd get lucky with a bed check.

Sue Sweeney: Was this with your roommate?

Lieutenant Daniels: No, see my roommate and I were very different people. We sort of became like sisters in a way. Because we always felt that we could trust each other. And we were supportive of each other. And so we talked a lot and we were very close. But we were not the same kind of people at all. She was much more—worked harder, very straight. She would always—the upper class when we were plebes would always piss me off. She would give them the benefit of the doubt, "Well, they're just doing their job."

"Don't they make you mad?"

"No, we shouldn't get mad." Oh, God, we always had all sorts of fun debates about that. But we operated very differently. She pretty much followed the rules, and that sort of thing. And I think I was trying sometimes to be rebellious in different ways. Usually in minor ways, I never did anything really major.

Sue Sweeney: What was the hardest thing for you during the four years?

Lieutenant Daniels: I mean for me, that I let it eat at my own self-confidence, so it took me a while to get that back. I allowed them to make me feel stupid and ugly, etc., you know, because of the way things were. So that was probably—"Gee, if I could go back with what I know now, I'd change things."

Sue Sweeney: Does something stick out as being the most satisfying aspect?

Lieutenant Daniels: Well, I found that sailing and I found that being the skipper of my own boat was the most satisfying leadership experience there. I mean they were always telling you to get involved in the battalion and all the military part of it. Well, I thought a lot of that was sort of fake, in a way, because there was this structure backing you up if you get this certain midshipman rank. Whereas if you were on a boat, it was going to be whether or not you could really motivate these people, who didn't have to be there, to really want to do what they were going to do, and get out there and really work at it, and enjoy it at the same time. So to me that was a more realistic challenge. I enjoyed it. I really liked it.

And I had a good group. I learned—because, you know, I was always learning. I was obviously no expert sailor either. I'd just done it since I'd been there a little bit. There's always something more to learn there. Going out and doing—the ocean racing to me was always the most exciting, because there you don't see your opponents for a lot of the days you're out there. So that was the most exciting. The Newport to Bermuda race, that was really exciting. Because within the first 24 hours, I mean there were hundreds of boats and all sorts of classes. And after the first 24 hours—you won't see a soul after that. And for several days as you sail, you won't see a thing, and then you all converge on the island, all these people start appearing on the horizon again. So that's very exciting.

Sue Sweeney: Tell me more about the social aspects of sailing for Navy.

Lieutenant Daniels: It was fairly casual. I mean the coaches around were often officers in the area, or maybe people who worked at the Academy or something. And usually they were sailors themselves, so they were pretty casual and they enjoyed partying themselves. The only real uniform we had was wearing our little blue shirts that said, "Naval Academy Sailing Team," and white pants or white shorts, depending on the season. For the most part you didn't have to worry about uniforms.

Sue Sweeney: Was there a lot of curiosity about you?

Lieutenant Daniels: I don't remember. I mean there's some in some places, like on *Mistral*, being in a foreign country—especially if there was a lot of foreign military—where they don't utilize women in their military at all. Or in much more limited fashion than even we do. So there you get a few curious people. But I don't remember that so much. I mean you just sort of became one of the guys. I think that's sort of how I look back on it. You never quite felt like a real girl, because you never were anybody's date. You were there on your own, anyway. You're just sort of one of the group. That's how it went.

Sue Sweeney: For what you're doing now, could you just as easily have gone to UVA? Are you better prepared, having gone to the Academy?

Lieutenant Daniels: Well, it's very different. You never really know. I think my life has sort of led me in a very different direction by going this route. If I had gone to UVA, I probably would not have learned how to fly. That's the one thing I'm glad I did. But at UVA, I feel like I would have done a little better academically, and would not have lost that self-confidence. And, you know, maybe I would have ended up premed. For all I know, I could have gone there and done terrible, and changed my major three times. It's really hard to say which way would have turned out better. This way—I have learned over the years to sort of make use of what good this has done.

Because, see, I never thought of it at the time, or personally, I don't see it as that much of a big deal. Because of the people I saw at the Academy, and the people I know from high school who do other things now, and are civilian types, I don't think the Academy people are special. To me it's like, so what. But to somebody else—there are a lot of other people who say, "Wow." So, you know, you kind of learn to make that an advantage and it looks great on a resume. Somebody else would be impressed by it. If they're impressed by it, great. I'll let them be impressed. It's sort of like, you know, people are impressed by certain schools or something. I hardly made it through, but I went there.

Sue Sweeney: Do you have any feel for whether a so-called "party school" like UVA would have done you in?

Lieutenant Daniels: Well, see, I was a pretty serious person when I was in high school and very goal oriented. And I think at the Academy, because of my little rebelliousness there and withdrawal, I think I lost sight of a lot of goals there. I'm only coming to terms with that now even that I want to—that maybe I can and I should get back on track. You know, one of my other goals has been to become an astronaut. I sort of—I dropped it because I just never felt that I could do it. For years I sort of, like, set it aside. While I may not become an astronaut now, I still have decided that I want to work somewhere within the space aspect of things. I'm coming back to where I was losing sight of having any goals at all. I'm coming back and feeling a little more confident, and will go and seek them out. There, I think I sort of lost sight, whereas I don't know how I would have changed there either. But that certainly is a big time for a certain amount of socialization. But I was pretty serious when I first started. I think I changed a little bit going through the Academy. I could have been a bag lady for all I know.

Sue Sweeney: Why don't I think so? What have you done since graduation?

Lieutenant Daniels: Well, I was a TAD [temporary assigned duty] at the Academy as the sailing coach.

Sue Sweeney: How was that?

Lieutenant Daniels: It was fun. You know, it was a really good duty as far as I was concerned. Sailed all through the summer, and sailed in the afternoons in the fall. Because I didn't get a flight school date until February the next year.

Sue Sweeney: Did you see a difference in the plebes you were training in the summer of '80?

Lieutenant Daniels: Well, you see a little bit just like, you know, looking back when you see high school people. High school people, don't they always look younger and smaller than you were a member in high school? "Gosh, did I look like that?" So I think you look back at it in those terms. As far as the women, there just weren't that many on big boats, so I never really saw that much of a difference. You know, and the only other women I knew on big boats really well were Allison, who ended up being Gid's [a yawl executive officer] wife. She sailed with us a little bit. She's very quiet, but a very good, competent individual. And Kay Hire in '81. I knew her because we had her on the boat.

In fact, she was in one of the squadrons I was with because she became an NFO. So those are the people who you know aren't going to let some snide remarks bother you too much. Even if it bothers you, you're not going to show it. You're still going to do what you really want to do. And a couple other classmates sailed with me a little bit—one of my other classmates for a while—but she wanted to do a number of other things in her spare time, so she didn't stick to sailing.

Sue Sweeney: Did you find Annapolis a lot more enjoyable as an officer rather than as a midshipman?

Lieutenant Daniels: In some ways, yes. But I think I have always had this big thing about Bancroft Hall. I still didn't feel comfortable going back. I mean I go to Annapolis, go into town now, you know, kind of the old haunts, and remember this, that, and the other. But as far as Bancroft Hall—I'm trying to remember—sometime after graduation I went back into the Hall. For some reason I went back to get something or do something. And I just remember feeling really weird—it's like, "Ooh, I don't want to be here. This place really depresses me." And I'm not sure I've ever been back. Like I say, I haven't been to any reunions, and I've been pretty local. I am not much of a football fan.

The only reason I'd go to a reunion is, I think, if I had half a dozen friends of mine go rather than—the other part that's sort of embarrassing to me is because when you're one of only one or two women in a class or doing something in particular, or even in flight school, guys remember who you are, but I don't remember a lot of guys. I'll recognize their face or maybe remember a first name or something. But they know who you are, and you never hardly remember who they are because, like I say, I tend to sort of just be quiet and withdrawn, for the most part, unless I'm with a group for a period of time. So that's sort of embarrassing to me. People would come up and, "Oh, Sandy, how're you doing?" And it's like, "Who are you? I don't know you at all."

Sue Sweeney: That should be good for your confidence.

Lieutenant Daniels: Well, you always wonder what they remember about you. Either that or at some party—and you wonder, "Was I standing on my head at the time? Was I wearing a lamp shade? I don't remember which party it was." If I had a group of friends, I suppose I might now. The first three years I think I just refused as a matter of course. I just didn't want to have anything to do with it. Just get me away. I gave away all of, anything that said "Naval Academy" on it—my old sweatshirts, everything. Gym clothes, uniforms, everything that I couldn't use in the fleet, I got rid of.

Sue Sweeney: You're not wearing your ring. Do you have one?

Lieutenant Daniels: Yes I do, but I don't wear it very often. I wear it if we dress up. To me it's kind of a gaudy thing, it's so big. So I just don't feel comfortable. Because I think so many people—"Aw, the old ring-knockers"—I'd rather just sort of fit in. If they find out I went there fine, if not I don't really care. It's no big deal one way or the other. I wear it if we wear mess dress, or something.

Sue Sweeney: Where did you live in Annapolis during that summer?

Lieutenant Daniels: When I was TAD, I got a little apartment out on West Street. It was in a house—top floor of the house. I just had a little apartment by myself and that worked out just fine for the summer and fall. I didn't get to flight school until February of '81. Because I was so—the way you get your slot, usually, is when you have service selection night, everybody goes in based on class rank. Well, me being at the bottom of the—the basement child here, you know, so I got the latest dates. So I had to wait a while, but that was okay. Then I went to flight school—that took about a year.

Sue Sweeney: Did you enjoy flight school?

Lieutenant Daniels: Well, I kind of actually have a lot of good memories about it because I think the challenge was right there. You knew what you needed to do. Of course I was scared to death of flunking out, just out of embarrassment, I think, everybody really feared it. To me it was like, "I'll have to change my name, move to South America," or something. So I really worked hard at it. You work hard at what you want, everybody does. And I remember, for the most part, enjoying it. There was a lot of hard work. That was all you had to concentrate on. That was your concentration. So you knew the direction you were going. You knew what you were striving for. And the feedback was very direct as far as how well you were doing and whatever. So it's pretty challenging, but very straightforward—that sort of challenging. I had a really good roommate there. She was not a flyer-type at all. I just accidentally met her. I didn't like living in BOQs, they always seem depressing. They're not very personal. So we ended up being roommates for a year and becoming good friends. So I had a good time, you know, at the same time.

Sue Sweeney: Were the academics harder there than you expected, or were you pleasantly surprised?

Lieutenant Daniels: Well, I don't know. See, I never viewed them much as academics. I mean you had certain classes, but most of it was the actual flying and studying for the flights and learning the procedures. It was challenging for someone who had such a poor memory. But I learned that I liked it. I liked the flying. I mean I had a really enjoyable time. It wasn't like a good-time fun, but it was rewarding.

Sue Sweeney: Did you go there knowing that you wanted to fly props?

Lieutenant Daniels: Well, actually, my original thing was I wanted to fly jets, really. This egotist here wanted to be a jet jock. But at the time the rules were, after the women went through basic, or primary—the beginning part with the single engine—everybody had what they call jet grades. It varied a little bit, but so many net above check marks, those were, you know, minimum jet grades, and then you could choose jets.[3] Well, the women weren't allowed to go directly to jets because there were so few billets. And because, I think, their thinking was a little screwed up. They decided that the women had to learn— to go through the prop syllabus first, and then go through the second half of the jet syllabus once they identified a billet for them. It was really weird.

That's why Chrystal ended up being the only one that went jets, even though Suzanne [Grubbs] wanted it. And at the time, I think I was just—I wasn't so thrilled with the Navy. And I thought, "Gee, I don't want to waste this many years just in flight school," by the time I get out there, because I started so late and everything, I'm going to be staying in half of my life, you know. And I had the minimum jet grades, but I didn't even try for it. I said, "I'm just going to go props and see what happens." Forget it. I didn't want to go through the rigmarole.

And then I always remembered, too, that at some point while I was in flight school—and I think it was while I was still in primary, maybe I was in advanced, in the summer or fall—a DACOWITS representative was advertised to be there to talk to the women in flight school about anything they wanted to. I made a point of showing up, and only one other woman showed up—I was really disappointed at that. I felt for sure, whoever else might be down there at the time might have something to say. And one of our biggest beefs was that particular rule. It was like, this is really stupid. It's wasting the

---

[3] Each item to learn was graded at three levels corresponding to pass, above, or below a pass. "Net above" indicated the total number of "above" check marks.

Navy's money. Why shouldn't the training be the same? There's no reason for it not to be the same.

And I think what finally must have clinched it, we don't know this for sure, soon after that a woman ejected from a jet—she had gotten into some uncontrollable configuration, or something. And she was fine, they just lost the airplane, which the Navy's never thrilled with. And so somebody thought that—the syllabus, the jets had been divided up into T-2, which is the easier jet to fly, and then the T-A4s which are the more difficult jets. Well, the women were apparently getting, if I remember correctly—Chrystal would probably be a little more expert on this than I am—but I think they were just getting the latter part of the training with the harder jet—you know, they weren't getting the whole complete syllabus—so they thought that maybe she got herself in that situation just for lack of training. That was her only choice, to eject. And maybe if the training was the same, that wouldn't have happened.

And finally it dawned on the Navy: Boy, this really is stupid. Why are we spending all this extra money on these women? So they made it the same. But it was after I had already made my choice, so I went with props. There weren't that many squadrons to go to, when you went through the list. I wanted VXE-6 as a first choice, which is off the West Coast. They're the ones who fly the C-130s down to Antarctica. That seemed like, to me, if I was going to be in the Navy, I wanted to do something that I would probably never get to do when I would get out. So, hey, land in Antarctica, that's something you probably won't get to do too much—and go to see big penguins, because

I'd heard about these big emperor penguins. This is a good reason to go. This is where I want to go. And this other poor woman, she wanted VXN-8, which is where I ended up.

Their nickname is the World Travelers because they're an oceanographic research squadron, they fly P-3s, and they travel everywhere. Wherever the projects go. They get a lot of traveling into a variety of places. She wanted that squadron.

Sue Sweeney: Where were they based?

Lieutenant Daniels: Patuxent River, Maryland. She wanted that squadron for the travel. A lot of people had told me to pick that squadron, but to me, Antarctica still sounded kind of exciting. So we had these reversed first choices, she and I. She got her orders first. She got VXE-6, which was her second choice. And then already after she'd left—it was too late for us to trade—I ended up getting VXN-8. It was like, "You people, why couldn't you figure it out? You could have given both of us our first choices, and still fit the billets." So I ended up in VXN-8 for the three years. And then came to NRL [U.S. Naval Research Laboratory] after that.

Sue Sweeney: Tell me more about the Patuxent squadron. Where did you fly?

Lieutenant Daniels: Well, we flew P-3s and we flew just about everywhere. I have this huge picture in the back with all these countries' names and places I'd been. One of the trips, one of the biggest ongoing projects they have is Project Magnet. It's a specially configured P-3 where from the cabin door aft, it's all nonferrous metal because they measure the Earth's magnetosphere. And you fly all night, because the sun is apparently less active then, so the measurements are more accurate. So, anyway, that one tends to be the most travel. And at the time, those were about two-month trips. And I went on about two and a half Project Magnet trips. One time I replaced someone who had sinus problems. And the very first one I ended up on was a round-the-world trip. We went to the Canaries, we went to Athens, Kenya, La Réunion, Sri Lanka, to Diego Garcia just to get a few parts, Philippines, Bali, Indonesia, Perth, Australia, Tasmania, Tahiti, and Mexico City.

Sue Sweeney: Were you the only woman in the crew?

Lieutenant Daniels: We had one woman enlisted on that trip. There were a few navigators, a few other pilots, and some women enlisted in the squadron. And we didn't always travel together. Sometimes one of the other women navs and I would travel together, but there was no real sense of, "You will always have a pair of women on these trips." Sometimes you were and it was no big deal. And you had a few people who might be somewhat negative or something, but for the most part it wasn't a major problem. Until the last CO.

Sue Sweeney: Where would you stay when you went to all these places?

Lieutenant Daniels: We stayed in hotels; we lived pretty well. A lot of places we went to there are no bases, so there was no other choice anyway. But most often we stayed in hotels. The only time it would become a problem was if we were in a very high-cost area and just to stay within per diem, we'd have to double up. So on that particular trip, in Tahiti, and I can't remember if at some other place, they wanted me and the enlisted to double up. Normally you wouldn't do that, but it was no big deal. And in some ways you do get a little lonely because you don't have friends—it depends on the guys. If you have a friend among the guys, then it's no big deal, but sometimes it can be a little lonely. Sometimes if the guys are out barhopping for the specific purpose of seeking companionship, you might feel a little odd. Or they may not even really want you along because then the other women they're seeking may think you're with them, you know. But not everybody does that. I had a pretty good time.

Sue Sweeney: How were your COs? It sounds like the last wasn't very positive about women.

Lieutenant Daniels: No, he wasn't very positive about a lot of things. He was investigated twice after we left. Once for fraud, waste, and abuse, and once for sexual harassment. He never harassed me; I wish he had. I would have gotten him good. But we didn't like him very much. And it was apparently obvious enough—you worry when you're in these situations, you don't want to appear too sensitive about, you know, taking insult or being paranoid and thinking that they're really against you as a group. So you usually learn not to complain too much, especially because there may be—we had one woman at the beginning of the time I was with the squadron. She was not that good a pilot, and she probably should never have become an aircraft commander. She's flying for Piedmont now; be careful. Hopefully she's still in the engineer's seat. She could do things if they were planned, but if you threw too much at her, I don't think she was quite right. But they gave her aircraft commander anyway, because they were afraid of her running around yelling, "prejudice," etc. And that was too bad because—and she would, she would have, I have no doubt—and that was too bad, really, because that makes the rest of us a little too afraid sometimes to say too much. Because you don't really want to be one of the complainers. You don't want to be a real weenie.

But I even had one of the chiefs in the squadron mention to me one time, "It's pretty obvious who that guy doesn't like, you know, women." He might give a person here and there a couple of token good deals, but for the most part—but he was also negative toward some of the guys. What his problem really was—at least in my opinion—was he had a very specific image of what a naval officer ought to be. First of all a man, so that kind of eliminates us. But also, there were some guys there that were really bright and talented people, but they didn't fit the image. They weren't big tall, athletic, macho men, didn't say the right things, drink the right things, or whatever. And so, while they were sometimes the most talented people, they weren't the halo boys. And you do find that even in regular, all-male type squadrons. It just depends on the CO and who he picks as his halo boys and whatever. He would have been a bad CO, I think, in any squadron.

Sue Sweeney: Was he Academy?

Lieutenant Daniels: No. In fact he had been jets before—and there were some rumors about why he wasn't the backseater in a jet anymore. He was also a navigator. He was a little strange guy, a little strange. He was pretty disgusting.

Sue Sweeney: Did you ever have cause to consider turning someone in for sexual harassment?

Lieutenant Daniels: Well, not so much specifically with me. I think because I tend to come across as a person who—a fairly big-mouthed, strong person. I think someone like him would know that I would turn his ass in in a heartbeat if he so much as, you know, did anything directly. I didn't find out about this until I had already left the squadron. What had happened with one of the other women was that she was duty officer and he was drinking at the BOQ—this was a big deal now, of course, drinking and driving. He had always said to everybody in the squadron, "If you need a ride, call the duty driver."

Well, he didn't want the enlisted duty driver to see him in that state, you know, the CO, so she was the duty officer, so she picked him up in the truck and was going to drive him home. He lived like 45 minutes away, it was a pretty good drive. And on the way he had to pull over to answer the call of nature there. And when he came back, he started——he got in on her side of the truck and started accosting her, and she, of course, pushed him off, and he finally quit and got back on his side. But she was so embarrassed by it, I think, that she didn't say anything about it. And that finally——that and some other thing that he had said, and whatever, you know, became part of the investigation. I didn't think much was ever done. The guy still made captain.

But he even said, while he was still XO——they had a trip where I was the aircraft commander and the another woman was the mission commander, the NFO. And so we had a trip together——he went along. Well, the whole thing was like having a [qualification] board the whole time. And he was constantly on our case. He didn't seem to like anything we did. And we never——I never had another aircraft commander trip again. She was leaving the squadron, so she never got one. This was like a good token deal. The CO had really wanted to do this for everybody. And, "Oh, isn't this wonderful," two women running the mission. Big deal, you know. He was not thrilling to be around.

I always remember we were all sitting around in the bar afterwards——I think the other woman had gone to her room or something——just a few enlisted, a few Os, and the CO. And he was just sitting there, you know, having a few beers and talking, and he's like admitting that he had a hard time dealing with us in a professional capacity. And his wife was in the Navy, second wife. She was a lieutenant in the Navy. She ended up getting out, I think, to please him, but that's all backfired, so I don't know how they're doing these days. But he is a weirdo. I feel sorry for his wife. I don't know why she married that jerk.

Sue Sweeney: Is that the worst case you know of?

Lieutenant Daniels: Oh, well, for me directly with him pretty much. I think we had other arguments, but I mean as far as having sexual harassment or any kind of woman attachment directly, yes, that probably would be. I'm trying to think of other people. You know, there were people—you get some resentment, especially when guys are getting in groups again or where the guys were sort of grouped together and, "Oh, all the women are this or that," because one woman had said something one way or whatever. So there was still a little bit of that sometimes, you kind of wondered if you were considered an equal.

Sue Sweeney: Do you still feel that way now?

Lieutenant Daniels: Well, it just varies with the individual. Most guys, I think, just accept me as whoever I am, I guess. And hopefully with whatever weaknesses or strengths they see through me as an individual. You still get a lot of people who, "Oh, I've never flown with a woman before." But as long as they find out you can do it, they really don't care. They don't have any heartburn with it. So for the most part, there's not too much of a problem unless—the only time you might find out about some people's opinion is if you get into the great debate of women in combat, and all the opinions start falling out onto the table here, as to wherever they stand. So that can be interesting. If I'm not in the mood to argue, I just—I don't even want to approach those kinds of debates—it's always the same old stuff, you know, I've heard it all for years. It's, you know, "I don't want to debate today, thanks."

Sue Sweeney: I'm almost afraid to ask for your thoughts about the Secretary of the Navy.

Lieutenant Daniels: Oh, Webb—Webbola—oh bring him up. We hated him. We did not like that article [James Webb, "Women Can't Fight," *Washingtonian* magazine, 1 November 1979] at all.

Sue Sweeney: How do you feel about him now being your boss?

Lieutenant Daniels: Oh, I had a big letter writing campaign to make sure he wasn't appointed. In fact Kay Hire had called me up from the West Coast because she found out that he was up for appointment. Because she had also been in VXN-8, so we became friends there. She called up and said, "God, we've got to do something about this. If this man gets appointed, I'm going to quit. I've had it." And she—I mean we were all there and for us, it slapped us in the face the most. We couldn't believe it that they were going to appoint this man. And so she called me up and said, "Okay, we've got to do something about it." And she gave me a few suggestions. And I got something started here where I wrote letters to everyone I could get addresses for. I got in contact with people to find out about stuff. So a bunch of us wrote letters to the congressmen, you know, everybody on the defense advisory committee, or whatever the heck they were called. They were going to be doing the questioning.

And I wrote—luckily I had the computer at work, so I just had to change the name, you know. But I sent out all these letters. And a bunch of us did and enough letters were gotten to most of the offices because we all got some response back. And they had told us, really, that for something to become an issue, you only have to send out 10 letters or something. If they receive 10 letters on the same thing, then the office will respond with a letter. So that was kind of interesting to learn.

Sue Sweeney: What kind of response did you get?

Lieutenant Daniels: Well, we didn't discuss it with too many male officers, I think, because a lot of the men—I don't think some of the men realized, unless they were Academy grads also and had been there during that time. I don't think they realized the reason for our resentment of him, because I mean the guy is obviously astute and intelligent, and good in other capacities. But our argument was, how can you have a boss who doesn't believe in the value of half of his employees, or a portion of his employees? If he had said some of the things that he said about women about Blacks or Hispanics, or some other group of people, you can bet that would have come out, and you can bet he would never have been appointed. I mean not even appointed for the appointment. I mean he wouldn't have gotten that far. But in this case it was sort of, well, it's the military, and the women—so that was okay.

And I think what surprised me the most was that he was actually unanimously approved. I mean, yeah, the senators and whatever all paid lip service to our idea and they brought questions up and all that good stuff. He, had of course, by now, learned to tone down his responses. He made it, though. I even told one of the—I went to a DACOWITS conference that they had in D.C. just out of curiosity to sit and listen. And one of the women that was in some of the meetings—a very intelligent young lady that works for one of the congressmen, I forget which one—but, you know, her dude had been on this committee, too. And I asked her a little bit about it and she said—or maybe I read it—that he had been approved unanimously from the group. And I just told her, I said, "Well, I hope the votes they traded somehow for all of that will really benefit somebody in the end." That kind of pissed me off. We kind of already knew—in fact when we talked to the [congressmen's] offices there we already knew that he would probably make it. I mean the offices, "Well, you'd be better to write about this, that and the other, and this bill for ships or whatever, because I'm sure—politically we already get the feeling

he's going to make it." Well, that's nice.

Sue Sweeney: Did you provide a copy of the *Washingtonian* article?

Lieutenant Daniels: Oh yes. We referred to it in the letter. I have copies of everything still

in my little file. But, oh well, can't win them all. So a lot of us just resigned ourselves.

Okay, he's there. He's got to deal with us. We'll have to deal with him. It's not our place

to carry around picket signs. But he did give a talk—I belong to WOPA, which is Women

Officers' Professional Association. It's set up in Washington now. And I just sort of

started participating within the past year. In fact, I sort of discovered them when I was

doing my letter writing campaign. This was another source for people.

Anyway, they had him—he came to give a speech. So of course we went to that.

We wouldn't miss that for anything. And here's this little guy that looks like a little boy

up on the stage there giving his speech. And of course he opened with a couple of jokes

and, you know—you can see how he got where he did because he's a very perceptive

individual. He even joked about the fact that he was a bit of a masochist for getting up in

front of this audience where he knew he was resented. So he brought it up, right up front.

But I think he did kind of dance around the rest of it and pay lip service. Just from body

language—at least my perception was—he's quite intelligent. A lot of people saw that

and everything. But I just got the feeling that he didn't quite take the issue seriously as far as—well, he knows what he's going to do with us already. And you're not going to change him.

In fact, they were asking him about, "Okay, how do you define combat then? And why can't the women be in it," etc. And see, he's got—his definition of combat is being right in the front lines, somehow, with real access to the enemy, and there was another criterion he used. Basically, based on his memories as a Marine in Vietnam, that's his way of viewing it. And even if you were to say, okay, you can't get beyond that rule with him, there's still a lot of other places, based on his definition, that you could open up. Like the VP, the patrolling with the P-3 aircraft, and that sort of thing. Because I can't fly any VP P-3s. I just have a couple of places I can go in P-3s or else I'd have to learn another airplane, because there's just no place to go. And the thing that's really bad is if I were to get out and go reserves, I can't go reserve VP. I'd have to learn another airplane, because there isn't any reserve squadron that does what I do now—research. I can't even fly there. And the navigators—one of the women that got out last year, she's a navigator and she's with a VP squadron, but she does administrative stuff—a reserve VP squadron. And she enjoys it for the most part. But sometimes they're so hurting for navigators, they get Air Force guys who don't know the airplane. And she knows the P-3 airplane, but she can't fly in it. That's a waste of manpower as far as I'm concerned. But even the VP guys that you talk to, they wouldn't care if women were allowed VP. It wouldn't bother them at all. It would suit them just fine, for the most part. So it's just kind of a waste of manpower. But, you know, everybody, "Well, if this happens—and this carries weapons . . ."

But I don't know. I don't think he sees it as really an issue. His mind is made up about what they can and can't do, and I don't think they're going to change him much.

Sue Sweeney: Do you feel any better about him now that some time has gone by?

Lieutenant Daniels: Well, I feel better in the sense that he knows that's he doesn't have total power. He can't change the fact that women are going to the Academy. He can't change the fact that other things are happening that he may not like. And so we're safe in the sense that we can't go too far backwards. But my only worry is that he can—and he's not going to be there that long in theory but he can adjust the people that work in his office. You know, it's like when a president comes in, he always surrounds himself with people who think the way he does. So that's what I'm afraid he'll leave behind. So even if he leaves, or switches jobs, that he'll leave enough other people behind and enough other things to where it may be harder to gain any ground. And a lot of the guys do like him.

Sue Sweeney: He's got a lot of charisma.

Lieutenant Daniels: Well, he does. You know, you can see that. And certainly he's intelligent. I'm not going to take away from what he does know, and the talents he does have. But I have reservations about someone who—you know, having a boss that doesn't see the potential of part of his employees, and really give them an equal shot. See, my argument has always been why not try everybody out on an individual basis. We used to have this argument at the Academy. I remember we argued this at the table one time. Because at that time we went through, there weren't enough women to really have too many sports. There weren't enough women for certain women's sports, to be on a team or anything. And so, you know, it was a little bit limited.

There was some argument—I don't know, just for grins they brought it up—about the football team. You know, why can't women try out for the football. So the guys' argument was always, "Well, most women couldn't make it."

"Well," I said, "most guys don't make it either, so what's the big deal?" But they never saw that as a point. That wasn't a valid point to them. "Well, you know, women can't do this, women can't do that," and what it'd come down to is most women can't make it. But my point is not all guys make it either. So why not let everybody try and fail or succeed on their own, and not have a preconceived—you know, you wouldn't want to be told, "Now, you can't do this because you have blue eyes, and blue-eyed people can't do this." That's stupid. But they would never see it because it's so ingrained in them, sometimes, about certain people's abilities. It's like people who may be incredibly prejudiced against Blacks, or Jews, or some other groups. In their mind, it's so ingrained that this group of people have this characteristic or can't do that, it's—I'm not sure how you ever change that, other than forcing the experience. The other side of the argument is, "Well, there'd be so many problems." Well, okay, but you don't deal with problems by not facing them. You're going to have problems putting women on ships. You have to face them, deal with them, do the best you can with them. I mean you can't avoid it.

Sue Sweeney: How long do you see staying in?

Lieutenant Daniels: Well, right now I'm looking at perhaps going into some of the space stuff, either going to PG School [Postgraduate School] or trying for the space command down at Dahlgren. Which is actually another shore tour; normally I'd be going back to a squadron. But there're so few squadrons, and the lifestyle—I don't need flight hours. There's not much new that I would be doing at that point because I'm not up for my department head tour yet. So, if they don't give me what I want, I may go ahead and just get out.

Sue Sweeney: You'd still pursue space, but as a civilian?

Lieutenant Daniels: Yeah. Yes, as a civilian somehow.

Sue Sweeney: With so few squadrons open to you, do you have the option to create a billet for yourself, as long as you can justify the manpower?

Lieutenant Daniels: It depends on the detail. The detailers aren't often very sympathetic to the differences. And they're encouraging me to do the things that would check the boxes for aviation command. And I'm not sure if I want aviation command bad enough to where I'd bore myself for all those years. It's like, I don't think I want it that bad. Thanks a lot, but no. So for me, being happy in my job is the most important thing, even if it's not, like, the career move to do. If you're doing a career move you'd have to go back to a squadron and do all this other good stuff. So for me, I don't know. But as far as—I think they're going to have to open VP up for women—the other P-3s—eventually. But I usually, from what I've read of the history of things, things won't really change until they're forced to by the manpower crunch. And I think the oddest thing that we're all looking at now is that, you know, they're looking at manning that 600-ship Navy, and yet each year now they're getting rid of so many officers and so many enlisted.

Another criterion, apparently, has come out for I don't know how many hundreds or thousands of officers they're going to get rid of, and 20,000 enlisted, or some ungodly number. So my question is, "Okay, how are you going to man all these billets? You keep creating more of them, and yet you're taking away people?" Well, they're going to have to realize sooner or later that the women are a resource there, and that they're going to have to open up. But I never see drastic change like that happening until the crunch comes. That's just about how you're going to see it.

Now they did have a bill, you know—I'm a little bit angry at myself, because I got so busy with classes this fall and I didn't do too much about a letter writing campaign for it. It's a Cohen-Proxmire bill—I've forgotten what number—that deals with number of billets for women in several services, as far as opening a few more things up, like opening up some areas on ships for women. I don't even know if it's come up, or I've already missed the whole deal. But, you know, there are some senators that are submitting things like that, sneaking them in here and there, where not a lot of fuss gets made, and hopefully they'll pass. So changes can be made slowly, but the Navy is the slowest.

The Air Force has allowed women to do more things, as far as flying and that sort of business, than the Navy has. And so much of it tends to be because of the ships, because so much is based on ships. And even with the ships, like some of the support ships that they want to put women on that they're not on now, women argue—some of them argue, you know, that we should be able to be on the ships. And the other guys say, "Yes, but they can also become part of the carrier task force." And the guy that's in charge of the carrier task force can say, "That ship has to be a decoy, therefore, it's a target. Therefore, we don't want any women on it."

So it's like, "Well, yes, but that doesn't happen very often." The other thing—I'm sure they've all discussed it—my question is, in the next war, given that it may be a large one—hopefully not—but if it gets to the scale that they all seem to be preparing for, tell me where the battle zones are. Tell me where they're going to draw the lines for combat. I don't think you can, not very easily. That's not a valid argument anymore, I don't think. But, anyway, I think it's just going to take a lot of time. And the other part is there are not that many women in power in the military—or even in other places with military experience. So I think that there is—it'll take that amount of time for certain changes to occur.

Sue Sweeney: Do you see it happening within your career?

Lieutenant Daniels: Not really. I mean, at this point in my career, I'm not sure I'd be interested in going VP. I don't know if I'd really want to change now. It would be such a late start. But it would help a lot if there were some changes to retain women. And one of the biggest problems, especially in areas like aviation and stuff, retention is really pretty bad for them because there are so few places to go, and you just get bored with it after a while. And a lot of women say, "Screw this mess," and just get out and go to the airlines. So now they're real good candidates for the airlines. They get to be the token airline pilot, so that works out well for them. And a lot of people just don't stay. They get sick of it, maybe they have a couple of bad experiences within the squadron and maybe the type of duty they get following, you know. Some of the women from VXN-8 that I know got really terrible orders after they went to VXN-8. And they said, "Hey, I don't need to do this all of my life, to be unhappy." Then they leave.

Sue Sweeney: Have your goals changed since you graduated?

Lieutenant Daniels: I never thought I'd stay in for 20. I've always decided to play it kind of by ear. I never really planned to be—you see for me, going there was practical: it paid for school and it taught me to fly. And I never really planned a career. I always thought, Well, I'll just see how it goes. Because I still had a kind of this space thing sort of in the back of my mind, anyway. I just sort of planned to see how it goes. The career path for women isn't quite as definite for men. I think if you work at it—what we have to do a lot is find—and really it works out that way for guys, too. If you want something really different, you end up having to do a lot of research on your own, then go to the detailer and say, "Oh, I want this particular job. And I know there's a hole there, and I know that I qualify for it," and beg for it. Naval Research Lab, they usually—the detailers have a lot of holes to fill, and they're under a lot of pressure. So they feel obligated to give you the party line about what the next type of duty should be. "Well, we got this, and we got this."

"Well, I don't want those. I want this." So I had to practically beg for NRL.

The guy was telling me, "This is a lieutenant commander billet, and you may not get it."

And I thought, "Put me down for it anyway." Sure enough, no one else wanted it, so I got it. I got what I wanted, but you have to do all the research ahead, sometimes. But that's all right.

Sue Sweeney: What has been your experience with detailers?

Lieutenant Daniels: Well, I just had the one because really after flight school, you just put down things on the preference card. You never really even go to D.C. or anything. You just get stuck someplace and from there, that's—usually after your first tour is when you actually negotiate orders. And maybe go and see your detailer, and that sort of thing. And that might—trying to get to NRL was the only other experience I had. Some of them—I mean, detailers vary—but some of the women I know have had some bad experiences with them because they didn't want, you know, to make a special case out of this particular woman. I think the hardest thing is for some people who are couples. You get to be married, and that gets to be kind of difficult. Because you can't always be stationed in the same place because of the aircraft you fly or whatever. You either put up with a lot of separation or you change your orders and try very hard to get a billet wherever your spouse—one spouse gives up something for the other.

Sue Sweeney: What are you doing now?

Lieutenant Daniels: I'm at Naval Research Lab. I'm assigned there as a pilot, so I fly P-3s again with scientists in the back, but the trips are shorter. It's a shore tour, so there're not as many hours. I fly out of Pax River, but I work up in D.C. at the lab itself. The first year I was there I worked over in the computation division. You can, if they don't need you in the operations section, work in the lab someplace. So I worked in the computation division for a while, doing a little writing for them and getting to use their computers. I didn't know anything about computers—still don't know a lot. I can log on and kind of edit on them. Not too much. But now, over the last year or so I've been working in the space sciences division with a satellite research project, looking at the ionosphere and all that stuff. So I've really enjoyed that, and that's helped me get back on what my real interest is. I've enjoyed the lab.

And the lab has been good because we've had some very good—you know, after VXN-8, which I found to be a rather negative experience, not only for the last CO, but the last couple COs were, in some ways seemed to encourage incompetent lieutenant commander department heads a lot. So from the junior officer point of view, all these lieutenant commanders—we had some good guys but they weren't always the halo boys. The halo boys always seemed to be the real jerks. So we didn't enjoy it there. And coming to NRL, and having a CO and chief of staff and other officers that are very competent, the sort that you actually respect—that's really a nice change. It's been a rather positive atmosphere, a real positive tour. So that's probably the only reason, in fact, that I've even considered staying in. Because after VXN-8, I wanted out. I thought,

"This sucks; I'm leaving." A number of the women—in fact, a number of the JO guys—wanted out just because of some of the ways the squadron was run. They wanted out, too. They didn't like the Navy; it wasn't fun. But NRL has been quite positive so far. It's made me actually consider, "Well, maybe, if things work out, I may even stay in for a little while longer." We'll see how that goes.

Sue Sweeney: What's a day like for you?

Lieutenant Daniels: Well, the local stuff is if you fly a local flight out of Pax—just in and around the area or something, out over the Bay or out into the ocean in the warning areas or something—you drive down and they pay you per diem to do that, and you fly or do whatever you're going to do that day. Other days are the days you work in whatever office you're in. You just go into work basically 8:00 to 4:00, but if you need to work later, it's up to you pretty much. When you fly, the passengers are scientists and other flyers, other aviators. The det—the maintenance people, a lot of the air crew, and there's a couple of officers down there that run the det. And the rest of us are all in D.C., either farmed out at a lab someplace or working in ops, doing the scheduling and all that sort of business.

And then it's the scientists. So they have a number of women scientists here and there, too. Here it seems to be pretty low key, overall. Before me I don't think they had another woman pilot or an NFO, because there just weren't any. There are just not that many P-3 drivers—not because it's anything spectacular. And now, just this last summer, there's a woman navigator now. So it's kind of nice, because I get a bit more of a companion, in some ways, to talk about things. It's pretty low key as far as—they didn't make that much of a fuss when we came in.

Sue Sweeney: How much longer do you have at this assignment?

Lieutenant Daniels: I got a short extension so I have until June. As a matter of fact, I'm trying now to negotiate orders. I'm trying now to get all my stuff together first, and then hopefully get the little blessing on the orders. We'll see what happens.

Sue Sweeney: You mentioned PG School. Are you working on your master's now?

Lieutenant Daniels: No, actually all I've done in the last couple years—I took one of the Naval War College seminars which is graduate credit free; you don't even pay for your books. It's a set of three courses that you either go to the War College in Newport, Rhode Island, to do or you can take one at a time because it lasts the whole year, once a week. It's sort of a seminar deal. They have them at the Navy Yard, and they have them sometimes in different areas where they give the classes. So because it was free, I kind of went for that. And also I took one computer course, but I decided I didn't like the idea of programming as, like, a way to go. I took Pascal [programming language], which is a little different anyway. And last semester I took a calculus course, this past semester, in addition to the seminar, to kind of review since I slept through my original calculus. So I figured, "Well, I need a review now."

Because I'm trying to up my score—you see for PG School they have a number score that summarizes your academic performance—the first number represents your grade point average within a certain range. Next number is representing how many calculus courses with such-and-such a type of grade average. And the last one was for any physics courses with such-and-such a grade average. And so mine, at first, because of the first number—because my overall academic score was rather low—that's why I never got the PG School in the first place. It's only in the last year that I sort of decided that maybe I'd want to, you know, look into getting in there. And maybe I would even stay in the Navy long enough to do all this.

And so the course that I took last year, I got a good enough grade to up the score. And so now I have the minimum criteria to get in, even though I don't have the minimum for the space major that I want. So that's why I took the calculus course, also, to try to bring some of those numbers up.

Sue Sweeney: Do you feel strongly about Monterey, as opposed to a civilian school?

Lieutenant Daniels: Not so much. I mean it's a free school, and they do have the space systems operations, which is not a major you find in other schools so easily. You'd have to try to put something similar together, but I don't know if you could at a regular university. So that's the reason for it. It's because of the particular major I want to try to get. But I'm trying now to get a space subspecialty code based on experience.

Subspecialties can be obtained through school, as well as experience if you can justify that, "Well, I've worked with this, and I've learned this, and I've done this," whatever. So I've drafted the letter being worked on now by my command. Because I'm not a lieutenant commander they won't have to do a board to approve it, they can review the package of information I provide. The office—the subspecialty people—will just have to look at it and decide whether or not I really know anything at all and approve or not. See, if I can get the code, I can perhaps even go to Dahlgren, down to the space command there. And in a way, that might even be better than going to school, if I could even swing doing a shore-to-shore. Because then at Dahlgren, if I decide that I am really unhappy in the Navy and that the space stuff in the Navy isn't really what I want, then I can still get out; whereas, PG School—it you finish PG School you owe them time. You have to be ready to be obligated again. One of the reasons I haven't had much schooling, or that I've always paid for it myself, is because I didn't want to have any obligation. I want to get free and clear to pick.

Sue Sweeney: When is your obligation up?

Lieutenant Daniels: Oh, I could have gotten out last January, this past January. But I always knew that I wanted to complete my tour at NRL because I liked NRL, and I like the science environment. There was no question about that.

Sue Sweeney: Was there ever any sense that if it wasn't working out, the Navy would have let you go without obligation?

Lieutenant Daniels: Do you mean get out free and clear or something? No, I never felt that even though—see, I always felt like if I went through and got the training, then no matter whether I liked it or not, I was going to pay it back. That's just the way you do things. And you hear once in a while maybe a—I don't know so much now, maybe it was more in the past—of a woman getting pregnant and deciding because of that now she wants out. To me I always thought that was a pretty poor excuse if you really owed them for an education or for whatever. I mean you knew that when you signed up, you know. You were an adult when you signed up, so you should be willing—I always thought it was pretty poor, if there were any women—which I don't know of directly during my time—who would get out without a real reason, you know, like somebody's physically unable to carry on their duties. Because I always kind of looked down upon that. And I think, obviously, most of the guys would. And I don't think they—I would hope that they wouldn't especially if it was just a reason like, "Oh gee, I just don't like it here any more."

Sue Sweeney: It seems to me that several of your classmates left the service before their obligation would have been up. I was wondering if it had ever been intimated that you were an experimental class, and that if it doesn't work out, you're not stuck.

Lieutenant Daniels: I never got that impression. Maybe it was because I never had the question in my mind. Maybe it was because I never looked for it anyplace. I never got the impression that we would be able to. I assumed it would be you owe them, and that's life, you know, and that's the way you do it. I never really looked for it, I guess.

Sue Sweeney: What are some favorite recollections of your classmates?

Lieutenant Daniels: If you get me started with anecdotes, I can tell stories all day. I don't know. There are amusing things, some things I've heard and some things I experienced. I can't think of anything particularly. One thing I thought was really funny was, apparently during plebe summer, supposedly it happened in some other company so I don't even know the individuals involved, but one of the women had discovered that sanitary pads made great polishers of shoes and belt buckles, by virtue of what they're made out of.

So when they came around for an inspection, she had this very neatly folded little pad that had the little Brasso stains on it, or whatever, underneath the sink where all the little cleaning gear was. And the upper class thought this was just atrocious, because they weren't quite sure how to deal with looking at this sort of thing. They made a big fuss about it. "Oh, gosh, you can't have this, and blah, blah, blah," because I think they were just too embarrassed. So what had happened was—and this is all rumor, again—but apparently she handed out pads to every one of her classmates in the company, male and female. So the next inspection everyone had one under there, so it was sort of like major protest, and I guess they really couldn't do too much about it.

The other things that were pretty amusing—oh, I remember this—I guess as we were there, whoever of the gods that be who were running the joint probably thought of more potential problems for us women here. It must have dawned on them that we're all wearing these little white uniforms—what if someone had a little accident? So one day we come back to our rooms, and on our desks—just the women's desks—are little white cotton things—pockets—that are made like envelopes with a belt loop kind of thing made through it and some piece of string so you could tie it around your waist. And at first we weren't quite sure what these things were. It's like, "What the hell is this? Did you get one?"

"What're you going to do with that?"

"Looks kind of like a wallet to me."

"We could carry things in it."

Well, it finally dawned on us that I guess they were issuing us little personal device holders or something, you know. And we thought this was a scream. We don't really need these. We're all pretty mature. If we need to do something we all have figured out little ways of getting our stuff to the bathroom without carrying it in our hands down the hall. Good grief, we thought this was a scream.

So apparently, all through the time they worried about these kinds of things. And they had another day where they decided for Sunday formation—we had just gotten our service dress whites issued, I guess, recently—and they wanted us to wear it to a formation. You know, we always form up in Tecumseh Court and other places, where all the tourists—we always felt—because, like the Academy's kind of like a park. We're not allowed to sit on the grass, to walk on the grass, or to hold class on the grass. And we're the squirrels in the park, you see, that the people come to see. We're kind of the entertainment there when we march in. So they thought it would be cute if we all dressed up in our service dress white uniforms, which meant skirts for the women.

Now you see, we had to still jog down the Hall. And if you gave a chow call way down in this wing, and you had to be in Tecumseh Court by such-and-such a time, and you had, like, two minutes to get there, you sprinted. In fact, you couldn't go through one place that was officer territory, and so you had to go upstairs, back down, all around, and this business. I had the chow call or something, you know. And I was like, "Oh, my God, I'm going to have to really haul butt to get there." And the skirt is just this little tiny thing. It's like a rubber band around your knees. So you couldn't run in it. I remember having to go upstairs, I just hiked it up, up the stairs and back down—and you couldn't run worth a darn. And then we got in formation, and you couldn't march because our stride wasn't allowed to be long enough to keep up with the guys.

So we were just always shifting around to keep in step. And after that we never had to wear skirts again in a formation. It finally dawned on them, this doesn't really look too good, you know. But that was a scream. The other thing was they didn't have—there weren't any women officers around, so we had no examples of how certain uniforms had to be worn. Of course the guys were clueless. They didn't know either.

Well, in your midshipman-held publications they had all the regs, uniforms and stuff, and they had these Xeroxed old photos of people in different uniforms. But you couldn't always see the details real well. These were Xeroxed old black and white photos. Well, we'd just gotten service dress whites again. My roommate, Pat, who was Catholic and fairly church-going, she was going to go to the chapel that morning and wore her service dress white. And it's hot in the summer and the Hall was not air-conditioned. And the service dress white consists of a blouse, a white blouse with this stupid-looking bow tie that we all wear—a Bozo tie, we called them—and then the white lined jacket, and a skirt, and nylons, and shoes and all this. And we're looking in the book, and we couldn't see that there was a blouse under there. And the jacket is buttoned high—it's not anything revealing at all—we just couldn't see the picture real well. So it was hot. We put her in the jacket and the skirt and off she went to chapel. She came back a little while later, "Oh, I don't think you can wear the uniform this way. I think we messed up." We learned you did have to wear the blouse and tie. But I thought that was pretty funny. You just didn't have too many examples, and the guys didn't know any better. It was pretty amazing.

I can't remember. These anecdotes always come to mind when you're in the middle of something else, and something reminds you of something.

Sue Sweeney: Did the underclass girls come to you for advice? Did you find you were big sisters?

Lieutenant Daniels: Not a lot. I don't think they came to us a lot. I'm sure it depended on different situations, different individuals. But I think that we were afraid of coming across as being too protective of our fellow women. And they probably were just afraid, so I don't think there was that much of it. I think—I'm hoping that after several years—because also you didn't always have underclass women in your company, because there weren't enough women. So there would always be some companies that didn't have women. Maybe you wouldn't have any for a year or two. I think we had some of '81 or '82, we had a couple of women, but other than that—then there was a time without them, so that they all got moved around.

Sue Sweeney: Was there any sense that you and your classmates had to carve your own niche in the company, while later classes of women were able to hang onto your coattails?

Lieutenant Daniels: There may have been that in some cases in the beginning, because I think anytime someone has suffered, they want to be sure the other person suffers just as much. The same thing with upperclassmen in general: "Well, when I was a plebe, boy, it was tough. And we're going to make sure it's just as tough on you." So that could have been part of it, but I think sometimes, too, there was just a general discomfort.

I think for me, I don't think I really knew how to be a role model because I didn't feel I had it all figured out yet. So I didn't really see it as that much easier, because the place hadn't changed that much. I would only hope now that there's more of a positive tradition of it and everything, that maybe people are a little helpful.

Because they say—you know, you read in business magazines about women who are out forging new places—that one of the things the women have a little difficulty with is reaching back down and helping someone else out. And sometimes because a woman has done it alone so much that she hasn't gained the kind of experience where she's been helped by someone, and therefore she knows how to become a mentor for someone else. So I think it just takes time for there to be more women, and enough of more women where it's more commonplace that they be mentors or mentees at different times.

Sue Sweeney: Would you ever want to be stationed at the Academy as a company officer or instructor?

Lieutenant Daniels: Not now. I have too much of my mind set on pursuing a particular course. And before this, no, I don't think so because I just feel—I think that there's still a lot of resentment. But I could see where, maybe in the future, if I began to feel a little more positive and everything sort of sets back into perspective, that, yeah, maybe for a different kind of tour, I suppose.

I think that's one of the reasons I really would have liked to do a little coaching on the sailing team, because some of the coaches felt like that would have helped a little bit, to have a woman who had been a skipper before, etc., to do that. But I don't know, it's mostly just time that I haven't really had to go back. Between traveling, or else taking classes, there hasn't been any time for that sort of thing at all. And maybe if I were to be back in the area here, I might try to make a point of that in the future, but I don't know. I don't know how much it would help, I mean I can't see it really, like, changing anything in particular. But it might do something.

Sue Sweeney: Are you getting any more nostalgic about the Academy as time goes by?

Lieutenant Daniels: No, not nostalgic as in "Gee, those were the good old days." Certainly not. I don't think I've lost that many brain cells over the last few years. I have enough of the not-so-great memories from there. But I think I'm putting more of it into perspective and chalking more of it up to experience, you know, what I've gained. Trying to look more at the positive side. What did I learn? What did I gain out of it, as opposed to, "I wish they hadn't done this to me," trying to be a little more mature about it, I suppose. And, I think, overcoming whatever the Academy did to the different individuals, whether it lowered their self-confidence, I think most of us are—obviously, you get to the point in life where you're going to have to recover from that and regain your own self-confidence.

Sue Sweeney: Could you recommend it to high school girls? Would you ever be a Blue and Gold officer?

Lieutenant Daniels: I think what I would present, for guys and girls really, but especially for women, for what you're going to have to put up with there—especially if you really want to be career, I mean still a good check in the block. It looks good, people within the Navy—the Academy still has that kind of fraternity, and it is a little bit of a fraternity in the sense of how you may get to know people and keep in touch with them—if you make the best use of it.

But you have to go in there realizing that it's not the same kind of fun and loose environment as a regular school. So it really depends on what you want out of it. If there's another school that offers you better academics in a particular field that you're interested in, you'd probably be better to go to where you're going to learn the most for your particular field. But if you really feel strongly about the Navy, and the sort of, maybe—I don't know how much of an edge it really gets you. That can be debatable. It depends on who you meet sometimes.

But at least on paper—and, of course, the school's free. They pay for you. And you do have access to a lot of things. I think if I hadn't closed my mind and eyes so much while I was there, I probably could have taken more advantage of the other things that it had to offer. So it can be a place—but I wouldn't recruit just blindly, like "Gee, the Academy's a wonderful place for everybody." It's not at all. It's a kind of different environment. If you're willing to put up with the things you do, and give up the freedoms that you give up there as far as the little everyday things, you can benefit. But a lot of people—that may not be the best place for a lot of other people. I think I'd probably try to give them a better view, a balanced view, of what it was like, and then let them choose.

Sue Sweeney: You'd have no qualms if your daughter wanted to go?

Lieutenant Daniels: Oh, no. I mean if she wanted to, and hopefully, she'd have a strong enough personality and everything, she could help herself. That would be great. But only if she's doing it—not for me—but for her own benefit, because that will benefit her life. Sure—have at it, go for it, whatever. But if she wants to be a super engineer, who knows, MIT might be better for her. Or she wants to be an artist, well, the Academy's no place there, so she should go someplace else. It has to make sense with whatever the end goals are.

Sue Sweeney: Sandy, I certainly do thank you for sharing your thoughts.

Lieutenant Daniels: No problem. I always enjoy babbling. I hope it makes sense when you have it all written.

***

Interview with Lieutenant Tina-Marie D'Ercole, U.S. Navy

Place: U.S. Naval Institute, Annapolis, Maryland

Date: 7 May 1987

Sue Sweeney: Thank you for coming to Annapolis, Tina. Would you start by telling me about your family and background?

Lieutenant D'Ercole: I was born in Hamilton, Ohio, on December 14, 1957. I have three older sisters. My mother's originally from Hamilton, and my father's originally from Waltham, Massachusetts.

Sue Sweeney: A civilian family?

Lieutenant D'Ercole: My father was 12 years active duty and 24 reserves—and my mother was in the Navy in World War II. That's how they met. But growing up from my time period, my father was an insurance salesman and my mother worked part-time, for a while, as a secretary. Then she worked as a bank teller. As I got older, she worked as a full-time bank teller.

Sue Sweeney: What did they think of you choosing the Naval Academy?

Lieutenant D'Ercole: They thought it was great for me. I was really lucky because they could have cared less, really, that I was in the first class. They liked me. And when I was at home with my sisters, it was almost like a haven because you didn't get all the questions and all the probes into your life. They just picked up where we left off. We'd go shopping and we'd have fun. And they couldn't have cared less. I think, sometimes, that that's what kept my sanity.

You can't blame people on the outside for being curious, but there was so much light shed on us from the inside that you didn't want it when you got away. So I was really lucky with my sisters. They were just glad that it was something that I wanted to do and they never had any desire to do it themselves—especially my older sister. She's a product of the '60s. She still, to this day, has a problem with me going in. You know, just the fact that I'm in the military.

Sue Sweeney: Did your family visit Annapolis often while you were there?

Lieutenant D'Ercole: My mother and father did, yes. But all three of my sisters are married with children, and jobs. So they came—it seems to me they always came for the June Weeks. Especially my first year. My last year, all but my oldest sister came.

Sue Sweeney: What interested you in the Naval Academy?

Lieutenant D'Ercole: I knew since I was in grade school that I did not want to live and concentrate myself in Hamilton, Ohio. I just thought that there was more to see. Not that Hamilton was bad. It was a neat place to grow up, but I just knew that there was more of a world than Hamilton. I knew I wanted to go to college. And I knew that I didn't want to do just one thing with my life. So, therefore, I saw the Navy offering, you know, a lot of that, because you change jobs every three years, and you travel around. And yet I'd still have a paycheck coming in, so it wouldn't be like I would be out of work. It seemed to all fit. I figured, back in junior high when it started forming in my brain, that, hey, I think I'll join the Navy. I really can't give you a bottom reason for it. I just got it started.

I figured I'd go in NROTC because the academies weren't open. There were two counselors who used to tease me and say, "If the academies open, are you going to go there?" And I'd say, "It's not going to happen in my lifetime."

Sue Sweeney: How aware were you of the Naval Academy?

Lieutenant D'Ercole: My cousin went here. He graduated in the class of 1963. So I knew there was a Naval Academy. I just figured that it would never open. And then, at the end of my junior year, a friend of mine contacted me and said, "You know, if you're really interested in the Navy, why don't you go into the Academy? They're taking applications for women this year."

And I figured, why not? I didn't give it much more thought than that. Growing up with three older sisters, Dad was very supportive of us. He never showed us there were things that we couldn't do. It just never occurred to me that people would have a problem with it. That's how naïve I was, growing up in Hamilton, Ohio, you know. And so I applied—I mean, there's a lot of paperwork, as you well know. But it was easy as far as—the paperwork came in, I filled it out, I sent it back. Then there were the interviews—and that was kind of it.

Sue Sweeney: From whom did you get your appointment?

Lieutenant D'Ercole: Tom Kindness is his name—and he thought it was great. I don't think he's a congressman anymore because he tried for the Senate and lost to John Glenn, the age-old senator from Ohio. It will take a lot, I guess, to unseat him. He thought it was great. I don't know whether, in the beginning, he thought it was a feather in his cap that a female from his district wanted to go. But I got to know him after the fact, and he was really supportive. He thought it was about time that we did this.

Sue Sweeney: How did you prepare yourself once you were accepted?

Lieutenant D'Ercole: Nothing! I guess I got my hair cut shorter, knowing that I'd have to have a short haircut. I can't honestly say that I brushed up on anything, because academics came very easy to me, so I didn't see any reason to take any courses to get myself more prepped for it. Math always came very easy and I took the honors courses in that.

As far as the physical side, I was not ready, mentally, for that. In my high school—when I was in high school—they offered tennis, swimming, basketball, and softball for women. And then you'd have gym class. And I always took part in that, but I really didn't do anything. So I didn't realize that maybe I could have prepared better for the physical part of it. But I didn't have any trouble with physical things. I'd ride my bike. I would go swimming, different things like that. I didn't have any trouble with physical things. It didn't frighten me when I got here. I just had to work to get into better shape. And that was just going through a couple of weeks of summer training.

Sue Sweeney: If the Academy hadn't opened to women in time, where would you have gone and what would you have majored in?

Lieutenant D'Ercole: I still would have majored in math and science—in that area. But I probably would have gone to Miami University of Ohio and joined the NROTC program. I didn't apply to that many other colleges—I don't know why. I guess I figured if the Good Lord wanted me to go to the Naval Academy, I will.

Sue Sweeney: Were you surprised to get accepted?

Lieutenant D'Ercole: I don't know—yes, I was. I can remember the day that the congressman called and said he had nominated me, and now it was a matter of waiting for the acceptance from the Naval Academy. I guess my parents—once again, it's my naïve attitude at the time. I didn't really realize how competitive it can get. I didn't realize that it was—and I still don't know that I feel it is—"special" may be the wrong term, but I just don't feel that people who go there walk on water. I realize that people that go there have a lot of talent, but I also realize that people who go to regular college have just as much talent.

It's just the different things that you want, you know, out of your college life. And so I never looked at it as something to go to my head. I don't know how to describe it. So when I got the notice, I was more than pleased just like anyone would be getting accepted to a college. I felt—I don't know—I felt in my heart that I would come here. I don't know how you should take that. I just knew that I'd come here. I don't know why. There have been things that have happened in my career that I almost knew that they would happen before they did. I just—when I'd hear about it, and I'd think, "Gee, I'd like to do that." And then the doors opened, or the paths came up that I saw that there was an avenue to do that.

Sue Sweeney: Sounds like competence and self-confidence!

Lieutenant D'Ercole: Well, maybe that—and a lot of prayers.

Sue Sweeney: What do you remember of I Day?

Lieutenant D'Ercole: Oh, golly. I can remember that I was looking around at some of these people, wondering about their reactions to me. I—once again, brought up in Ohio—I was never an oddity. So coming here, all of a sudden being treated like one, I thought that this is really a strange feeling. I can remember thinking little things like, "Gee, I'm glad I got my hair cut." I was really hot that day. I had a pantsuit on that I'd just made. I felt dumb because I had to put the T-shirt on over it.

There I was in this pantsuit with this T-shirt over it. I just felt like—and there was one point at which I did start to get nervous. And because I was, when we were carrying our luggage to our rooms—I was very nervous—the plastic handle on my luggage kept slipping out of my hand. So I kept falling behind, and I felt really stupid. All of a sudden I started thinking that—not that I had made a mistake—but that people were going to think I was weird or something. You know that when you're 18 years old, a lot of things go through your head.

Sue Sweeney: Do you remember being conscious of the media?

Lieutenant D'Ercole: To a point I do. I remember them being in the background that day. I can remember the reactions of the guys to them. And I can remember thinking in my brain, "Don't these guys understand we don't like it either?" But I'm not a person to be deliberately rude, so I wouldn't be deliberately rude to the guys—and yet, I wouldn't be deliberately rude, at that point, to the press. By the time I got to be a senior, it wasn't that I was rude during the interviews, I would just refuse the interviews. Because I thought, "Wait a minute, this is my life, too, and I've had it!"

Sue Sweeney: How often were you asked to do interviews?

Lieutenant D'Ercole: As a senior, you mean?

Sue Sweeney: Throughout the four years.

Lieutenant D'Ercole: There seemed to be a number of times where they would ask me, quite honestly, "Would you give this interview," and I would say, "No, I really don't want to." I don't know if they focused in on a few of us. Maybe I answered the first questions correctly. I found that in answering questions from the press, the less specific you can be, the better. And that's only because they seem to—it wouldn't even be that they'd misquote you; they'd just take a few words of what you said, put it into their own sentence, and it sounded like dirt. And too often, I can remember classmates taking the interview, you know, taking the newspaper and shoving it at you and saying, "What the hell is this? How could you say this? I thought we got along great." I remember thinking, "If this is what the press does, I don't want any part of it. I just don't want any part of it."

Sue Sweeney: Did the Academy urge you to do interviews?

Lieutenant D'Ercole: Well, the Academy was kind of caught between a rock and a hard spot because were they to take a hard stand and say, "No, leave the women alone, they don't want to be interviewed," I'm sure the press would rip them apart for that. So they toned it down. I'm sure it was our senior year where the commandant promised us that we only had to do one interview—unless you were willing to do them. Normally it was for the paper from your hometown, but you were only required to do one.

And so I wouldn't do more that time. The only other time I remember doing an interview was plebe summer when I was on Plebe Detail. And I felt like—it's funny, I sat through the same interview that Sandee Irwin was in. And Sandy and I differed in our opinions about a few things. And one of them was what to say in an interview. I sat through the same interview, in the same amount of time, and we answered the same questions. My answers were a little more vague, and all her answers got in the interview. The only part that got in the interview from me was when they took the time to meet the guy that I was dating and they talked to Greg and myself.

I had warned Greg beforehand, "Please be very general in your answers. Not that I'm old hat at this, but they'll rip us apart—they'll look for something because we date each other and live in the same hall." And they did take out of context some of the things he said, so that after the interview he looked at me and said, "I didn't mean it that way."

Sue Sweeney: This was in the *Washington Post*?

Lieutenant D'Ercole: Yes, naturally. I said, "I know you didn't mean it that way, but this is what they do." You didn't do a bad interview and don't feel bad. Some of our classmates reacted to him for some of the things he said. It was said in innocence—just kind of answering the question.

Those were the things that got me angry. I can remember thinking that none of our classmates understand that we hate interviews just as much, but I felt like it was also our responsibility to, kind of, calm the press. Okay, they want an interview, so give then an interview, but don't give them anything that reflects badly on the group.

Sue Sweeney: How did your answers differ from Sandee Irwin's?

Lieutenant D'Ercole: Sandee and I were really close friends our first year here. We didn't really have a falling out, but we just changed because of our experiences here, and how they affected us. We just kind of had different philosophies of life. Not that she was wrong and I was right, or vice versa, but we just changed. She—I don't know, this is just personal opinion—for example, when they did an interview, and they would ask questions about how do the guys react to you in the Hall. Well, I would say to you that guys prior to us coming here knew women as their girlfriends and their sisters and their mothers. And now they had to react in a different way—and that I think sometimes that's frightening to them. And sometimes, it's just as frightening to us. But it's a learning experience and you had to work through that.

She would take it one step further to maybe use an example. There's this one guy that I was close to—we used to sit up at night and talk. I can remember in the article—I can't remember exactly what was said—but they kind of twisted it. And the guys, then, were personally hurt. It's like, "What do you think we are, babies? You have to babysit us—mother stuff?" You know, mother and apple-pie stuff. So I just found that I would never give specific examples. I just didn't like the attention that it drew to us. And that's just personal.

Sue Sweeney: What memories stick out from plebe year?

Lieutenant D'Ercole: Plebe year . . . I can remember—I have to preface this with the fact that I'm a very idealistic person. And that comes from growing up, I think, in a fairly sheltered environment. I grew up—my parents were one of the couples that didn't get divorced. A lot of my friends had divorced families. My family seemed to always get along. I don't remember arguing, so I think I had—and still do—an idealistic view of the world that people can get along, that people can work through things.

So when I would meet up with a—what I would call a dirtball—I would just make them not exist in my mind. I would concentrate on the really positive people that I met throughout plebe year. You met up with guys who liked you, or the guys who didn't, or the guy who couldn't care less. I always concentrated on the guys who liked us—you know, were supportive of us. The guys who didn't like us, I just stayed away from. I figured I'm not going to waste my time on somebody like that. They'll either change by my example that I set, or they'll just go through life feeling this way—and that's fine.

Sue Sweeney: How difficult was it to just ignore people who weren't in favor of women being there?

Lieutenant D'Ercole: Well, I mean especially as a plebe, if they're going to pay attention to you, they're going to pay attention to you. I was successful—it's all how successful you're going to be in your own brain. There were men who came up to me at the end of plebe year and said that I had made quite an impression on them, or that maybe their feelings had changed somewhat. Or maybe they still felt that women shouldn't be in combat, but I proved to them that women could, in fact, do the Academy, and perform even better in a supportive role because of the things that went on here.

There were the guys who kind of wavered, depending on the crowd they were with. And those were the ones that I termed—they just don't really care. They'd just take on the colors of the people they were with. And some of those people I can remember coming up and saying to me—either they'd apologize for something they said before, or I had shown them that, you know, women can work just as hard as men. I don't know. I certainly wasn't out to prove anything to them. I'm more a person that, I figure, examples are better than words. I don't like angry confrontation, I guess, because I didn't grow up in that kind of environment. I just think it doesn't get you anywhere.

I can get really angry, and really say things that are mean. In junior high school I recognized that I can have a pretty wicked tongue. After I had hurt a friend of mine, I realized that I could never take the words back. No matter how hard I tried to say I'm sorry, it wasn't going to change anything. I thought, what I have to change is my reaction to things. I've got to change that about myself. So I work on that. And, I think, I became more of an extreme—I keep my mouth shut even more, rather than let the words come out of my mouth that can really pierce right through someone.

So I found that to be the same thing here, where I just figured, okay, they're going to say these things, and I'm just going to go on with my life. At least in my mind, and in my close friends' minds, they'll know that I wasn't involved in that, or that I didn't handle it that way, or that I did work and passed the stuff in the men's times. That was my goal.

When I realized that they did put different physical standards on women—and that was always the first thing the guys would fight at. "Well, if we're equal, well why don't you do the same thing?" It was just the opposite for the women. The majority of women didn't have a strong sports background, so they too needed time to catch up. Once we could accomplish the requirements, then tighten the requirements and see what we can accomplish. So, you know, you had to explain to them, give us time to get going here first—to come up to speed and then change the requirement. But early on I got it in my head—and that just comes after four years, I guess. By golly, I'm going to pass it in the men's time, so that I can look at them and say, "Now, wait a minute. They may have had these standards, but I passed them within your time." That was just a sword I took on myself. Not that I got anything for it.

Sue Sweeney: Except well-earned self-respect! Were many of the other women able to meet the men's standards?

Lieutenant D'Ercole: I honestly don't know. We graduated with 55, and I do know of some who just were really physically fit and could do it. And some who could have done it, but were so intimidated by the time we were seniors of, say, going out and running a mile, that they would just be sick. I mean physically sick when they had to go run the mile. I'm sure it affected some of the guys the same way, but a guy is less apt to show it because guys aren't allowed to. That's the way it is. I think we were more lucky in that if we showed it, people would react, but at least we were still allowed to, you know. One of those things—the age-old, "Women are allowed to cry, and men aren't."

Sue Sweeney: What do you remember about the attitudes of officers and professors?

Lieutenant D'Ercole: I found that the officers were honest in that, "Okay, I don't necessarily agree with this, but I'm a naval officer, and these are the rules now, and therefore, I'll go on from there." And I respected that attitude. There were a couple civilian professors that I could have smacked. Had I not been a midshipman, I probably would have.

Sue Sweeney: What reaction were you getting?

Lieutenant D'Ercole: Oh, very negative. One in particular—I had him three times a week. I was the only woman in the class—he would always take five minutes out of the class to talk about women. And I can remember thinking, you know, "It's only an issue if you make it one. Would you just shut up and teach your class?" To this day, I cannot stand the subject he taught. I have no interest in it, and that disinterest is partly due to the instructor's influence. The guys were starting to notice his behavior. If the guys notice it, then you know that you're not halfway off your rocker. Finally one day we got a test back—I was just livid—I probably should have turned him in. But that's where I still have a tendency to hold back. I felt if you turned him in, it would be the same old reaction from most of the people, that it's just a woman crying wolf, and I thought I've got to deal with it on my own.

Sue Sweeney: What did he do?

Lieutenant D'Ercole: He passed this test back and had just really ripped apart my paper, which I agree with—the fact that some of the things were wrong. But I was comparing with the guy behind me, and we had worked the same problem the same way. I got no credit, and he got 75 percent credit. So I went up to the professor afterwards, and I asked him, you know, why I hadn't at least received partial credit, because I had worked it correct up to the point of the last two lines—I forget the ultimate answer.

And his first reaction—he got angry—and the first thing that came out of his mouth was, "Just because you are a woman doesn't mean you are going to get away with getting a better grade." And I looked at him and I said, "I don't think that's the issue here." And that made him even angrier. And I can remember just looking at him, and my classmate looked at me and he said, "This is worthless."

I just walked away from him. I got a C in the course. The only reason I got a C was because—I mean, I didn't try on the final at all. I thought, "This man's sick—I don't care if I flunk. I don't like this man. I don't like this course. I have not learned anything—I ought to flunk." You know, that type of reaction. I got a C out of the course only because I think that he must have realized—or someone talked to him, or something—because I was ready to take my classmate and go to the dean and say, "This man is so unsatisfactory, it's ridiculous."

Sue Sweeney: Do you care to say who he was?

Lieutenant D'Ercole: I'd rather not.

Sue Sweeney: Was he considerably older?

Lieutenant D'Ercole: Oh, he's older. Then it seemed like the older ones did kind of—it was hard for them. They were used to teaching all guys and I guess they looked at it as a slap in their face, too. I don't know.

Sue Sweeney: Do good experiences with professors stick out in your mind?

Lieutenant D'Ercole: Yes. That's the thing. No matter what question you ask me, I can give you examples of the good, the bad, and the ugly. And I tend to concentrate—for instance, the only time I think about that previous course and professor is when I'm asked very specific questions. Otherwise, I never think of that man because I concentrate on the ones who I liked, who were supportive, and who I learned a lot from. I'm not going to look back on four years of my life and remember all the bad. That's just the way I am. I prefer to look at the positive. I met a lot of neat people here, you know, mids, officers, and civilians. And that's what I'd rather focus on.

Sue Sweeney: Does anyone in particular stand out?

Lieutenant D'Ercole: Professor? That's a tough one. Professor Buikstra taught me a lot as far as mathematics goes. He was a fun teacher to have. I don't know if I'd call him the best. I think the class I enjoyed the best was a psychology class—I guess it was our youngster year—and we had an instructor named Lieutenant Brunza. His classes were really exciting for me because he discussed the really hard issues. He got down to the cold, hard facts of—I guess the issues between men and women. And the guys in the class just reacted positively. It's almost like they wanted to discuss it too, but in a mature light, rather than how sometimes—like when James Webb's article came out in our senior year.

The first day that stupid thing came out, that's the only thing that was taught in any of the classes. And I felt like, "Oh, I don't want to go to class today. I don't want to hear about this freaking article again." It was discussed in a very, I think, immature way, taking things that he said and saying, "Oh yeah, this is the way it is, isn't it?" It just created a lot of hate with this thing. So I found in the psychology classes, where they discussed it on a much more mature level, and looked at things a little differently, I really enjoyed that. Because it helped me—at least the classes that I had the guys that were in those classes were also very up, so it helped me understand that kind of thing. And that was why I always felt I needed to be here, in order to understand some of the things that went on. You could understand them better—because if you don't do that, you could become pretty bitter.

Sue Sweeney: In your opinion, did James Webb have any valid arguments?

Lieutenant D'Ercole: No. I really didn't like it. I thought it was a really disjointed article. I've had a lot of other people read it even before he was nominated to be Secretary of the Navy. And even some of the men who have read it were appalled at what was written. Don't decide for me what I want to do with my life. Don't do that. He has no right to do that. I don't know. I just felt it was really more an ax to grind for him than a well-written, substantiated article. That's probably also through my eyes, because I read it.

Sue Sweeney: What are your thoughts on women in combat?

Lieutenant D'Ercole: Same as they are for men. It frightens the heck out of me—both for men and for women. I don't like to see anyone go to combat. I think that because of the lack of training, women find a lot of—for instance, in the Army, where you're on the ground, backpack and that type of stuff, I think women could be trained to handle this kind of stuff just like small men are trained. I don't think it's an impossibility, but I think that the motivation has to be there inside the woman, and that's where I draw the line. If a woman is motivated and willing to give it her best shot, then let her try it. Otherwise, she's not going to do a good job. She's not going to pull her load, and then I think you have a legitimate concern.

I don't like to see anyone go into combat and I recognize that with the training that American men have, they are protective of women. And I appreciate that in my personal life. I appreciate that. I feel safe with my fiancé when I go somewhere, and I like it that he opens the door for me. But out of politeness, sometimes I open the door for him if I'm the first to the door. I mean it's not that we have arguments over it. So I know there's a lot of social things that men and women learn that would have to be changed. When they come with the argument that, "What if you were a prisoner of war and they'd rape women?" Well, that's true, but you can get raped walking through the center of Washington, DC. And I see people dealing with solutions for that, you know. So it's a hard thing—hard issues. I'm not saying that—I'm not a women's libber in that I think men and women are equal completely. I don't use the term for men and women, because there are things that I can do easier, and things that he can do easier. But that doesn't mean one or the other is less equal.

And, once again, with the attitude and the background I had growing up, my father's point was always if you're going to do it, do it well. Be honest with yourself. If you can't do it, then let somebody else who can do it better. And that's kind of the way I feel about it. Combat—it's a hard thing, an ugly thing. But it is for men, too. I don't like to see the men dismembered, or getting bombed, or shot at, or anything like that.

Sue Sweeney: Do you think the laws about women in combat should have been changed before women were admitted to the service academies?

Lieutenant D'Ercole: I think not. I used to think that they should have—that Congress did it backwards. And I guess there's still a part of me that does think that way, because you come here as a female—and it is to train combat officers here. But if in fact it should be how James Webb's article put it, where it's to train men morally, mentally, and physically to be officers—combat officers, whatever—then by golly, don't have any people who have waivers. And there are plenty of men in prior classes who went Supply Corps, who went cryptology, who went intel. If it's going to be that, then make it completely that. Don't give me this stuff that we can't send women here and have them go into the restricted-line field, because there are men who did not go surface line, aviation, Marine Corps, or submarines. And I found, for me, that not only do I have a better understanding of what the men need to do for their career, but since I experienced a lot of it, I am better able to support them in the jobs that I do.

When they say, "The fleet doesn't need that," or "Well, this is what the fleet does need," I can go fight for it or use the correct channels. Because one aspect, if you want to look at it that way for women, for instance, they can be in the Washington, D.C., area for more than one tour. So they can get to know the ins and the outs and what you need to know to get things done. And they're not coming back in and learning, when they're a commander, how to deal with politics in Washington, D.C. And that can be an asset. So, I don't know—the training that I went through here—the only thing they did not let us do is go on submarines. There isn't anything here that a woman couldn't do—and that a woman shouldn't do. And that's just how I feel about it.

Sue Sweeney: How often does this discussion come up?

Lieutenant D'Ercole: Well, where I work now, the people are so, so mature. I just feel like I live in a fantasy world again. They're aviators—most of them are—or they were aviators, and now they're aviation duty officers or engineering duty officers. I work in Space Systems. Nobody's been to space, or is space-qualified. So it's just not an issue. It's just not brought up. I do my job. They do theirs. It's great, you know. The only time it's brought up is very rarely with close friends—they'll tease. And then, you know it's only teasing. Where I find it's brought up is when I go to a Naval Academy function, and there are old Naval Academy graduates. And depending on his attitude, tone of voice, or whatever, that's when I determine in my mind, is it worth talking to this person or do I not want to risk a fight. Are they going to hear what I have to say, or are they going to look at me politely and not let the words sink in.

If I feel like they're listening to me, then I truly listen to them. I don't have a problem with their own opinions, but I have a problem when their opinions stop me from doing something, I guess. You know, I mean, there are some things that—and I have to fight it with myself, too—there are some prejudices or opinions that you grow up with, that you've got to allow the other human being to try or to show whatever they want to do with their life. I can't force my opinions on some one else. I can have them, but I can't force them.

Sue Sweeney: Are you disappointed with the pace at which attitudes are changing?

Lieutenant D'Ercole: Sometimes. Depends on my mood. Sometimes I think it changes so slowly. It's like, "Wait a minute, it's been how many years now? Come on, now, women and men are not a new thing. Let's grow up here." And other times I get surprised that— for instance, each duty station that I go to, it seems that more and more people are accepting that it's not an issue. You go, do your job, and go home.

Sue Sweeney: Were you able to count on emotional support from your female classmates?

Lieutenant D'Ercole: No. And the only reason I say that is I think the class of '80 weren't intended to. We're closer now than we ever were here, because we tended to stay with our company. I found—I was in 21st Company and moved to 2nd Company. When I got to 2nd Company, I found the guys were very supportive and they liked us. When I got to know the girls in my company—and there was one other girl I got to know really well. She was over on the other side of the Hall, in 29th Company.

Other than that, you knew who they were, but we really tended to stay away from the other women. We hated when they'd have an all-women meeting or something because it brought attention to us. And the last thing that we needed was attention brought to us, mainly because of the press, and things like that—the attention that was brought to us was negative, and what we needed was some positive attention. We were very much afraid, I think, overall as a group, to get together. I mean it was like pulling teeth to get us all together for a group picture the day we graduated—we felt that if the photographer can be here at such-and-such a time and take a picture, then we'll do this, but we just didn't even want to be there then, and that's something to remember. It did get taken and, you know, I never did get a copy of it. We were supposed to. Some of the girls got copies of it. I don't know what it looks like for my follow-on address may have not been correct.

Sue Sweeney: One of your classmates mentioned she thought the Academy intentionally limited interaction between the women. You would agree?

Lieutenant D'Ercole: Well, that's true. And I think that their intent was that it was important to put us into the brigade. And I don't know how you would have balanced it, if they were to get the women together at times in order to have that support group. A lot of time when the women got together it turned into a bitch session. And, you know, you need that also, I think, just to find out that other people are having some struggles, too. But it never seemed to have the other side of the coin, where you were able to say that, "You know, I do have a friend or I do have a group of friends." And I think that the Naval Academy did it correctly as far as women are concerned. I don't know now that having a company of women—all that would have done was give the class of '80 35 companies of men and one company of women. I don't know that that's the answer. I think that what they did was good.

Sue Sweeney: Why did you switch companies?

Lieutenant D'Ercole: I switched companies because the company I moved to needed a roommate for one of the women. The Academy really tried to keep at least two women to a room and two of the same class. They wanted to make them two and two. And I was still—the company I came from, there were still three women there. I figured the guys who were my friends in the 21st Company would remain my friends, then the others—I could get along with.

Sue Sweeney: Who initiated the change?

Lieutenant D'Ercole: She approached me, actually, the one approached me.

Sue Sweeney: One of the women in 2nd Company?

Lieutenant D'Ercole: She said that she needed a roommate and she could set it up, so I said yes.

Sue Sweeney: Were men allowed to change companies?

Lieutenant D'Ercole: Well, the thing is—that's where, in a way, the guys were a little understanding. A guy could easily switch within a company, and that was allowed. I mean, if it got bad, I suppose anyone could. So they were kind of understanding in that. There weren't many people who could switch with you.

Sue Sweeney: You were a cheerleader, which counts as a sport. What other sports did you play here?

Lieutenant D'Ercole: Cheerleading only counted for one semester. Gee, I tried a lot of different things. Since I grew up in an atmosphere where there really wasn't that much for women, I liked having choices. I did a lot of intramural things: tennis, badminton, and running. My last year here I did the track team, because I found that that was kind of the niche I wanted and enjoyed. And although I didn't have the background to be a good competitor and really bring the team into first place, I talked to the coach and said, "You know I would be a senior on the team and therefore I could get some leadership experience, and I could offer, you know, 100 percent dedication to the schedule," and told him that my personal goal was to run a sub-six-minute mile.

And he said, "Great. I'll get you the personal goal if you'll support the team." So I said fine, and I worked my senior year with the team. I love baseball. I grew up going to baseball games with my dad. So I was baseball manager.

Sue Sweeney: For the men's team?

Lieutenant D'Ercole: For the men's team, yeah. And I enjoyed that. I traveled with the team. They used to call Coach Duff and me "Beauty and the Beast." The guys were really good.

Sue Sweeney: Did the men treat you differently when you were on the road with them at civilian schools?

Lieutenant D'Ercole: Oh, yeah. All of a sudden I got a lot of attention. And that's where it was hard, because my classmates were really jealous of that.

Sue Sweeney: Your female classmates?

Lieutenant D'Ercole: No, male classmates might have been jealous of the attention I got from the upper class on the team. One of the pressures was often having male classmates interpret the attention we got from upper class as different . . . even though they too were receiving attention.

Sue Sweeney: Did the ball players revert when you got back to Bancroft?

Lieutenant D'Ercole: Yes.

Sue Sweeney: They were civil—just not as friendly?

Lieutenant D'Ercole: They were civil, but not as friendly, yes. It is a hard thing. Let's face it, 18 to 22 years of age, if you're at a regular college, for a guy or girl, you're going to be going out and dating. There's not going to be anything taboo—who you can't talk to or anything. And rightly so. You know, they had the rules that you didn't date the upperclassmen or anything like that, but you also didn't have to treat them like dirt. And not that everybody did but—I mean, it was a struggle for both the guys and the girls. If they'd been regular guys, you'd have gone out and dated. And whether people want to admit that those feelings exist or not, they do exist. You see yourself through other people's eyes.

Sue Sweeney: What are your memories of socializing here?

Lieutenant D'Ercole: I didn't. I hung around my classmates. I did, and found that many could really be friends. I have many close friendships, and I value them. If anything, that's really one of the assets of going here, because you really find that you can be friends. I didn't party much or anything. I kind of stuck close to my sponsors—you know, we have sponsors here. I was lucky with the sponsors I got.

I had them all four years, and so I tended to spend hours there. I sew and I do crafts, and I found I could kind of slip into the other world when I was at my sponsors', come back here and do the professional things, physical things, and the academics things. I needed a break from that. I didn't find my break going out and getting drunk all the time. I'm not a heavy drinker at all. I'm practically a non-drinker. Not that I don't like it, I just don't drink much. So I'd go to my sponsors' and kind of slip into my other little role where I'm creative and make things and spend time by myself.

Roger [then-fiancé, now husband] says I analyze too much. He says he's never met someone who analyzes as much as me. But it really helped me when I was here to understand them and me. Otherwise I think I probably wouldn't have taken the time to get involved with another person.

Sue Sweeney: Are you engaged to the guy who talked you into doing the *Washington Post* interview?

Lieutenant D'Ercole: No. This guy went to a regular college. He's an NROTC graduate of Illinois Institute of Technology in Chicago. He's one year ahead of me.

Sue Sweeney: How difficult do you imagine it will be to synchronize your two careers?

Lieutenant D'Ercole: Not difficult at all.

Sue Sweeney: Do you intend to make the Navy a career?

Lieutenant D'Ercole: Yes.

Sue Sweeney: Are you surface line?

Lieutenant D'Ercole: No, I'm general unrestricted line, and my specialty is Space Systems.

Sue Sweeney: When you were at the Academy, did you consider other possibilities—air?

Lieutenant D'Ercole: Yes. The first three and a half years here I wanted to be a naval aviator because I figured that was the way to do it. I didn't want to go surface line, and submarines weren't an option, and I knew I didn't want to be a Marine Corps officer, so that narrows it down. And since the mission of the Naval Academy is to train officers of the line, I figured that that was my only option.

Then I realized—somewhere in the back of my mind, somebody said to me, "Tina, you go through this life once—what do you really want to do? Do you want to do what everybody else thinks you should? Do you want to stay on the bandwagon and do what line officers are supposed to do? What do you, as an individual, want to do? Where can you be an asset to the Navy?"

And suddenly I realized that the career path for aviators and surface line officers for women stops at lieutenant. And I thought the Navy's going to be stuck with me longer than lieutenant rank, because I want to stay in as a career. Now, going on that premise, what designator in the Navy offers me a career? Well, I could go intel, but I didn't know much about intel. You don't learn much about it. They do maybe now, they go though a whole thing for the women, and they started to with us, they realized that they needed to, because they only took five aviators and five women into the Women in Ships Program, and I guess five or six Marine Corps women—and all of the rest of us had to do something. So I didn't know much about intel. I really didn't know much about cryptology, and I wasn't trained to be a Civil Engineer Corps person, so I thought, what can I do?

And so I saw this general unrestricted line, and at that point I saw it as being really kind of disjoint, but yet I knew that they were trying to come up with a career pattern, and I knew that I could make it through admiral if I remained a general unrestricted line officer. I knew that I didn't want to keep fighting the same old battles.

When you get to lieutenant as an aviator—and a lot of my friends are feeling this right now, the ones who are still in—what are they going to do? They just don't have anywhere to put them. And I think, to me, I didn't want to always have those frustrating feelings. You can be the one—the real good one—that the Navy will use as an example and say, "Yes, this is what we're doing with the women." But until it truly changes, you've really got to fight to be that one they use as an example. And I thought, "Do I really want to do that with my life? What do I want to do?" And I thought, "As soon as I answer that question for myself, then I think I'll be happier."

And I figured I'd go general unrestricted line and I would get as technical as I could. I knew that in general unrestricted line, my sellable point would be to get as technical as I could. And I knew I could do that, because I'm math-oriented. So that was kind of my dream. I thought I want to do a career in the Navy, and I want to be an asset to the Navy. And I don't want to fight the same old battles. Somebody else can do that who's more motivated. And there are women who are more motivated for that. And I respect them for that.

I kind of, I guess, wanted a little more freedom to design my own career, and I've been able to do that, getting more technical and then finding out about the space engineering curriculum. That opened up, and I graduated in the second class of the Space Engineering Program, electrical engineering with a space systems concentration. I'm in a field where no one's space-qualified. It's very challenging and very technical. And the Navy is not only getting the benefit of the education that I earned at the Naval Postgraduate School in Monterey, but I'm also using many things from here. And they're using—all the time and money that they've invested in me, they're using, I can say, 100 percent in this job. And I think that that's great. You know, I think the Navy has really benefited from the time and money they invested in me. And they have to do this for the guys.

The guys that I graduated with who were aviators went back to fly. They're not using that education at all, as far as Postgraduate School. They are using their flight school education. And that's the way it goes in the Navy. But for me as a general unrestricted line officer, the Navy is getting 100 percent of what they invested in. And I think that that's really good. And I think that's a good checkmark for the Navy.

Sue Sweeney: You've carried your weight—and it seems you follow a pattern of not taking the easy way out.

Lieutenant D'Ercole: No, a lot of people would think that general unrestricted line *is* the easy way to do it, you know. The feeling of the general unrestricted line community, especially when I first entered it, was that's where all the dregs go—that's where all the dropouts go. If a man doesn't make it in aviation, he goes to surface line. If he doesn't make it there—but he still has a commitment. They often make him a general unrestricted line officer and he completes his commitment. But it's not that way with the women. It's very competitive. They're suddenly realizing that, but it's taken a long time.

Sue Sweeney: What was your reaction when the new Secretary of the Navy was announced?

Lieutenant D'Ercole: My heart just broke when I realized—I guess to me it told me, on one hand in a very subtle way, on the other hand in a very loud way—how those men up there really think. And that disappointed me—that *really* disappointed me—because I just thought that we'd come so far. And that they would consider a man who very openly has the feelings he does really hurt me. I really struggled for about two months. I had given all that I have professionally to the Navy. Not that the Navy chooses the person for that position, but I've given the Navy 100 percent.

And to me, to have those men choose him and put him in that position, really made me have to reevaluate myself, because I thought I don't want to give them anything anymore. If anything, I want to get out of the Navy. My first reaction was I will get out of the Navy—this angers me, this is not fair—you know, that syndrome. And I was very angry about it, and then I realized that I didn't need to cut off my nose to spite my face. The bottom line coming through all that—you know, getting over the anger and getting over all that stuff and also trying to give benefit of the doubt that people can learn, people can change—in my heart I was so very disappointed because that really just tells me I was wrong. People haven't changed very much.

Sue Sweeney: Do you have a sense of how your male peers feel about it?

Lieutenant D'Ercole: Oddly enough, they were just as disappointed—maybe not for the exact same reasons. I was just at a wedding this past weekend, and I was sitting with some of my classmates and somehow his name came up. And their reaction—I was just going to be quiet, and I did essentially remain quiet, just agreeing now and then—but they were just as disappointed. And that made me feel good inside. I thought, "Well, maybe these older men are scarred—not capable of change, or in their mind they think they're not capable of change. But at least my classmates have learned. At least the guys my age are more human, I guess." And they are. I think they're more feeling and more understanding, and they're much more giving and able to take people for who they are, rather than man, woman, Black, White.

Sue Sweeney: It must have been a blow.

Lieutenant D'Ercole: Oh, it was. It really was. You know, I was talking to my parents and they knew—both of them knew—exactly how serious I was. That when my commitment's up, I was going to get out of the Navy. And I wrote to 25 senators, congressmen, and I got two answers back. Only two. And it was the first time in my Navy career that I really took any action. Usually I feel life is cyclical, you know, and you've just got to work through this. For every three steps you take forward, there's going to be a step back. Maybe I'm too easygoing normally. But I reacted to that. It really hurt me, personally. Because that article he wrote was about *us*—me. And I just—he'd have to do so much convincing to me that he's changed. And he doesn't give a damn about me. He doesn't, you know. He could care less that some lieutenant is troubled that he is Secretary of the Navy. And I refused even to read his books. I've never read his books, because I know some of that money will go to him. I just won't do it. So, yes it did, it hurt, because it shows what they think. And if it was the easy way out for them, if he was the choice for them, then my respect is even less.

Sue Sweeney: Were you surprised by the length of time it took for him to be approved?

Lieutenant D'Ercole: You know what I was surprised on—I remember reading this one article—I read it and then I was so angry when I read it, I essentially forgot it. It said something about, "After the hearings they were so—the senators and congressmen were so impressed by his answers, that they were all 100 percent backing him," or something like that. I just got nauseous, you know, it was like—I have never felt so adamant toward something that might harm my career. One of the reasons I went in the Navy is I think this country is really neat and it's given me a lot. It's given me a lot of opportunities. And I know nowhere else in the world would I have the opportunities that I do. That's why I like being in the Navy—it's kind of to give something back to it.

When they chose him, I just thought—it's like a few years ago when they were voting on a raise for the military, and one of the congressmen had the audacity to say something about, "If the military were really dedicated, they wouldn't worry—or you wouldn't have to use money to entice them to stay in." But, you know, you've got to live somehow. I recognize that the job I do, I could maybe make three or four times as much on the outside—hands down. I could be hired tomorrow and make three or four times as much, but I'm not in it for the money.

And when I think of it—not to sound self-righteous—but when I think of my dedication and a lot of my classmates' dedication to the Navy and the United States—and then to have people like that get voted in? Or to have the audacity to say that we're not that dedicated, or we're taking the easy way out or something? I think, "Come on, where is *your* dedication? Can't *you* give some back?" And in the letter that I wrote I said, "Respect goes both ways. It's got to go up the chain of command and it's also got to go back down the chain of command." It's very hard for me to work for people who I know do not respect me back. And that was the bottom line when I was discussing it with my parents. I don't feel any respect back. So then I had to go through the old, "Okay, but you've got to be happy with your actions." No matter about all this other dirt that's filtering down you've got to be happy with yourself and your actions. And that's kind of how I dealt with it.

Sue Sweeney: Tell me what you've done since graduation.

Lieutenant D'Ercole: I went to the Naval War College and I was assistant to the dean of administration there. They didn't know what to do with an ensign. The next closest rank was commander on this staff. So I created my own job. I knew, having gone here, that I needed to get leadership experience. So there were enlisted people attached there, and I created a division. And I was lucky enough to work for a captain there who—he had spent all his life on ships, and I was brand new. He was like, "What am I going to do with this female ensign?" So he essentially let me take the ball and run—many, many different projects. He was there if I fell on my face, or to give me a few pointers, but otherwise, "If you can do it, do it." And he was great to work for, because he did allow me to just run the place. It was great. And I worked with budgets and stuff like that.

From there I went—just for a short period, I went out to Hawaii. It was the worldwide military command and control system. It's a joint effort, consisting of all the services. It was very computer oriented —programming and computer stuff. And from there I went to the Naval Military Personnel Command, and I was a detailer.

Sue Sweeney: The dreaded detailer!

Lieutenant D'Ercole: That was an experience. And I'm glad I had it young in my career. It was really different—one of the hardest jobs I had, because I wasn't really happy in the job. I found it quite political. I'm not a real political person, as I guess you've noticed. And I found it very political, so within the scope of that I tried to be as fair as I could with the constituents. And I realize where they get the old, "Your detailer talks with forked tongue," because you would be honestly working up a person for a job and an admiral would tell you, "No, that person is not going there, this person is." And so you had to call back the original person. And you can't say, "Well, Admiral So-and-so wants his lieutenant to go into that job. I'm sorry." You had to create a story. You had to. So I found that very frustrating for me, and I would try as hard as I could not to lie.

And from there I went to Postgraduate School and got my electrical engineering master's, and concentration in space systems. This past year I've been at the Naval Space and Warfare Systems Command.

Sue Sweeney: How did the experience at Monterey compare to your time at the Academy?

Lieutenant D'Ercole: I found the academic environment very hard—mostly because I didn't really have the electrical engineering background. I had an engineering background, but not electrical. So I was kind of in a loophole.

Sue Sweeney: Was it a much freer environment?

Lieutenant D'Ercole: Oh, yeah. It was nicer; I enjoyed it much more. The academics were certainly harder, but my time outside of academics was certainly fun.

Sue Sweeney: Did being a member of the class of '80 attract attention?

Lieutenant D'Ercole: They didn't know. People could care less.

Sue Sweeney: I notice you don't wear your ring.

Lieutenant D'Ercole: Well, that's funny. The Academy has, with a lot of people out there—has the old ring-knocker reputation. And it's funny to let the people get to know you first and then you lay it on them that you happen to be a Naval Academy grad. Usually the reaction is, "You don't act like one."

And then you ask what one acts like. And I think that's one of the reasons I don't wear my ring. I don't wear it because my taste has changed. I don't really like the ring I chose anymore. And it's not my life. I'm proud of it and glad I went here, and it means a lot to me, but it's not—my life doesn't revolve around that ring.

A lot of men, you know, use it as their wedding ring. I'm not married to this place. It's a great place, but I am not married to it. There's more. And they—a lot of the people who come into contact with Naval Academy grads—I think maybe there's a small, small percentage who think they walk on water because they went here. They think the Navy owes them something because they went here. And it's unfortunate when that's their first contact with a Naval Academy grad, because that's, to me, a minority. You've got the silent majority—you truly have the silent majority when it comes to the Naval Academy—because there are far more sharp people, and nice people, and human people who graduated from here than jerks. And yet it seems like when an officer is really a jerk, you can say, "Did you graduate from the Naval Academy?" and nine chances out of 10 they're going to say yes.

And you think, "Hmm, and I went there, too—I have to admit that." So, I think, the silent majority are the ones that realize this is a special place, but it's not the only place, and you're not God's gift to the world because you went here. It just happens to be the way you chose to do it. And, yes, it's competitive, and yes, there are things that are harder, but yet, on the other hand, they make a whole lot of decisions here for you that are hard decision if you're outside at a civilian college. So I think it evens itself out.

Sue Sweeney: What does your current job entail?

Lieutenant D'Ercole: I'm in an area called Advanced Concepts. So I look at the way we can do things now in communications, and things like that, and try to find a way to do things better. With microprocessors and Silicon Valley out in California now, you know, where an old-time computer, the first one, took up three rooms, three stories high, and now it's down to one chip. The satellite that was built 10 years ago can be built more efficiently now. More can be done. So I like being in Advanced Concepts because I kind of look out to the future. Not only is the Navy getting 100 percent of their investment back, but I'm able to keep current with what's going on in and around the business areas today and can apply that, but I don't have to work back with technology from about 10 years ago. That's the gist of my job now. It's very much engineering. It's about 40 percent engineering and 60 percent contracts, and it's been all on-the-job training. It's been fun, and I've had some very supportive people that, you know, I'll come in and say, "Do you have about an hour to teach me this?" So we'll sit down and they'll say, "Watch out for this. This is where they can get you on this contract." And different types of contracts, firm fixed prices, cost plus fixed fee, and all the stuff in between. So, it's been really a wonderful job.

Sue Sweeney: How much longer will you be there?

Lieutenant D'Ercole: Two years. I was teasing them that they're stuck with me until April of '89.

Sue Sweeney: Sounds like they're lucky to have you! You're getting married; will you do that here?

Lieutenant D'Ercole: Yeah. Roger gets the biggest kick out of the fact that I went here because he says somebody has to—because he wouldn't have. And that when he asked me to marry him, when we were talking, we realized that this would be neutral territory, and we can both be involved in the planning of it, rather than have it at home in Ohio or at home in Chicago. I didn't want to have it in Ohio, and he didn't want to have it in Chicago. If we would have it in Chicago, my mother wouldn't forgive me, and if we would have it in Ohio, well, I just didn't want to have it there. So we thought, and he said, "Well, you rate the Naval Academy Chapel. Why don't we do it there?" So I was like, "It's not going to bother you?" He said, "Not at all—let's do it." So, yeah, August 15th.

Sue Sweeney: Do you plan to start a family?

Lieutenant D'Ercole: I don't know—I guess we'll cross that bridge when we come to it. We want a few years to ourselves, which probably brings us to around 34 to 35 years of age. And both of us don't necessarily think that we want to start a family then. Adoption certainly isn't out of the question, but at 35, I don't know if I want to have my first child. He kind of feels the same way. Maybe we're both kind of selfish. We really want time to ourselves. We've had enough time apart.

Sue Sweeney: Your fiancé is also interested in making a career in the Navy?

Lieutenant D'Ercole: Through commander, he is. He really—and the guys are geared that way—he'd love to be a skipper of a squadron. That's his goal in life. And after that, you know, he'll stay in if it's fun—if they're challenging him and he's being able to utilize something. But after skipper they don't fly anymore, and what he loves to do for the Navy is what he does inside the E-2 when they're up there operating. He loves that. That's what he wants to do. And if he can't do that anymore, I don't know that he'd be an asset to the Navy.

Sue Sweeney: If he gets out, is he content that you may stay in?

Lieutenant D'Ercole: Oh, yeah. As a matter of fact, he's always teasing me, "You have such a great chance at O-6—just don't blow it."

Sue Sweeney: Tell me about your classmates. Who were the women in your company?

Lieutenant D'Ercole: Janie Mines, Liz Sternaman, and Barbara Morris. Janie Mines and I don't keep in contact at all. I've only seen her once since we graduated.

Sue Sweeney: As the first Black woman, would you say she had an extra layer of stress?

Lieutenant D'Ercole: That's a tough question. She was my roommate. Janie was a very strong person. I have no idea what she looks like now, but I always thought she would be very attractive. Most of the people liked Janie. Some of them kept their distance from her because she would tell you what she thought. I haven't kept up with her since graduation other than, as I said, I've seen her once. She hadn't changed much when I saw her last.

Sue Sweeney: Do you think that she identified more as a Black midshipman than as a female midshipman?

Lieutenant D'Ercole: She really had some issues to deal with, obviously, because she put the checkmarks under "minority"—both Black and female. And yet she handled it pretty well. She was more apt to jump at something that you said rather than trying to understand how the person meant it. Sometimes you may say something that just doesn't come out exactly as you meant it, you know. I don't know—it's hard to say. She kept to herself. I was her roommate, and she kept to herself.

Sue Sweeney: She's the one who brought you from your original company?

Lieutenant D'Ercole: Yes.

Sue Sweeney: Tell me about the other girls in your company.

Lieutenant D'Ercole: Barbara Morris and Liz Sternaman. I was just in Liz's wedding last December. In fact, we lived together out in Monterey. She's a sweetheart of a lady, and so is Barbara Morris, who's now Barbara Ives. They have two children and she's out of the Navy. I don't know of anybody who didn't like them, especially Liz Sternaman. There is something about her that every single person liked. And I just don't know any of the guys that did not like her. She held her own here. Sometimes we'd laugh and say, "We want to get out of here." She's from California, and very easygoing and, you know, just held her own. She really did a good job.

Barbara was a sailor when she was here—she was on the sailing team. She was always off doing sailing things.

Sue Sweeney: What other classmates stick out in your mind?

Lieutenant D'Ercole: Peggy Feldmann. I have always had the utmost respect for her. She's just really a neat lady. To meet her, you'd think that she was really focused and very athletic. She is a swimmer, and well respected, and well liked by everyone. She's married now to a guy from the class of '79. They live in San Diego—a really neat marriage.

Sue Sweeney: Is she still in?

Lieutenant D'Ercole: Yes. And she's one of the neatest ladies, I think, that graduated with us. I have no idea what Sandee Irwin does anymore. Lynn Rampp—I don't know. Beth Leadbetter—I understood her really well, and knew her background from seventh grade on, so I knew what drove Beth. Beth did not stay in. She thrived in her jobs she got as a civilian. The Navy's jobs are not for everyone.

Sue Sweeney: What were the circumstances of her resignation?

Lieutenant D'Ercole: Oh, she got out on a medical discharge, but there's a lot involved in that. And it was best that she did get out. Marjorie Morley, I guess, is out. She went aviation, and I understand she's doing a really good job. Sandy Daniels, I got in touch with. We've talked periodically for the past few months—really a neat lady. She's had some hard times. She's an aviator and is looking at, "What do I do now? What can they offer me?" There's nothing she can do. Go back to the squadron she was in before—well, guys don't do that, you know, and it's just not challenging. But she's neat. I've gotten to know her better since we've been out.

Cheryl Spohnholtz is out at the Postgraduate School. She's in the space operations curriculum. And she seems to be doing real well. Her sister just died, oh, nine or 10 months ago, and that was kind of tragic for her. She's had to work through that, but otherwise she's doing real well. She's just going to need some time. Sue Stapler's out of the Navy and got married a while ago.

Sue Sweeney: Do you go to reunions—get together with the other women?

Lieutenant D'Ercole: The first reunion I came to was this past year.

Sue Sweeney: Was it well attended?

Lieutenant D'Ercole: There was a good crowd from the class of '80, but I don't know that there were many women. I saw Melissa Harrington, but I don't know that I saw any other women.

Sue Sweeney: Is there a real inclination to stay away?

Lieutenant D'Ercole: I was afraid to come to it, because I didn't know how they'd react to me. I knew how much I'd changed and I really wanted some positive reaction. And in all honesty, it was great up until the last five minutes. And then there was a classmate who just was an idiot. And I left. I thought, "I'm not going to let this spoil the day—or I'm not going to let him spoil it more."

Sue Sweeney: Did he try to rehash the issue of women at the Academy?

Lieutenant D'Ercole: No, he was doing something to me that I thought was pretty rude. And everybody stood there to see what my reaction would be. And for a split second, my feelings were hurt that none of my classmates stepped forward to say, "That's enough." And yet, I knew every eye was looking at me and what is my reaction going to be. I just turned my back on him and turned to the person I was talking to and said, "Well, I think it's time for me to go. Nice to see you," and I left. So, you know, there's always one who'll never grow up.

But it was great seeing everyone. And they were all happy to see me. And they all remembered me. Some remembered me and I didn't even remember them, you know. And that was a really neat feeling. Everybody was just really genuinely glad to see me. So I think everyone, when they get away from here, reevaluates and realizes what's important and what's not.

Sue Sweeney: Are you encouraged to come back again?

Lieutenant D'Ercole: Yeah, I'm encouraged—I'm encouraged to bring Roger if I ever see that guy again. I'm encouraged, because out at the Postgraduate School, I got to know wives of guys I graduated with, and that's the first time since I graduated that that's happened. These ladies could have cared less I was a classmate of their husbands—we just had a blast. Their husbands like me and we get along great. And they're anxious to get to know Roger. So it's very encouraging, because it's just not an issue anymore.

Sue Sweeney: What do you consider your greatest success so far?

Lieutenant D'Ercole: I think my faith has really grown—my faith in God. That, coupled with how honest I can be with myself. I don't know. I guess, you know, maybe I would have become that honest with myself prior to—but with all the issues you have to deal with, you've got to really learn how you feel about them, and go on from there. I think that I've gained a lot of things personally. The professional things, I think, I could have gotten anywhere. The education I could have gotten anywhere. But not the education about people, and that's been the most rewarding.

Sue Sweeney: Tina, I'm glad we could finally get together. Thanks for giving me this time.

Lieutenant D'Ercole: Thank you.

***

Interview with Lieutenant Maureen P. Foley, U.S. Navy

Place: U.S. Naval Institute, Annapolis, Maryland

Date: 15 November 1984

Sue Sweeney: Maureen, would you start with some background on your life before you came to the Naval Academy?

Lieutenant Foley: I was born here in Annapolis. My father was a seamanship and navigation instructor, and he's a Naval Academy graduate. He's still active duty, so I've always moved—there's no real home. I went to three different high schools and several different grammar schools. I have no real roots there.

Sue Sweeney: Was he the biggest influence on you coming to the Naval Academy?

Lieutenant Foley: I think just the familiarity with the Naval Academy and the way it's run and what it stands for. He wasn't really much of an influence, except that I saw the lifestyle and I liked what he did. He didn't push me in any way to come here.

Sue Sweeney: Throughout high school, were you keeping an eye on the Academy to see if it would open to women?

Lieutenant Foley: Actually, all through school—high school especially—people would ask me where I wanted to go to college, and I would say the Naval Academy. It's something that I wanted to do since I was a little girl. But it wasn't open, so they would pat me on the head and say, "What else would you like to do?" Some of my dad's friends used to say that. So when it did open up, just by chance, several of them wrote recommendations saying, "I know her and she's wanted to come since she was a little girl, so this isn't just a whim or fancy."

Sue Sweeney: If it hadn't opened up in time, would you still have gone into the Navy?

Lieutenant Foley: Yes.

Sue Sweeney: To what other colleges did you apply?

Lieutenant Foley: Princeton and University of Virginia. They signed the legislation opening this up about the time I was starting to make decisions, so that time was right.

Sue Sweeney: What aspects of Navy life appealed to you?

Lieutenant Foley: I think the variety. I think that it wasn't a nine-to-five thing every day, there was always something different. And camaraderie and esprit de corps between the people.

Sue Sweeney: How did you feel when your acceptance to the Naval Academy came through?

Lieutenant Foley: I was thrilled because I think I was a little bit naive, in that I thought that women going here would just be like everyone else going here. I didn't understand there was any distinction between male midshipmen and female midshipmen. So I didn't recognize that at all until the publicity started, because I was one of the first ones. There was the newspaper interest and, of course, Induction Day, the place was just crawling with newspaper and camera people.

Sue Sweeney: What was that like for you?

Lieutenant Foley: Well, it started the night before. My mother brought me down. I think my dad was on deployment. We stayed in Annapolis and walked around, just like a lot of other people did. I had short hair already, because I didn't want to come here and get my long hair all cut off. And so I had short hair. People would point and say, "Do you think she's one of them?" It was really unnerving, because I didn't know what "one of them" meant. That's when I had an inkling that it was going to be different.

Then Induction Day itself was just a zoo, beginning about 6:00 in the morning. There was a big gaggle of people, and the girls sort of gravitated together just because we all looked around and were glad there was someone else doing it. We felt as though all eyes were on us, which, I guess, they were.

Sue Sweeney: You walked through the field house door and then what?

Lieutenant Foley: Actually, it started before we even got to the field house. I remember standing out in the parking lot in front of the field house and there were about three other girls and my mom took a picture of us. I think only two of us graduated. We were all standing there, looking bewildered. We walked in the field house and they, I guess, took our names and then put us where we were going to be up in the bleachers with other people in our company. Immediately the girls gravitated together just because there were three of us and 100 guys. We just wanted to know a little bit about each other. I guess we figured out right away that we'd be rooming together. So we just got to know each other a little bit. We were all in the same company and squads together. We weren't mixed in with any of the other girls in the other companies, so it was just the three of us for the whole day.

Sue Sweeney: Were you getting much reaction from your male classmates at this point?

Lieutenant Foley: No, not from my classmates, because it was every person for themselves on I Day, because it was such a new environment that you were thrust into, and no warning, actually. So we didn't get any word from the guys. The first class were extremely wary, sort of "I don't want to get too close or too involved." They'd been briefed, obviously, endlessly on how to deal with the women and to treat them just the same as anyone else. So I think it was new for them, too, and it was an awkward position for everybody.

Sue Sweeney: Were you offered any help with the heavy bags?

Lieutenant Foley: No, I didn't have any trouble with that. I looked sort of foolish because I wore a skirt, and we had to put on the ProKed sneakers and the Naval Academy T-shirt and the Dixie cup, and I had this skirt on. So, of course, I looked ridiculous. Then nothing fit of the uniforms. They gave us the whiteworks, which everyone gets, but they didn't fit. They were men's sizes, 32, 34, 36. And so in order to get the right shoulder size—most of the women wore about 34 or 36—they wouldn't go over our hips. So it was all bunched up around our waist and wouldn't go over our hips. And the sneakers were too big because they didn't have real tiny sizes, and then the arms and legs hung about six inches too long on all the uniforms. My squad leader was appalled. Before the induction ceremony, he made me stand on the desk in our room while he stapled up hems in my shirt and trousers. He wasn't real pleased about that.

Sue Sweeney: The men in your squad made out all right with their uniforms?

Lieutenant Foley: Everybody else's seemed to fit because the uniforms were tailored for men. I guess I had short arms and little shoulders and big hips, and nothing fit right.

Sue Sweeney: Has that been fixed since then?

Lieutenant Foley: They fixed it for that year. They started putting panels in the hips. It would just fall straight down like it does on the guys.

Sue Sweeney: Much better.

Lieutenant Foley: Much.

Sue Sweeney: How intrusive was the media?

Lieutenant Foley: They were there from the first moment. Even while we were standing around trying to get the big bags and the little covers and everything that we needed to do, and signing on the dotted line, there were photographers everywhere. That was hard, just because of the fact that you didn't want to stand out. You just wanted to be a midshipman, but that's difficult to do. And I think some of the resentment with our classmates started on the very first day, because it was a big momentous thing for them, too, and yet they felt that it wasn't being recognized.

Sue Sweeney: Did you feel the Academy wanted you to give the interviews—hoping for some positive PR through the women?

Lieutenant Foley: The first day we didn't really interview, as I recall. Some of the women may have, but I think it was more of a catch-as-catch-can type thing for the photographers and the newspaper people themselves. "There's one, can we talk to her?" Because I didn't give any interviews, and I don't think the other girls in my company did either.

Sue Sweeney: In general—throughout your four years—do you think the Academy wanted the women interacting with the media?

Lieutenant Foley: I think they felt the less said the better. There weren't any real problems until Christmastime, when the women went home. A lot of the home papers wanted to do interviews, and some of those turned out rather poorly. My roommate Pam Wacek's sort of backfired, with out-of-context quotes.

Sue Sweeney: Pam mentioned what a bad experience it was.

Lieutenant Foley: Yes, that was very bad. And so I learned early on, and I never gave an interview.

Sue Sweeney: Then you never had a similar experience?

Lieutenant Foley: No. That was definitely a learning experience. I'm sorry for Pam that it had to be, but that just showed the rest of the women that you can't say anything.

Sue Sweeney: When the academic year started, what was the general attitude among your civilian professors?

Lieutenant Foley: I didn't have any problem with the civilian professors. They seemed to accept things as just another change. Most of them had been here so long that they had seen change, and this seemed to be one more, although it was a highly visible one. I had a few problems with military instructors.

Sue Sweeney: Male or female?

Lieutenant Foley: Male. I never had a female instructor.

Sue Sweeney: Anything that sticks out in your mind?

Lieutenant Foley: The one that absolutely sticks out in my mind—there're two—the worst one was in an engineering class, electrical engineering. I was not a whiz student by any means, but I happened to get the highest grade on one of these quizzes that he gave, and he proceeded to berate the class for letting a female—who would obviously never need or never utilize an engineering education—get the highest grade. It was like a big embarrassment.

And then in a PE class on personal conditioning first-class year, when the instructor was saying the reason we need to be concerned with personal conditioning was that otherwise you ended up looking like all the women at the Naval Academy— "basketballs with arms and legs"—which I found somewhat offensive. There were a few instances.

Sue Sweeney: Did comments like that stay in the classroom or did you hear about them later?

Lieutenant Foley: The "basketballs with arms and legs" one, I was sort of irate about. That afternoon I had an interview on the integration of women into the brigade with a consultant who was working on—Edie Seashore, that's her name—she was working on making sure that the women were being integrated into the brigade, and so I just happened to bring that up, and I think that was taken care of. For the most part, they took all the things in but they didn't do anything with the information. We kept all these things to ourselves.

Sue Sweeney: How about your company officers? Did you feel they had your back?

Lieutenant Foley: I had two. The second one, we didn't have much dealings with. The first one—he was trying very hard. It was obviously a new thing, so it was a hard position for him to be in. He made some mistakes—what we thought were gross errors in judgment—but I think he did have best intentions.

Sue Sweeney: Can you tell me about them?

Lieutenant Foley: The one that really sticks out in my mind is when we were youngsters. We weren't plebes anymore, we were free to do whatever we wanted with the upper class—be friendly, date if we wanted. He and the company commander decided there were too many guys hanging around our rooms, so he had a sign-in log. If a male midshipman came into our room, he had to sign in what time he got there and the reason he was there and then sign out again. So we were completely ostracized because nobody wanted their name in the book that the company officer was going to see. Which hurt one of my roommates who was having academic problems, I think, because no one would come and help her, even her classmates.

Sue Sweeney: Were you free to go to the males' rooms?

Lieutenant Foley: Yes, but there was such a stigma, because the impression he was giving off was that it was taboo. Plus the fact that you had to have your door open if there was a male midshipman in your room.

Sue Sweeney: Was that the rule all four years you were there?

Lieutenant Foley: No, I think the first two. Plebe year—I guess I can understand it, even though it's really difficult. Because we were such an oddity and a tourist attraction even in Bancroft Hall, if you will, that by seeing your door open all the time, you invited people basically just to pop in and shoot the breeze or just to look in. That's unnerving when you're trying to study and there are people in the Hall staring at you.

Sue Sweeney: Anything else about your company officer that sticks out?

Lieutenant Foley: He really tried hard. I'll give him credit for that.

Sue Sweeney: You mentioned a consultant that you talked to the day of the basketball comment. Were the women asked for feedback very often—about how things could be improved?

Lieutenant Foley: We had meetings with her scheduled a couple of times and I didn't go except once. I was requested to go several times and avoided it because she would have female midshipmen and male midshipmen and she'd ask the females, "What do you think?" And then she'd ask the males, "What do you think?" And it turned into a bitching session, basically, back and forth. It got sort of ugly, and so I thought it did more harm than good.

Sue Sweeney: You'd think the first thing they'd figure out would be to ask separately! Could you ever convey that the coed talks weren't working?

Lieutenant Foley: Yes, but they were extremely wary of ever having segregated-type meetings, and that was a thing that started early in plebe year. I don't remember the circumstances, but the women tried to have some sort of a meeting where they could just get together and talk to each other, because we were so isolated that we were really the only ones on our floor. To talk to other women, you had to go someplace far away. So we decided to have a meeting. That didn't work out. That was nixed. So they were very leery about having just women and just men.

Sue Sweeney: Not nixed by other classmates, but from higher up?

Lieutenant Foley: Higher up.

Sue Sweeney: What was the camaraderie like among the women?

Lieutenant Foley: Well, I think it varies. For the most part, I think there's a very strong feeling between all the women, and there was a lot of trying to help each other out. And yet if one of the women did something which reflected badly on all of the women—then that was a problem. Because there were so few of us that sometimes that one woman would be the only one that male midshipmen ever saw or got to know, so if she was a bad representative, it was likely to reflect badly on the rest of us.

Sue Sweeney: Can you give me examples of things that reflected poorly?

Lieutenant Foley: Basically just conduct offenses, things that were obviously against the regulations and practiced by some people.

Sue Sweeney: What were the easiest aspects of being a midshipman?

Lieutenant Foley: Academics were fairly easy, and sports. I was a varsity athlete the whole time, and that made things much easier.

Sue Sweeney: What did you major in?

Lieutenant Foley: Oceanography.

Sue Sweeney: Would you have studied oceanography at a civilian school as well? Is it something you've always been interested in?

Lieutenant Foley: It's something that if I had gone to civilian school, I probably wouldn't have been able to, so that was a plus for coming here.

Sue Sweeney: Have you been able to use it in your career?

Lieutenant Foley: A little bit. Basically I guess I just wanted to know more for my own personal satisfaction.

Sue Sweeney: What did you letter in? What were your sports?

Lieutenant Foley: Fencing, the whole time.

Sue Sweeney: Had you done it before?

Lieutenant Foley: No. That was a lot of fun.

Sue Sweeney: What was the most difficult aspect of being a midshipman?

Lieutenant Foley: Attitudes of male midshipmen.

Sue Sweeney: Did you ever see a thaw in male attitudes? Could you see progress being made?

Lieutenant Foley: There was definitely progress made as the all-male classes started to graduate and there were more [female] midshipmen in the brigade. At first, when there were 4,000 of them and 50 or 60 of you, that's really difficult to make any inroads, but as there were more women, it became more commonplace and less of a fishbowl effect, and it got easier. But I think the hardest part was negative attitudes from our classmates, because they had no reason, we felt, to be negative.

Sue Sweeney: Were some of your classmates more negative than the upper class?

Lieutenant Foley: It was the case that the upperclassmen were worse as all-male classes, but I couldn't understand the reason for any resentment among our classmates. I just thought that was uncalled for. They weren't there when there were no women, so for them to say that women don't belong at the Naval Academy—that was sort of an ignorant thing for them to say. So there's supposed to be the big camaraderie thing that you look to your classmates for support, and most of them really were supportive, the guys in the company, but there were some that weren't. And that was more painful than the upper class, because you got to the point where you would expect upper class to be resentful or cruel or whatever—to speak as if it was their institution and we were intruders—but our classmates came the same time we did, so we weren't intruding on anything they had.

Sue Sweeney: Did attitudes start changing as they saw the women performing?

Lieutenant Foley: One-on-one, yes. It was very easy to win people over just in a one-on-one friendship. But in groups, it was not socially acceptable to be overtly nice to the women.

Sue Sweeney: What was dating like?

Lieutenant Foley: Very difficult. I mostly dated the same person the whole time I was there. I felt very badly for him because it was difficult for him. Well, I know it was extremely difficult. He was a varsity football player and was sort of ostracized by the other football players.

Sue Sweeney: Did any of the women keep civilian boyfriends through the four years?

Lieutenant Foley: There may have been one or two, but not many. Because that was awkward, too. I dated a civilian guy, I think, at one concert or something, one month out of high school. It was plebe year and I felt funny—and he felt funny—because he felt like he was in an all-male environment and yet he wasn't one of them—which is true—which would mean that I was supposed to be the one.

Sue Sweeney: How did male midshipmen react to your civilian date?

Lieutenant Foley: Just comments, sort of snide things, nothing real overt.

Sue Sweeney: Did you ever think of quitting the Academy?

Lieutenant Foley: Daily.

Sue Sweeney: Did it ever get serious?

Lieutenant Foley: I think youngster year, because plebe year—I expected it to be horrible. It's supposed to be horrible for everyone, so I thought youngster year would be better. And when it wasn't much better—and in a lot of cases it was worse because the resentment could really come out without the midshipmen being afraid of being fried for plebe violations. Youngsters were pretty much fair game. I thought that was discouraging and I thought about leaving. Then it got to be sort of a personal challenge when they'd tell you over and over again, "You'll never graduate from this place. I'll see that you don't."

Sue Sweeney: Did you share with your father what was going on? Was he able to offer moral support?

Lieutenant Foley: He did, because he knew it was going to be difficult. I think he was a little bit reluctant to egg me on towards coming here because he knew it was going to be really difficult because he knew about the traditions and that there would be resentment. I was naive enough to believe that there wouldn't be. So I think he knew that it was going to be like that. But once I made up my mind to come, he was very supportive. I'd call up and say, "This place is horrible."

He didn't say, "I told you it would be," or anything like that. They were just supportive.

Sue Sweeney: Would you ever encourage friends to apply? Could you imagine yourself as a Blue and Gold officer?

Lieutenant Foley: I think I could see myself as a Blue and Gold officer—to tell people what it's like from firsthand experience, to be sure that people don't come with the wrong idea. I think some of our classmates came not really knowing what the Navy was and what to expect when they graduated. It's bad enough not to know what the Naval Academy is about, but to not know what you're getting into long term, I think, is a shame. So I'd like to be a Blue and Gold officer from that respect, just to educate people so that we get more educated midshipmen rather than ones that don't want to be here.

Sue Sweeney: Could you counsel a sister or daughter to come?

Lieutenant Foley: If I really cared about the person, I think I would tell them all the pitfalls and let them make their own decision, just like my parents did for me, because I think that's important. You can't tell anyone, "You should go there," or, "No, you shouldn't go there."

Sue Sweeney: What were your summer programs like?

Lieutenant Foley: Youngster cruise, women weren't allowed out on ships so we went on the YPs. It was a lot of fun. I suppose I learned a lot. Mostly it was nice just to go in to the fleet and not feel the resentment that we felt as midshipmen at the Naval Academy— because of, I guess, the curiosity out in the fleet. People were really interested in what we were doing and what we had to say. There was no animosity that I could feel.

Sue Sweeney: Where there other aspects of the YP cruises that made them enjoyable?

Lieutenant Foley: I guess the feeling of being responsible for your own time, because we would do our duties during the day and then, if we were in port at night, we were free to go as long as we were back by quarters the next morning. That was very different from being a plebe at the Naval Academy. So that made us feel a little bit more mature and more or less grown up. We could stay out all night if we wanted to. You were foolish if you did——but just to know that you could if you wanted to was nice.

Sue Sweeney: What were your duties?

Lieutenant Foley: The shipboard duties, we navigated the YP and took care of basically everything aboard the boat. We did all the cooking and cleaning and the navigation and the charting and the communications and everything from here to Norfolk first, and then up the eastern seaboard, to New York City; Cape May, New Jersey; and Newport. It was a good experience from that point of view. We learned a lot about navigation, but we didn't really learn anything about how the enlisted structure is and what enlisted people do in the Navy because we really didn't see many.

Sue Sweeney: Had you gotten enough of a navigation background as a plebe?

Lieutenant Foley: Pretty much. We had some courses before we went out. I guess there was a week that we were taking classes before we actually went to sea.

Sue Sweeney: Was it easier being around your male classmates at sea than in Bancroft Hall?

Lieutenant Foley: Yes. It was much easier, and I think they appreciated the fact that we were women, because there was a lot of socializing on the cruise, and yet when you came back from the cruise, it abruptly ended because we were back in the Bancroft Hall environment. But while we were on the cruise, it was a lot of fun.

Sue Sweeney: Was there initial resentment about being on the girls' cruises?

Lieutenant Foley: I don't think so. I'm sure there was in the beginning because they were the subject of ridicule for going on the "Love Boat" cruise rather than a real fleet cruise, but I think most of them really had a good time. The ones that I was with, anyway, they enjoyed it, but they would never come back and say that they really had a good time or anything like that. But while we were out there, there was no trouble.

Sue Sweeney: One-on-one, could you discuss why they treated you differently when others were around?

Lieutenant Foley: Well, I knew why they did it, because of the pressure that they got in Bancroft Hall, and so I could accept that, because I didn't want to make it any harder for them. It was the same way with dating people. I got to the point where I didn't want to publicly date anyone—especially the one person I was dating—because he had such a hard time, and so I felt badly that I was the cause of that. That didn't really bother me. I'm sure it hurt deep down, but I would never make an issue of it because it wasn't their fault.

Sue Sweeney: What was second-class summer like?

Lieutenant Foley: That was a lot of fun, too, except we had a few bad moments. We went to Quantico, and that was great—we played GI Joe and jumped out of helicopters and all that. We had the surface portion, but women still weren't allowed to go on ships. So the men would go out on a day cruise and we would have to go down on the bus, stand on the pier, watch them get on the ship, and they'd be gone for the day. We'd piddle around Norfolk for the day and be back on the pier when they came back in, which I found sort of degrading.

Sue Sweeney: What did you think of Pensacola?

Lieutenant Foley: Pensacola was a lot of fun. I didn't get to go in a jet because I'm too small, but I enjoyed the helicopter and I went in a T-28, which I guess they're phasing out already. It was a lot of fun; I had a long ride. Then propellers—we did a lot of acrobatics and all that stuff. The pilot really wanted to make me sick but he couldn't do it. That was my own feeling of satisfaction, not throwing up.

Sue Sweeney: Did they modify the summer program for the women—highlighting service areas that were available to you?

Lieutenant Foley: They didn't modify most of it. Most of the commands that we went to, though, threw in something, knowing that the women were going to be there, and they'd throw in something about what the women could do, or say, "But you can't do this." We did have one week when the men were on the submarines, which we absolutely couldn't do. We went to either Norfolk or Washington and had a female running mate and followed her around to see what her job was. That was interesting. The first time I ever met her, this female lieutenant said to me, "Oh, you're from the Naval Academy?"

I said, "Yes."

She said, "Well, I'll just have you know that because of you, I'll probably have to go to sea some day."

"Because of me?"

Sue Sweeney: What did you say to that?

Lieutenant Foley: "I don't think it's because of me. Perhaps it's because of Congress." She implied it was all my fault, so there was a little animosity there, whether it was professional jealousy or whatever.

Sue Sweeney: Have you encountered animosity toward Naval Academy graduates from non-graduates? Or does being from the Academy open doors?

Lieutenant Foley: I think it has opened doors. It did in my first command, in that when I went down there I was supposed to be assistant legal officer, which is sort of a nothing billet. It wasn't even a billet. They were creating one. I went down there and I did that for about a month. The CO finally called me in and he said, "I realize you're from the Naval

Academy. You're obviously fairly competent. Is there something that you would rather do?" So I told him that I wanted to go to the maintenance department and be a division officer, and he let me, so I'm sure that was only because I had been to the Naval Academy and he felt I had the professional experience.

Sue Sweeney: Had the Academy prepared you to lead a division?

Lieutenant Foley: I had enough confidence that I'd built up over the course of the four years in dealing with people. I didn't have the aviation maintenance expertise. I had to acquire that in a hurry on my own time. But as far as being supervisor, I think the Academy prepared me for that.

Sue Sweeney: Did second-class summer influence your choice of service selection?

Lieutenant Foley: No. I didn't really know what women could do. Even after second-class summer, I wasn't sure what they could do, because everywhere I went, they said, "You can't do this. Someday it might open up." That sort of thing. And so I wasn't sure at all what I wanted to do. For service selection, we didn't even know what we were going to be able to do until very shortly before service selection.

Sue Sweeney: What was that night like?

Lieutenant Foley: It was a lot of fun because we'd all gotten together beforehand, the women, and we knew what the billets were, so there were only 50-something of us, we decided that rather than cause hate and discontent on service selection night, we would get together beforehand and tell each other what we wanted to do, according to order, so that if you and I both wanted the same billet but you were higher, I knew that I would have to pick something else, rather than waiting until service selection night and saying, "Oh, my goodness, my billet's gone." So we all knew exactly what we were going to do before service selection night.

Sue Sweeney: Were there 55 billets and 55 women? How much choice did you have?

Lieutenant Foley: There was quite a bit of choice and there were a lot of billets, so it was just a matter of where you wanted to go and what you wanted to do. And I think everyone pretty much got what they wanted.

Sue Sweeney: What was your choice?

Lieutenant Foley: I went 1100 general unrestricted line to a squadron in Pensacola. That's what I wanted to do.

Sue Sweeney: What was your first-class summer like?

Lieutenant Foley: I was on an oceanographic research ship for a cruise out of Japan with one other female midshipman and two male midshipmen.

Sue Sweeney: What ship?

Lieutenant Foley: The USNS *Dutton*. That was a great time.

Sue Sweeney: Tell me about your cruise.

Lieutenant Foley: We went to sea for 28 days, then we went to port. We couldn't receive mail or send mail because what we were doing was very secret. It was in a very cold place—which we hadn't anticipated—because they didn't tell us where we would be going because it was secret. But we had a very good time. I learned a lot because we used our oceanography. We were all oceanography majors.

Sue Sweeney: Other recollections from that cruise?

Lieutenant Foley: I guess just feeling responsible and being at sea, that was the real Navy. The Naval Academy is not really the Navy, but we felt that it was being out there at sea. I love ships, I love going to sea, so I enjoyed it.

Sue Sweeney: You said that during youngster cruise you didn't really experience the shipboard enlisted structure. Did you have more interaction with the crew on board the oceanographic ship?

Lieutenant Foley: The crew was MSC—Military Sealift Command—so they weren't even really Navy, but the Navy unit attached was an oceanographic unit. If you'd just gone on those people, you'd have gotten a distorted perception of Navy enlisted people because they were all highly technically competent and mostly petty officers. There were only about 20 people together in the unit, I think. So we did have some dealings with them, but it was more dealing with oceanography and how that part of the Navy works than actually dealing with the enlisted people. They all had a job and they were under supervision.

Sue Sweeney: Were you midshipmen the only women on board?

Lieutenant Foley: And a female ensign they sent as liaison because there'd never been women on the ship.

Sue Sweeney: What was the reaction of the crew to you? Were you a curiosity?

Lieutenant Foley: Yes, and it was fun for the other midshipman and I because the crew were "old salts." A lot of them had been doing this all their lives, and their reactions to having women aboard ranged from—we were sort of daughter figures to "Women don't belong on ships, that's the reason the engines are breaking," and all that sort of bad luck.

Sue Sweeney: Did you really get some of that?

Lieutenant Foley: Yes.

Sue Sweeney: How did you respond?

Lieutenant Foley: Basically the comments were behind our back, and so we just didn't pay any attention to them because it was the same sort of thing we were used to. So it was certainly nothing that you'd want to confront, and you're not going to take this 48- or 50-year-old salty old guy to task for him not believing that women belong on ships. We'd learned early on that opinions are something you just really can't change. If it's a deep-rooted opinion about something, you can talk until you're blue in the face.

Sue Sweeney: What was your reaction when the Webb article came out in November of your first-class year?

Lieutenant Foley: I was extremely offended just because of the fact that we'd worked so hard and we were starting to make inroads, I felt, to being accepted. That just intensified the animosity because now it was down in black and white, it was someone other than midshipmen saying it, and it was something midshipmen could look at and say this is a highly decorated Vietnam veteran, obviously he knows what he's talking about, and he doesn't think we should be here, so why are we here.

Sue Sweeney: Had you ever met Webb or been in one of his classes?

Lieutenant Foley: No, I never had. I'm extremely grateful that I hadn't, because I wouldn't have wanted to have been in the article in any way, shape or form. The male midshipmen pinned up copies on all of the bulletin boards, and wrote comments next to it and everything. And a lot of guys would say, "This is true, and this is true." He has some good points; it's just the way that he presented them, the manner in which he did it, the elitist, narrow-minded, sort of chauvinistic view that he took of everything that was so offensive; basically ignorant, I felt. I have since been asked to do sort of a point-counterpoint article between me and James Webb. I would never do such a thing, as I didn't think it would reflect well upon myself or the Academy to do that sort of an article, because there's some animosity between myself and James Webb.

Sue Sweeney: Who asked you to do that?

Lieutenant Foley: A St. Petersburg reporter last year. I said, no, I would absolutely not be in the article. He called me about 10 times. He called me at home. I said I don't think so. He said, "Look, if you disagree so violently with what this man has to say, perhaps you would like a chance at rebuttal."

And I said, "No, thank you." And I put him off. Finally the article came out and it said that they tried to interview Lieutenant Maureen Foley, stationed at the Naval Academy, the first female graduate stationed there, and that she was so vehemently opposed to everything that James Webb had to say, that she refused to be in any article that he was in. Which is exactly true.

Sue Sweeney: That's about as safe as you can get.

Lieutenant Foley: I guess I came out as the hysterical female that was just so irate she wouldn't speak. That was better than speaking.

Sue Sweeney: What are your thoughts on women in combat?

Lieutenant Foley: I think there are some physiological limitations as far as upper body strength that may preclude women from doing some combat roles. I don't agree that across the board women can't perform in combat. I think women can fly airplanes and women can drive ships the same as men can. I think women can sit in foxholes the same as men can. I don't know that they could lift machine guns or something that was extremely heavy, although some men can't either. And I think that the way he presented it was that men wouldn't follow women, and men would be more concerned with saving the lives of women and being chivalrous than they would killing the enemy, which I find ludicrous. I mean, having been through the all-male environment and sort of blending in and finding, especially plebe summer, that everyone was so concerned about themselves, that they certainly would never stop to be chivalrous over taking care of themselves. Of course, it's a survivalist thing. The women worried about the women and the men worried about the men, but it wasn't that there was any sexist thing in it at all. It was just purely personal survival.

Sue Sweeney: Do you see combat opening to women anytime soon?

Lieutenant Foley: I don't see it opening up for a very long time just because of the social situation. I don't think Congress is ready to vote such a thing. I don't think the public is ready for it.

Sue Sweeney: Do you see it happening with the stroke of a pen—the same way the Academy went coed?

Lieutenant Foley: I don't think it'll happen overnight, but I think just like the Academy, it's an evolutionary process. It's a very strange transition period, but it eventually gets to be commonplace. It's like any other big social change, it takes a long time for acceptance.

Sue Sweeney: Do you believe it will happen within your career?

Lieutenant Foley: No.

Sue Sweeney: Have you experienced unexpected pockets of support?

Lieutenant Foley: Occasionally someone would walk up from out in town. I remember especially the night after Herndon, which is the plebe recognition ceremony when we weren't plebes anymore, you weren't allowed to drink or anything plebe year, so now you were allowed to go out in town and drink and date and do whatever you wanted. My roommate and I went out in town and we went in to a restaurant, had a huge dinner, we were treating ourselves to a big dinner and a lot of wine, and we went to pay the check, and the waitress said, "I'm sorry, it's been taken care of."

And we said, "Well, who took care of it?"

"I'm sorry, I can't say." So we just walked out. Our dinner was paid for, and everywhere we went, we didn't buy a drink, we didn't pay for anything. And so that was refreshing, but those were mostly civilians. I think some of them were old grads. There was some animosity with the old grads and old grads' wives who felt that we didn't belong in their Navy, but there was also some nice feedback.

Sue Sweeney: What was homecoming like when the old grads come tearing through the Hall?

Lieutenant Foley: That was pretty funny the first year. When I was a plebe, I had the duty on homecoming as company mate of the deck. We lived right next to Dahlgren Hall, which is where all the alumni go for their big cocktail party. These elevators would open up and they'd all pour out and I was standing there with my little watch cap and watch belt. "Oh, my goodness, a female mate of the deck." I felt like a tourist attraction as I stood there at the elevators telling them to get back in and go away, so they thought it was sort of funny. But homecoming—everyone's in a jolly mood and it was fun.

Sue Sweeney: What other reactions did you get from grads?

Lieutenant Foley: A lot of them, I guess, felt grudging admiration. Like, "I really have to respect what you're doing." That I never minded at all. If someone said, "I don't believe women should be there, but I really respect you for having done it," then I could really respect that. The ones that respected and recognized that it was difficult for me to do, they got a lot of respect from me, whether they thought I should be there or not.

Sue Sweeney: Were there people back home that surprised you by their opposition to women at the Academy?

Lieutenant Foley: I think my parents did more than I did. Because of my father being on active duty, some of the old grads that he knew, classmates and people that he worked with, there was some animosity there, and so they would tell him, "I don't think women ought to be at the Naval Academy." My mom would sometimes run into it at cocktail parties or with the other women and wives. But that's just the generation, because they were brought up differently than us.

Sue Sweeney: How did you interact with women who came to the Academy in subsequent classes? Was it easier for you all when there were hundreds of women, rather than a handful?

Lieutenant Foley: It should have been easier for them, and maybe it was in the way that they had someone they could look at and say, "She's done it, so I can do it." But in a lot of cases, it wasn't any easier because the upper-class women didn't make it any easier. There was some feeling in my class that, well, it was hard for me and nobody helped me, so these women will have to make it on their own. And that's sad. I didn't appreciate that, and I'm sure the young women didn't appreciate it either, but I think it was sort of a natural reaction because it was so difficult for us that there was almost a resentment for the women coming in that they had it easier.

Sue Sweeney: Was there a sense of wanting to make sure the women had a true plebe year like all midshipmen?

Lieutenant Foley: Well, yes, but even the plebes, I think, need someone to every once in a while to say, "Hey, I had the same problem when I was a plebe. You'll get through it." I think that's what youngsters are for, to be sort of a support network, and we didn't have one. So I think a lot of the women in my class found it hard to be that way for the plebe women coming in.

Sue Sweeney: Do you think the Naval Academy should have phased women in more carefully——taken more time preparing the Academy community for your arrival?

Lieutenant Foley: I don't think so. I think when you're going to make a change that drastic, you have to say, "Okay, this is the way it's going to be," and you just do it, and people adapt. It's a sink or swim thing. The women are coming. If you don't like it, you can leave now, that type of deal. When you do it as a long educational process, people start to resent it even more before the women get there, because there was an educational process before we got there, even in that short time, and I think the guys resented that. They had to spend time learning about women and how to deal with women. I think the longer you make that educational process, the more they resent the big change that's coming. If you don't give them a chance to resent it, then they won't.

Sue Sweeney: Was there more pointed animosity by members of the classes of '77 or '78—mids who had made their service commitment before the women came and felt the rules had changed in midstream?

Lieutenant Foley: I don't know that any of them would have done something else had they known women were coming, because that's sort of a cutting-off-your-nose-to-spite-your-face-type reaction. They would have been doing themselves more harm than good. A Naval Academy education is something that anyone can pride themselves in, and so to deprive yourself of that just because women were doing it, would be a very petty thing.

Sue Sweeney: What sticks out in your mind about first-class year?

Lieutenant Foley: I guess it was the best year in that it was just us and there were women in all the classes, and no more of "the last male class" and all that stuff. It was still difficult, in that some of the women who were put in leadership positions weren't always given the respect that they should have by underclassmen. And that was a difficult thing to be in a leadership position and to have underclassmen, who had absolutely no idea what it was like before they even got there, to say, "I don't have to follow you," and, "I'm not going to pay any attention to what you say."

Sue Sweeney: Did you hold rank as a first classman?

Lieutenant Foley: I was the company adjutant, in charge of taps boards and accountability.

Sue Sweeney: What did that entail?

Lieutenant Foley: Well, it was an administrative type duty, so that was accepted. It's okay for the women to do that. It wasn't a big leadership position or anything like that. I had a good rapport with the people in my company, so there was no problem.

Sue Sweeney: James Webb thought some women were arbitrarily groomed for stripes. Would you agree?

Lieutenant Foley: I don't know that they were being groomed, as such. I think there were some extremely capable women who were recognized as being capable, and so were not pushed into stripes, but were given the opportunity to perform in a striper position. That's the same with male midshipmen, you recognize early on who the potential stripers are. And then if you want to call it "groomed for stripes," you can. They're given the opportunity to be in a striper position. I can't see that they would have had a woman brigade commander in our class—since they still haven't—just because that would be a big change and maybe it would look like they were taking it too fast.

Sue Sweeney: How far up were any of your female classmates?

Lieutenant Foley: There was a company commander and there was a battalion commander—four stripes. The year after us there was a deputy brigade commander.

Sue Sweeney: After graduation—how did your career start?

Lieutenant Foley: Thirty days' Basket Leave and then I went to Pensacola to be in a squadron. That worked out really well because of the fact that the CO gave me an opportunity to do what I wanted to do. I wasn't just being an administrative person.

I had 60 enlisted people who worked for me, and so I was their—they called it branch officer. Basically I was just a supervisor. I didn't get involved in the actual technical workings. I had to know what they were supposed to be doing, so I needed an overview of the technical stuff. So I read up on all the technical manuals and their jobs, talked to the guys about what they were doing, and they'd explain it to me. Then on a day-to-day basis, I just took care of things that came up, that always come up with personnel supervision, signing chits, granting days off, emergency leave, taking people to Captain's Mast.

Sue Sweeney: Were your enlisted personnel aware you were a Naval Academy graduate?

Lieutenant Foley: They knew I was, but I think most of them really didn't know what the Naval Academy was. We had very few Naval Academy graduates in the squadron, only a couple. So for them it was no big deal. I'm sure they said, "Then that's why she's down here, because she went to the Naval Academy, whatever that means."

Sue Sweeney: How often, in general, does that come up? I see you wear your ring—do people recognize it?

Lieutenant Foley: They never assume. Especially in this area, they never assume that a woman went to the Naval Academy. Even being stationed here, they presume that I'm ROTC because there're so few Naval Academy grads. I do wear the ring and occasionally people will say, "Oh, your husband went to the Naval Academy," and I say, "No, I went to the Naval Academy." Because I got a miniature. I didn't get the big class ring because my hands are smaller, and I couldn't bend my knuckles. I didn't think that was too attractive, and I want to wear it forever, so I got it smaller. But the ring, I guess, means more than anything. I don't care whether people notice it or not. That's why I have a miniature, because I want to wear it all the time.

A lot of my female classmates said, "Well, anyone can wear a miniature. People's fiancées wear miniatures; people's mothers wear miniatures."

I said, "I don't care what other people think, because I know it's my class ring."

Sue Sweeney: What happened after Pensacola?

Lieutenant Foley: I came back here.

Sue Sweeney: How long have you been back?

Lieutenant Foley: Two and a half years. I wanted to come back here. I was only in Pensacola two years. I wanted to come back here, because ever since I was a midshipman, I thought they needed female Naval Academy officers back here, because that was one of the most difficult things as a midshipman, was looking around the yard and not really seeing anyone that I wanted to emulate. "She went here, and that's the kind of officer I want to be." There were a few women officers scattered around the yard, but there wasn't that feeling of, "Yes, she knows what I'm going through because she did it too." That's how the guys feel, because there're so many Naval Academy grads around. The role model thing—there weren't any. So I thought they needed some, and I asked to come back.

Sue Sweeney: What is your job?

Lieutenant Foley: Teaching in the leadership department.

Sue Sweeney: How much interaction do you have with the female mids?

Lieutenant Foley: That's what's good about being a leadership instructor. The way the course is set up, there's a great deal of discussion between the instructor and the midshipmen, and they get to voice their opinions and then I can voice mine. So that's a good forum for me to sort of prove myself as a Naval Academy graduate and say, "Yes, I went to the Naval Academy and I went in the fleet and this is what I did, and I'm back here." So they get to see what a female Naval Academy officer is like. That's good for them. And I do see a lot of women midshipmen. They seem to gravitate to me just because, "Was it like this when you were here? You know what they're doing." And that sort of thing. There's a bond, I think, just like there is between the guys.

Sue Sweeney: What changes do you see?

Lieutenant Foley: I think it's getting better. The animosity has decreased tremendously. I think the women in striper positions are being accepted better. There's always going to be a little bit just because, I guess, it's not socially acceptable quite yet for men and women to think equally of each other. But after a while, after kids are brought up that way, I think it'll get better.

Sue Sweeney: Have you seen any backslides?

Lieutenant Foley: Last year the women came to me several times when James Webb was coming here as a speaker. There was a lot of teasing going on back in the Hall that, you know, the Naval Academy must think highly of what he says or they wouldn't invite him to be a speaker. And then they circulated the James Webb article. A lot of them hadn't read it, and so they didn't understand why there would be this problem with James Webb. And that was ugly. But other than that, I haven't seen much backsliding.

Sue Sweeney: When you were a midshipman, did you receive many demerits?

Lieutenant Foley: No, I didn't get many and I didn't give many either.

Sue Sweeney: Was it hard for a female mid to fry a male? Did that happen often?

Lieutenant Foley: No, I don't think it happened often, and I think it would have been hard, because the women just wanted to be left alone, basically. We knew we weren't accepted, and so we were trying to keep from being less accepted, if that was possible. So I think we tried to avoid situations where we would be speaking out against somebody else. I don't think the women spoke up much in class. I know I never did. I think I went through four years and never raised my hand in class. And I think most of them were that way, just didn't want to be recognized at all.

Sue Sweeney: Would you have preferred it if the Academy had put all the women together, as they did at the Air Force Academy?

Lieutenant Foley: No, I think that would have made it even worse. I was really glad that they didn't do that, in that we got to be—especially plebe summer—just other plebes to the guys in our squad, and I think if they had set us aside, there would have been more resentment. Anything that the women got was because they were women. This way, if the squad got something, it was because the squad did it, some sort of a reward, it was everybody in the squad. Or if we all got in trouble, it was because all of us did something wrong. There was more of a camaraderie thing than if they'd set us aside.

Sue Sweeney: You mentioned that the administration frowned upon attempts to get the women together. Among yourselves, did you get together informally?

Lieutenant Foley: We did a lot of lunches on Saturday. Just a few women, maybe six— the women in the adjoining companies would get to know each other. But for the most part, we really didn't get to know the other women in the brigade real well because of time constraints and distance constraints. Going over to first regiment, if you were in second regiment, was like going around the world, it was so far away. It took 10 minutes to walk there, and that was out of your study time. That was a problem. You tended to associate more with the people that you lived right in close proximity to.

Sue Sweeney: Where do you hope to go from here? Will you make the Navy a career?

Lieutenant Foley: No. My letter of resignation is in already. I'm going to be getting out in May when my obligation is up.

Sue Sweeney: Do you have a job lined up?

Lieutenant Foley: No. I'm getting my master's degree now at Johns Hopkins. I'll be done with that in a couple of weeks. That's in business. I think I'd like to go into business.

Sue Sweeney: In this area?

Lieutenant Foley: No, I have no geographical preference.

Sue Sweeney: Where is your father now?

Lieutenant Foley: Hawaii.

Sue Sweeney: If you could be 18 again, would you still want to come to the Naval Academy?

Lieutenant Foley: Yes, because I think I learned a lot about myself and also about surviving in a male environment. The world is still, I think, despite everything, a male environment. Business is a male environment, and I think I'll be in good stead in that regard.

Sue Sweeney: What's been your greatest satisfaction so far?

Lieutenant Foley: My greatest satisfaction in life is definitely graduating from the Naval Academy because it was so hard. You always appreciate the things that are hard. That's the hardest thing I've done and so that's what I appreciate the most. I think it'll always be that way.

Sue Sweeney: Thanks very much—and best of luck to you.

***

Interview with Lieutenant Chrystal A. Lewis, U.S. Navy

Place: Officers' Club, Pensacola, Florida

Date: 1 November 1985

Sue Sweeney: Thanks for agreeing to meet with me this afternoon, Chris.

Lieutenant Lewis: My pleasure.

Sue Sweeney: Will you start by telling me where you were born and grew up?

Lieutenant Lewis: I was a Marine Corps brat. My dad is a retired Marine colonel—26 years. I was born in Hawaii and moved pretty much every year growing up.

Sue Sweeney: Is he an Academy graduate?

Lieutenant Lewis: No. He was NROTC at Stanford University.

Sue Sweeney: How much influence did he have on your decision to come to the Academy?

Lieutenant Lewis: He was the one who initially gave me the news that day—I think it was October 7, 1975—when President Ford signed it into law. He said, "Guess what, Chris? It's legal for women to go to the Naval Academy," or any of the academies. I had applied to three civilian universities, so I went ahead and submitted applications for the Naval Academy, Air Force, and Coast Guard Academy. I was accepted by all of the places by the following February and decided on the Naval Academy.

Sue Sweeney: Had you thought about the service before?

Lieutenant Lewis: Yes, I had my ROTC application in already at that time. I was going to try to go ROTC. Then the Naval Academy opened up, and that was just a tremendous opportunity. I couldn't pass it up.

Sue Sweeney: Did you come to the Academy wanting to go into the Marine Corps?

Lieutenant Lewis: No. Marine air wasn't an option for women.

Sue Sweeney: What was your major?

Lieutenant Lewis: I was a mathematics major.

Sue Sweeney: Is that what you would have aimed for at a civilian school, as well?

Lieutenant Lewis: Probably so—either that or engineering.

Sue Sweeney: How did your mom feel about you going to the Naval Academy?

Lieutenant Lewis: She thought it was great. I'm the oldest of four kids. They were very excited. I was glad to be doing something historical. I was thrilled about it. They were, of course, very proud. It's kind of funny, even though we're mostly women in my family, three girls and my little brother, I was pretty unexposed to the women's lib movement. That's not the reason I wanted to go to school there. I wasn't out to prove anything at all. The first year it was startling to come across women my age who were fired up to break a mold and were mentally prepared to face sexism. I felt a little naïve. My parents were behind me 100 percent. I was a big jock in high school, and thought, "Boy, this will be the best place to be able to be athletic all the time. I'm sure we will have the best teams and the best facilities." I was very excited about it.

Sue Sweeney: Where was your family stationed when you were in high school?

Lieutenant Lewis: I spent my senior year at T. C. Williams High School in Alexandria, Virginia. Dad was at Op 05 with the AV-8B Harrier program.

Sue Sweeney: How did your classmates react to your choice of the Academy?

Lieutenant Lewis: They thought it was great and were very supportive. Five people from my high school went to the Naval Academy that year 1976. I had four buddies from my high school at the Naval Academy.

Sue Sweeney: All males?

Lieutenant Lewis: The other guys were male. Four of us graduated.

Sue Sweeney: You visited the Academy before applying?

Lieutenant Lewis: I had never been there before applying. I had heard about the Army-Navy Game and all that stuff, but as soon as I submitted the application, Mom and Dad and I drove up to look at the campus to see what we were getting into. I fell in love with it the first time. It's a beautiful place.

Sue Sweeney: Did you go through with candidate guidance or just on your own?

Lieutenant Lewis: On my own. My next-door neighbor my senior year of high school in Alexandria was from the class of '21, an old diesel submariner. I went to him. He was kind of my grandfather, my surrogate grandfather from years before. We had lived there twice—once before when I was a small kid. So I went to Admiral Barbaro and said, "I'd like to go to the Naval Academy. Would you please write me a recommendation?"

At first, when he heard about women going to the Academy, he couldn't believe it. He just had a cow. But he said, "Yeah, yeah, okay. I'll write you a recommendation." I have it to this day. I wish I could read it to you. It basically reads, "Well, you jerks, I can't believe you went and let the women in our institution. You really screwed it up this time," and used all sorts of colorful language. "I can't believe you did this, but if you're going to let them in there, I think you ought to let this one in." That's the way it read. It was really neat.

Sue Sweeney: I bet he was awfully proud of you.

Lieutenant Lewis: Yes. He came to I Day. He was there at my graduation.

Sue Sweeney: Start with I Day. How did your career begin?

Lieutenant Lewis: My folks drove me there. It's only an hour from Alexandria. I wore some comfortable slacks and brought my little suitcase, because admissions said don't bring anything else.

Sue Sweeney: What time did you have to be there?

Lieutenant Lewis: It was pretty early in the morning, 7:00. They gave you a specific time to be there, because they ran people in shifts through the field house, according to your reporting time and date. You can't have all 1,200 kids show up at once. It would be bedlam. So I got there pretty early in the morning at the field house, they checked me in, gave me a couple of cards, and we sat in our place in the bleachers in a designated spot. Pretty soon you saw other people like you sitting around, mostly guys. There were three of us. We just sat there. For some reason, we were all not together. They were checked in that day in a squad form, which was not necessarily the permanent squad we ended up in, so I didn't really see my roommates until I actually made it into my room.

Sue Sweeney: What did you think?

Lieutenant Lewis: Not quite like UVA might have been.

Sue Sweeney: Do you remember what was going through your mind? Were you very nervous?

Lieutenant Lewis: I wasn't nervous, no, because I said good-bye to my folks, but I was going to see them later that afternoon after the check-in. As a military brat, I was used to being alone and making friends. I'm not too uncomfortable in a strange place. It was interesting. Pretty soon this first-class white uniform came up and herded us all in a line, and they paraded us all around the Academy, filling out papers and getting shots. There's a picture of me on the front page of the *San Francisco Chronicle* in my little Dixie cup hat, with my pants and the Academy T-shirt on, one sleeve rolled up and this guy is giving me a shot, with a stunned expression on my face. It was also on the front page of a Tokyo paper, too. I got letters from people overseas who saw them.

Sue Sweeney: They were able to track you down?

Lieutenant Lewis: They addressed it to "Midshipman Chrystal Lewis, Naval Academy," and they got to me. I got some wild mail.

Sue Sweeney: Just from the caption of the picture?

Lieutenant Lewis: Yes, based on the caption. I got a couple of letters from students at the Korean Naval Academy.

Sue Sweeney: What did they have to say?

Lieutenant Lewis: It's funny. It was kind of Pidgin English. They knew English pretty well, but you know how it's not quite right? They said, "We just think you look great. We don't have women in our Navy, but we do have some Navy nurses. You look a lot better than they do." And all that sort of stuff.

Sue Sweeney: How hard was it to live in a fishbowl?

Lieutenant Lewis: That first day—early in the morning, I was aware that this was going to be a big media blitz. It had been building up. I had done a couple of interviews already, even before I'd gotten there. So the press followed us all around. We were carrying our suitcases, and the cameras were all over the place, just focusing in on the squads with women as they marched by—but nobody got very close. I pretty much got all checked in and got the old haircut and shots. That's when some of the TV station people wanted to really get close to us gals and talk to us, so the squad leaders had to make special time. "Okay, Midshipman Lewis, come over here. We'll meet you in the library in 20 minutes. Do your spot."

I sat there, and all my buddies went trotting off. I was standing there with lights on my face, people talking. It was exciting, but at that point, my mind was a million miles away. It was with my classmates, contemplating our futures, and just feeling pretty nervous, because there were all sorts of weird things going on at Bancroft Hall, people running around, screaming and yelling. It was exciting. I enjoyed it. I didn't realize the impact that the press attention was going to have on my classmates until further on into the year, especially around Christmastime. Since everybody got cut loose on vacation, there was a good opportunity for newspapers to do stories on the hometown kids. A couple of my girlfriends got burned pretty badly—were misquoted in the *Chicago Tribune*.

Sue Sweeney: Pam Svendsen.

Lieutenant Lewis: Oh yes, Pam. That poor girl. You know, I read the article and I said, "There's no way that Pam said this. There's no way. She's not crazy. She's not a masochist." The papers simply invented corny and ridiculous quotes to make us look like idiots. And so stuff like that followed her and others around for years, a couple of years.

Sue Sweeney: Was there resentment within your company that first day when you were singled out to give an interview and the men were not?

Lieutenant Lewis: Yes. I wasn't aware of the resentment. I wasn't looking for it. Like I said, I was this green, 17-year-old kid out of high school. I had no idea that the guys would take it so hard. I'd been doing things like the guys all my life, like cutting grass for Dad and playing basketball all four years—lettered in a bunch of different sports. I never had any problem with the man-woman thing. I wasn't even aware of it. People kept talking about it so much. And so because people talked about it, I started to kind of look for some things. Of course, very soon the resentment became obvious.

Initially, I don't think my classmates cared one way or the other, but the tone of the upperclassmen, I think, changed their attitudes. Especially the first class, who the previous year had been required to go to numerous lectures and encounter groups lecturing on topics like, "Okay, what are you going to do if she cries? Okay, here's what you're going to do if she's got her period."

This was such BS. And they were threatened right and left by the administration: "Okay, if you're caught dating one of these girls, you're out of here. You get caught kissing one, you're out of here. Holding hands—or you get caught abusing one of them or swearing at one of them—you're out of here. Kicked out." You know, these guys, I think their attitudes went from shock and surprise to disgust, then hate over these threats.

The firsties must have thought, "Come on, buddy. I put four years of sweat in this place. You're not going to kick me out for yelling at a girl. Come on." But they did make these threats; they were very serious about all that stuff. This is what the first class told me after that first year when they were all graduated. So it's no wonder they had a really horrendous attitude when we arrived. I'm not blaming that entirely on the administration. I mean, the Navy did the best they could to prepare everybody for our entrance, but I think it was overkill and carried out without enough thoughtful planning.

Sue Sweeney: How did the resentment from your classmates manifest itself?

Lieutenant Lewis: The first class made snide comments in the Hall. Classmates sensed it a little bit. There were times initially when you looked for some mutual support, like the things you do as a squad to help each other out if you've got problems. In the girls' room, our classmates wouldn't check up on us to see if we needed help. For instance, there's one guy who went to prep school, he knew how to clean belt buckles faster than anybody, so he taught his roommates, of course, about cleaning belt buckles. Eventually the gouge gets around to all the other rooms. We, as women, would have to seek out this information. No one was going to come to us and help us out like the other guys had been helped. One of the NAPS [Naval Academy Prep School] graduates, a company mate (prior enlisted), went around to the plebe rooms and said, "Hey, I know how to polish belt buckles, let me show you." Not to us. We women got bypassed on that route and many others.

Sue Sweeney: Did many of the women go to NAPS?

Lieutenant Lewis: I don't know the exact number. I think we only had one NAPS graduate in our class. Kathy Shanebrook was her name—prior enlisted. She's an oceanographer somewhere right now.

Sue Sweeney: That certainly put the women at a disadvantage. Were there more obvious signs the men were unhappy about you being there?

Lieutenant Lewis: For me, later on, I'd say I had the most problem with my classmates in my junior and senior years, unfortunately. For other people it was different. In my particular case, I was a jock and no academic wizard. I mean, I did all right. My primary focus by then was to be the best captain of the varsity women's crew team I could be, which I finally got to pursue senior year. That was my goal.

Sue Sweeney: What sport?

Lieutenant Lewis: Crew. I played basketball and volleyball the first two years then went on to row crew. I rowed in high school, too, so I had a little experience. Because of rowing, I wasn't in the Hall very much. We worked out twice a day during spring break. In the spring, fall, and winter we worked out every afternoon, and I was absent from Bancroft Hall. I missed a lot of formations due to playing a varsity sport, and we had our own training tables where the team got to eat meals together. So except for the time I was a platoon commander. I pretty much stayed with the team and away from the company area. That hurt me socially. I can certainly see how classmates might not be endeared to you if you're never there, but that certainly wouldn't be enough reason to hate you. Many men were playing varsity sports as well.

Sue Sweeney: Male varsity athletes did the same thing.

Lieutenant Lewis: Sure they did. There were guys on the crew team that were in the same situation. Charlie Kanewske was at the next table, a company mate. I don't think he experienced the resentment that I felt. Senior year, I was assigned as a platoon commander, which increased the amount of time I spent with guys in the Hall. This was a position of responsibility leading 36 people of all classes within the company.

Sue Sweeney: Were you assigned here first-class summer with the plebes?

Lieutenant Lewis: I was squad leader in the summertime and I got 15 green plebes to train, which was a lot of fun. During first-class academic year, I was assigned as a platoon commander for the first semester.

Sue Sweeney: What kind of attitudes did you get from the male plebes in your squad?

Lieutenant Lewis: The plebes we trained that summer were very gung-ho and anxious to please. I felt very little resentment or skepticism from these guys and girls.

Let me mention first my trouble with the platoon when academic year resumed. We as a platoon had to do mandatory platoon drill for competition. It was a required thing in the afternoons. We had to memorize and practice a 25-minute sequence of steps, manual of arms and marching. As a platoon commander, you did the sword manual of arms. Three of my classmates were the squad leaders who marched at the head of the platoon [and they] had a real problem with my presence. I didn't know these guys very well. They were classmates, but they hadn't ever tried to be friendly. I just didn't understand why they didn't like me. They would cut up in ranks, be deliberately sloppy. They'd miss a step. They'd make everybody stop and crash and bump up behind them. This doesn't sound serious, but it was a serious business, because we had a bunch of underclass midshipmen in this group who were wasting their time out there drilling when they could be studying. They wanted to get it done and over with and get out of there.

These first class were screwing up and trying to make me embarrassed, when, in fact, what they're doing was wasting everybody's time. So finally, it got so bad, I made a command, "Right turn and march," and they'd do the opposite. So finally, I said, "I've had enough." I kept my cool. I was not going to lower myself to these guys. "Listen, you guys, perform or get out of here. You're wasting everybody's time." I finally had to embarrass them to get them to shape up, and they chose to leave. I had told the company commander the problem I had, and when it came time for the competition they were absent. We placed well, third out of the whole brigade. But anyway, finally, two years later after graduation, when I was in flight training going through jets two of those guys were there also. Both of them apologized to me. Years later—years later, finally.

Sue Sweeney: I would think that would be maddening—to make it to first-class year and have classmates still giving you a hard time.

Lieutenant Lewis: The hardest thing on me was those guys—about the most bitter memory I have. But then you asked about being a squad leader for the plebes that summer—what a gas. I wish everybody could have a chance to do something like that: take a bunch of high school graduates, still seniors, really, in their hearts—big men on campus—and then you get the opportunity to teach them how to walk, talk, salute and learn about the traditions of naval service. They were great. I remembered when I was a freshman, how you looked up at a firstie and thought, "Gee, I just want to be the best midshipman I can be. I'm going to tear this place up." They were in that mode. And they didn't care if I was a girl or a guy; or if they did, they hid it pretty well.

Sue Sweeney: Do you think they were as afraid of you as you were of your own squad leader?

Lieutenant Lewis: I think they were pretty intimidated just by the entire system. All squad leaders kind of worked as a team, so if I was walking at one end of the squad harassing somebody, then the other squad leaders would cover the other end and make sure no one was goofing off. We all worked together, pretty much. One plebe who had been a NAPSter—had gone through the Naval Academy Prep School, pretty salty—he gave it to me a little bit, but it didn't last long. His professionalism prevailed.

Sue Sweeney: What did you do?

Lieutenant Lewis: Just looked him in the eye and stayed dead serious. I didn't react emotionally or show how I felt. Just maintained a dead serious manner. Just stayed the strict professional—the guy didn't have a leg to stand on. If you made him look bad professionally, what can he do? Guys usually hang themselves. The best defense is just to be professional. Everyone wanted to succeed.

Sue Sweeney: Did you have a female role model—or did you pattern yourself on your father?

Lieutenant Lewis: My dad, yes.

Sue Sweeney: No female role models?

Lieutenant Lewis: It would have been nice to have a female role model to observe every day. Lieutenant Sue Stevens was there, but she didn't make herself available to me anywhere I was. I wasn't around her too much. I kind of wanted to talk to her, but she was busy and had a lot to do and Bancroft Hall was a big place.

Sue Sweeney: Was she a company officer?

Lieutenant Lewis: I don't think so. I think she might have been a conduct officer, something like that, in Bancroft Hall. But she looked great; she just had an immaculate appearance, she was trim, slim. She was always out running or something. I thought just that in itself—just knowing she was there, knowing that she seemed happy—that was enough for me to emulate her. And I emulated my father, my dad.

Sue Sweeney: Do you remember other female instructors?

Lieutenant Lewis: Later on there was a Captain Mayer—promoted to major and now she's a lieutenant colonel. I can't think of her first name. I want to say Shelley [B.] Mayer, but I'm not certain. She's down at Parris Island, a stalwart Marine, a tough gal— deep-selected twice. She must have done something right. She was there as a company officer. She was the first woman company officer there, I think.

Sue Sweeney: What about her did you admire?

Lieutenant Lewis: She was really neat—real tough. I thought maybe she was rougher and tougher than I would have been, but she was effective, and the guys liked her. She was gruff and straight forward. Boy, the guys in her company had nothing but great things to say about her. I kind of watched her just to see what she did that was so admirable. She had such a great rep . . . you wanted to know how she did it. She was a complete professional, and yet a good listener.

Sue Sweeney: Do you remember any civilian female instructors?

Lieutenant Lewis: A couple of civilian math profs. They were sympathetic to the conditions in the Hall. They gave us all a break on homework; they wouldn't pile it up on you like at Georgetown University or some place like that. They had to take into account that your time was limited, so they wouldn't pile it up. I didn't get really closely involved with any of the profs.

Sue Sweeney: Did you ever experience resentment from male officers or alumni when you were here?

Lieutenant Lewis: No, not at all. If anything, the company officers I had were the good guys. They were mostly all aviators. One guy was a boat driver, but the other guys were aviators. They were laid back and anxious to make everybody happy and work together. Of course, you see, women were already in the fleet, so it wasn't any big deal to them to see a woman in uniform, whereas for these midshipmen who'd been there in an all-male environment, it was kind of shocking, I guess.

Sue Sweeney: Did the Academy administration ask for feedback—what was working and what wasn't?

Lieutenant Lewis: Yes, they did. They were constantly making changes. As a matter of fact, we kind of called ourselves the guinea pig class because they tried so much on us. It's a good thing, a good thing to keeping trying new ideas. We would have these meetings. I can't remember how often they were—I remember we had them too often. Once every six weeks or so we'd hear the announcement in the dining hall, "Okay, all women midshipmen—this is when we were freshmen—will meet in the Mitscher Hall auditorium at 2000 tonight." Of course, in the wardroom, where all 4,000 are eating at one time, everybody goes, "Ooh, WUBA meeting! WUBA meeting!"[4]

---

[4] WUBA, working uniform blue alpha, devolved into derogatory slang for female midshipmen.

And we thought, "Geez! Why don't they just leave us alone? Why do they single us out like this so often and make us go to these stupid meetings, where it's only women going into the building." To be constantly singled out in the most public manner possible seemed to be a sadistic pleasure of the brigade and its officers. That's the time you just wanted to crawl under a rock. So we went.

One of the speakers, Lieutenant Pat Garvin, had a master's or doctorate or some incredible education in psychology, raised in New York City—you can imagine what a character she was. She gave us so much good advice. I still remember some of the things she said in those meetings, asking us questions and giving us her viewpoint. Every once in a while, we'd get emotional. A gal would stand up and tell of an experience, and all of us would go, "Oh, yeah." I was actually glad nobody else (male) was allowed in there. It was pretty neat, and it helped us to understand ourselves. There were some girls who had some really horrible experiences.

I thought, "Gee, I must be pretty lucky. I haven't had anything like that happen to me at all." But it helped you keep in touch with everybody, because in the Hall, as a freshman, you were in your own little room, and your world was as big as your company area, and that's it. You didn't know how everybody else was doing.

Sue Sweeney: Can you remember any of her advice?

Lieutenant Lewis: I don't know if you want to print this. She discussed dealing with men, how to deal with men successfully.

Sue Sweeney: What is the trick to it?

Lieutenant Lewis: She said—I don't quote her exactly, but just what I remember—"Anytime you have dealings with a man or have contact with a man—speaking, looking, handing him something, passing in the hallways—any time you have some kind of contact with a man, you're saying something sexually. And a man's ego is very delicate. Any man. All men's egos are very delicate, and you can never, ever insult a man sexually. I mean even in the most subtle way. You can't do it. If you do, you're finished in having a productive relationship with him. So any time you have any type of contact with a man, you must give him the feeling that he is sexually appealing."

Sue Sweeney: Oh, no!

Lieutenant Lewis: Now, don't take this in extreme. This is very subtle. She was NOT talking about flirting or initiating a romance. The minute you act dismissively towards a man—that you let him know that you don't think he's sexually appealing—he's not going to like you, he's not going to want to be around you, he's not going to want to hear what you have to say. So she gave examples of certain behaviors. It sounds extreme, but it doesn't mean flirting, but you have to—gee, it's tough to portray. Here's an example—you go to your company officer, and he says, "Good morning, Chrystal."

I say "Good morning, Sir." In a friendly, professional way, but you have to look him in the eye. You can't look at your feet, you can't avoid his glance. Heads and shoulders up, you know. "Good morning, Sir," and not avoid his gaze.

Sue Sweeney: Does it work?

Lieutenant Lewis: I've kept it in my mind ever since she told me. It really helps. When you're checking into a squadron, the way you meet somebody is important. You never talk about anybody behind their back. Boy, in the Navy you just don't do that. That helped a lot too, because if somebody hears you speaking badly about another guy, say, if I'm in the ready room and I said, "Gee, old Joe Smith, boy, he's just a real weirdo," they're going to think, "Gee, I wonder what she says about me behind my back. Does she think I'm a weirdo?"

See, you have to be real careful. Again, with sexual intonations, you can't allude one way or the other about anybody, because they'll take it the wrong way, and the guy will think you don't like him if you blow him off or are rude. You just don't do that. You can get yourself in a corner. Women must behave in a super-professional manner while also being seen as open and friendly.

Sue Sweeney: Did you compare notes? Did other women employ the same tactics?

Lieutenant Lewis: I think so. Yes, we talked about this at length. Dr. Garvin was a fascinating lady. The crew team would talk in the crew locker. "Dr. Garvin said this. That's first class." I tried to be a little nicer to males in the way she described. Not flirting. That's not what I'm saying. It's not flirting at all. It's not smiling and batting your eyes. It's being more acceptable or open to people, even if it's a man you can't stand. Say you've got a boss and you can't stand him. You can't let him know that. You're going to have to smile and be pleasant. A woman has to do that to get along. A man doesn't have to do that as much.

Sue Sweeney: Did you resent having to behave differently?

Lieutenant Lewis: Yes, because we all role-play. You role-play in everything you do. You behave differently with your boss than you do with your buddies. It takes emotional energy.

Sue Sweeney: Whose advice was the most important to you in getting through the Academy?

Lieutenant Lewis: My dad—my mom and dad, of course—but militarily, my dad.

Sue Sweeney: You were able to cry on his shoulder and tell him what it was like?

Lieutenant Lewis: I called him. There were a couple of times when I had a really bad experience. We all did. I don't mean to sound like, "Oh, woe is me." For example, the volleyball team. Oh, gosh, I'm telling you. There was some favoritism on the volleyball team. This was an intercollegiate team. This wasn't high school volleyball; this was the real thing. It was giving me some heartaches, because I had been a jock, a good jock, all the way through high school, and here I found myself in a situation where I was getting treated like I'd never been treated before. I just didn't understand it. It shook me up inside. I was getting treated like crud in the Hall, and didn't need to get treated like that in volleyball practice.

After a particularly bad experience, I called home to Mom and Dad and said, "Mom and Dad, things just aren't going well." And Mom, of course, she's great, she said, "Oh, Chris, don't worry. If you don't want to stay there, we'll pay your way to Stanford," even though I knew they'd just bought a new car with their college savings. There was no way they had money to send me to Stanford. But there was no pressure. She'd say, "You just come home anytime you want. We'll pay your way to college. We're proud of you." It was really nice support.

Dad would get on the phone, and I'd feel kind of silly crying to him, so I'd quit crying by the time I talked to him. "Dad, this place sucks, you know."

He'd say, "Yeah, yeah, it doesn't surprise me a bit. You wouldn't catch me in that place," just teasingly, making it lighthearted. It made me realize that nothing is that bad. He always has had the ability to lift me up and start talking about the future serving in the fleet, in the Navy. "Well, yeah, you know, you start flight school and you're going to need to know how to keep your cool," and all that kind of stuff. That made me think of the future, of how the lessons I learned now were going to be of use later on. He's a really good guy.

Sue Sweeney: Did you ever seriously consider quitting?

Lieutenant Lewis: I never thought of quitting. It never ever entered my mind to leave that place. Are you kidding? I wouldn't let those guys beat me. No way! I really wanted to be a naval officer.

Sue Sweeney: Was there a best thing at the Academy?

Lieutenant Lewis: The most fun?

Sue Sweeney: Something you enjoyed the most.

Lieutenant Lewis: The athletics. Rowing was just the best. Gosh, the best team, the best group of girls, a real intelligent group. I had them over to our house in Alexandria a bunch senior year. We traveled a lot together and became good friends. The sport itself was so neat. Not many women get to compete in rowing nationwide because it's expensive.

We had a tremendous boathouse on the yard. That's one great thing. The boathouse was about a mile from Bancroft Hall. We took off after class and spent the whole afternoon on the water or in the gym and even maybe went back there to study after evening meal, because they had a huge living room upstairs with a stereo. And the guys, when they were there, kind of forgot they were mids, too. We could all sit around and have a kind of fraternity-sorority type atmosphere, though still very regimented, you can imagine.

The summer cruises were a blast. We got out of the Academy and into the real Navy. My youngster year, we all were on YPs, which are yard patrol boats, 80 feet long, twin diesel engines, and we zipped up and down the eastern seaboard, had about eight ports-of-call—Newport, New York, Philadelphia, down the Intracoastal through Delaware and the Chesapeake Bay.

Sue Sweeney: What duties did you have?

Lieutenant Lewis: We all rotated around. You were cook for a while, then navigator, and OOD [officer of the deck]. We just had a great time. There were six or eight YPs. They mixed the crews up, half men, half women on the boats, so this summer training wouldn't turn into an all-girl cruise. There weren't plans in place at that time to do coed summer cruises on board operational Navy vessels so the YPs were organized to facilitate our training. There were several poor guys from the class of '80 who got drafted into going onto YPs that summer—they all bitched. "We want to go on the carriers and battleships!" They got teased when they got assigned to the YP cruises, because they were the "girls' cruises." It turns out these cruises were the best ones, because we got to do our own navigation, drove our own ships, picked our own courses and cooked our own food. We ran the ship, whereas the other guys who got stuck on ships like the *Francis Marion* going through the North Atlantic to the Queen's Jubilee chipped paint the whole time. They couldn't do a darn thing. They got two days' liberty in England and that was it, and came right back. That was funny. We got a great deal and the guys who went with us ended up having a super summer.

Sue Sweeney: Was there a particular duty you liked best on the YPs?

Lieutenant Lewis: OOD. Yes, up on the bridge conning and navigating was the best. It was especially thrilling coming into New York City past the Stature of Liberty early one morning.

Sue Sweeney: Did it make you think twice about air?

Lieutenant Lewis: No.

Sue Sweeney: You didn't like it that much.

Lieutenant Lewis: No.

Sue Sweeney: How about your other summers?

Lieutenant Lewis: The second summer, of course, everybody spent a month going to different places, to get exposure to the different warfare specialties. We did all the things the same as the men with the exception of a submarine tour. Of course, I had a blast in Pensacola, the best summer I think I've had in a while, or at the Academy, anyway. The week where the men go on the submarines, we weren't allowed to do that, so we were assigned to a shore job of our choice for a week. I chose to find out about women Marines, and went to Marine Corps Headquarters in D.C. I was assigned to a first lieutenant admin type, a lady. I was convinced very quickly that the Marine Corps wasn't necessarily where I wanted to be.

Sue Sweeney: Do you think she viewed you differently as a Naval Academy midshipman?

Lieutenant Lewis: I don't know. She had been divorced, and then after her divorce went into the Marine Corps. She was a nice attractive lady, who was very good at her admin job. Of course, to put this in perspective, I had just finished three weeks down at Fort Benning going through parachute school. I was one of the first three women at USNA to go through Jump School. We volunteered to go to Fort Benning, Georgia, during our leave time. It was mandatory for the other service academies. My two buddies and I drove down there on our summer leave and completed the course. So here I was with my brand-new jump wings on my chest with my little pistol "E" ribbon on, and my little "E" for lettering in sports. I was so proud to wear my whites.

She later mentioned that she was a little bit intimidated by me. Her military attitude was so different from mine. I had operational goals, and she had administrative goals. It was different. She said, "The first woman Marine general is stationed here. Would you like me to arrange an interview with her?"

I was thrilled. "I would be honored. I would love to meet this woman. She must be incredible." So she made the arrangement. I wore tropical whites with pants, not a skirt. I just never wore a skirt except to church or when I was forced to. She said, "Well, the general would like you to wear a skirt."

I said, "I'm sorry. I don't have it with me."

"The general, she doesn't think it's ladylike or proper for women to have medals, ribbons."

Lady, I thought to myself, I just sweated blood and risked my neck for these things. I'm not taking them off.

I went to see the general in my pants and wearing my ribbons. So I went in there and met her. She was very polite, and she was very, very nice, very nice.

Sue Sweeney: Do you remember her name?

Lieutenant Lewis: She was Brigadier General Margaret Brewer. She served in several capacities that helped the Marine Corps integrate women and was the first director of public affairs. Her first tour was as a communications officer then as an inspector-instructor of a Women Marine Reserve Unit. She was definitely from another generation of women Marines.

Sue Sweeney: What did you talk about?

Lieutenant Lewis: She very politely asked me what my goals were. "I want to fly in the Marine Corps. My dad's a Marine. That's what I want to do."

She said, "Well, you can't do that."

"Yes, ma'am, I know that now, but I'm hoping that it will be changed in the two years before I graduate."

She went, "Oh, no way." Then not only did she say that, but she proceeded to tell me why it was a bad idea, which is not what I wanted to hear at that moment. I thought if she had any sensitivity at all, she would have not said that, and she would have known that in time I would have found that out anyway. But I didn't need her to tell me that women had no place in jet aviation. I didn't need her to tell me that.

So half of my ear clicked off and waited for the conversation to continue. I asked her about her background. She just really had a different idea of what women officers were in the service. She was still from the old lipstick and powder puff school. That's just not where today's women officers are at all—not just me, but everybody. Everybody is operational these days and forward-looking. We're not all bra burners. Yes, there are a plenty of gals that would not care to go in a combat area and fly airplanes, but they still are a little more forward-looking.

She was very intelligent, extremely intelligent and very poised. She had a lot of presence. I was proud that she was a general. I was proud that she represented us. I just thought that operationally she was just ancient history.

Sue Sweeney: Did the admin officer who told you that the general didn't like women wearing ribbons say why?

Lieutenant Lewis: Because it presumes. I think she thought that if a woman officer, especially a Marine, a woman Marine, wore medals, it would allude to the fact that you thought you were combatant or infantry or something like that. It's a joke, because women Marines are not operational in that way, not in infantry or artillery, flying or tanks. I think she thought it was a little bit of a "Who are you trying to kid" thing. That's my opinion. Of course, it wasn't like that at all. My peers and I had very real operational aspirations.

Sue Sweeney: What else did you do while you were in Washington that week?

Lieutenant Lewis: Just pretty much tag after the lieutenant, and that was not real exciting. She was a nice gal, but her job—whew! Watch somebody push paper all day. So I walked around the Pentagon, roamed around, poked my head in offices. I had a good time. My folks live there, so I saw a lot of them.

Sue Sweeney: Did you stay with them?

Lieutenant Lewis: No, I wanted to be on my own.

Sue Sweeney: You stayed in the BOQ?

Lieutenant Lewis: I stayed at the Fort Myer BOQ.

Sue Sweeney: Was that your first time in a BOQ?

Lieutenant Lewis: Not by that time. Actually, frankly, growing up with Dad, we stayed at BOQs a lot, the whole family. I'd been around the military for quite a long time.

Sue Sweeney: What about Fort Benning? What was Jump School like?

Lieutenant Lewis: It was great. The way midshipmen went to Jump School was that you had to go through a screening process at the Naval Academy. It was a volunteer program, and the Academy had 100 percent completion rate down there from all the midshipmen sent to Fort Benning. They never had anybody wash out. That's a pretty good legacy.

To make sure everyone is successful, the Academy has their own PT screening program and airborne program they run at school through the dead of winter in icy February in Annapolis, to make sure that you can do all the PT tests and you're mentally motivated to complete the course. I think it lasted about three and a half or four weeks long, where we'd get up at 4:00 in the morning, shine your boots up, you had to wear infantry boots, and fatigues, military pressed, and your hat all starched up for inspection.

This was on top of crew workouts, three hours of running and lifting in the afternoons. We got up at 4:00 in the morning and ran down to the frozen field by the seawall, with about 100 guys or so initially and they pared us down as the weeks went by. It was pretty tough. They inspected you, they PT'd you left and right, and then you went for a big long run around the Academy. The bottom line was, the first year you had to be able to do 10 pull-ups. Well, for anybody in pretty good shape, you can do it, but here we were with all the gear on, too. That was pretty hard.

The first year that women were permitted to go to Jump School, one of my good buddies, Suzanne Grubbs, who was killed last year in an aircraft accident, was the first gal to go out for it. She had been a parachutist free-faller back at UT, University of Texas. The pull-ups were a big obstacle for her. There was no way a woman can do 10 like that with all the gear. You just couldn't do it unless you were Peggy Feldmann, All-American swimmer, with super strong upper body. Unfortunately, she successfully finished the runs and technical training, but they washed her out because of the pull-ups. She stuck through the whole thing, and they wouldn't let her go.

Sue Sweeney: Was it every man for himself in the training program?

Lieutenant Lewis: Pretty much, yes. It was so arduous, you didn't have time to think or do anything to help anyone else.

Sue Sweeney: She didn't get any kind of—

Lieutenant Lewis: They didn't give her any kind of a break. The Academy modified its physical fitness standards when women were admitted. Women didn't have to run the mile as fast as men and we used a timed flexed arm hang in lieu of pull-ups because we were physically not equal to men. However, the airborne screening program that first year did not modify its standards—very disappointing. Suzanne was really motivated to try out anyway, and she hung in there for the three weeks. The other recruits kind of admired her for staying with it that long. They still to this day remember, "Yeah, ol' Suzanne Grubbs, she was out there that very first year."

Well, the next year I wanted to do it. I was involved with sports, and the coach wouldn't let me have the time off because it would ruin my basketball shot, which wasn't very good anyway. So the next year I persuaded two other gals one year behind me to try out also. "They might change the standards this year. Why don't we three do this?" We all went out for the three week screening course, and lucky for us they changed the pull-up rules. By that time, Suzanne was disgusted with the whole thing, and I did not blame her for not feeling motivated to prove herself once again. It would have been real bittersweet to do the whole darn thing again. She had proved the point, and it paved the way for the next year.

I just wanted to parachute. So we successfully went through all that pre-training and headed down to Fort Benning. The guys we went with were really good. We spent a lot of time mornings and afternoons running and running around the yard. I remember that very last run, we had to finish with the pack (not lagging), with the platoon, about three and a half miles all around the snowy Academy, in boots. This was with everybody. It was after you'd PT'd really hard. I remember Sue Cowan and I were running together, and you could see the end of the street, and everybody kind of started breaking up and just going for the end, because everybody's psyched because they're almost done. We just were dying. I was in good shape, but I was starting to die. The guys were really shouting for us to finish, "Come on you guys, you can do it! You're in!" I felt somebody shoving on the small of my back, giving me a little push forward, just to keep the momentum going. "Keep the ol' legs moving!" That was just the biggest shot in the arm. It was great.

We drove down to Fort Benning, and I was one of the first people to arrive, so they made me in charge of the entire women's barracks [*grimace*]. We three Navy gals arrived in our dazzling summer whites—you know, those are dazzling uniforms—and all these zoomie [Air Force] and woop [West Point] girls showed up too. They were going through this program too, only because they had to be there. They were not volunteers like us midshipmen. They said, "How come you're in charge?" "Chrystal, how'd you get put in charge of all this?"

"Come on, you guys, shut up."

We had to scrub the place down and clean out a bunch of lockers and closets that hadn't been used in months in the barracks. These gals said they're officer material— "We don't do that."

"Come on, guys, we've got to do this."

"Who put you in charge?"

I put on my best Colonel Lewis (dad) tone of voice. You had to be real professional. You couldn't be wishy-washy. You just had to lay it on the line. "I didn't put myself in charge here, but this is stuff we've got to accomplish, this, this, this, and this. Questions, anybody? I'd be glad to help. Just let me know what you need."

Sue Sweeney: Was that your first meeting with West Point and Air Force girls?

Lieutenant Lewis: Pretty much, yes. It was fun and interesting. After that first initial meeting—everybody settled down but they all stayed in their little cliques, though. All the Air Force girls slept here, all the woops slept over here, and Carol and Sue—there were just three of us, we had no clique, so we hung out with the guys (mids). We ran in platoon formations. Crooks [Carol Crooker] and Sue [Cowan] and I could run circles around them. We were having a ball at Fort Benning, because no one yelled at you in the same way they did at the Academy. They just made you do push-ups if you messed up. That's fun! We'd do them all day! Almost . . .

There were several platoons of cadets and mids. They sent 500 people at a time through the program. They mixed the women in with the men on the runs.

After a while, some of the zoomie ladies started groaning, "We can't keep up with the men. They run too fast. We want our own platoon. We want a women's platoon."

Crooks, Sue and I were not happy about this. "You're crazy! What do you want to do this for?" We worked so hard to do as well, and they want their own separate platoon. Oh, gosh. So it got up to the major in charge, and he made it happen. Well shoot, great. Just what I wanted, you know. So we grudgingly ran with an all-ladies platoon after that.

Sue Cowan, Carol Crooker and I led songs (jodies) while running to keep everybody talking and breathing. We started rival military songs. We'd start singing this great song that everybody would repeat and repeat, and then the stinger punch line would be a slam-dunk on their community, like, "Army wings are made of lead." Also we'd do crazy stuff, like break out and run circles around the moving platoon, while all the cadets were wheezing and puffing. It sounds kind of stupid, but it was fun.

Sue Sweeney: Were you able to do much comparing notes with them?

Lieutenant Lewis: A little bit. That was kind of fun. They were a proud bunch of women in that group, all class of '80, an unusual group of women. They were completely independent, too. "You don't tell me what to do. I don't need any help." Just a real domineering outgoing bunch of gals. It was fun.

Sue Sweeney: Had any women from the other service academies made it the year Suzanne Grubbs tried?

Lieutenant Lewis: I don't know. Maybe they did from that year, I'm not sure. I don't think so, because the other service academies normally go their second-class summer, so that might have been the first year for all.

Sue Sweeney: Did a different type of woman go to Air Force and West Point?

Lieutenant Lewis: Yes, I think so.

Sue Sweeney: Obviously the best went to the Naval Academy!

Lieutenant Lewis: Obviously. We had some smart women.

Sue Sweeney: Were there a lot of ROTC women?

Lieutenant Lewis: Yes, there were a couple of ROTC gals there. As a matter of fact, my roommate was one. She's a pilot now. I ran into her once years later. "I know you from somewhere." It was Fort Benning.

Sue Sweeney: Was there a lot of interest in the service academy women by the women from other colleges?

Lieutenant Lewis: I think they were pretty fascinated to hear some of the stories.

Sue Sweeney: How about you? Did you yearn for the carefree life of a civilian school?

Lieutenant Lewis: No. I needed a lot of discipline to study. I probably would have not done very well academically at another university. I don't know. That's one thing very attractive about the Academy—the discipline. I mean, the regimentation. Some people say that's what they hated most, but I kind of needed that discipline.

Sue Sweeney: Did you ever see a thaw in the attitudes of male midshipmen during your four years?

Lieutenant Lewis: I'd say after second-class summer, which is the first summer where you go to the different communities, the first chance you really got to get out and be with people from other companies and meet some other new friends. I made friends that summer who I wouldn't have crossed paths with ever in the future because they went to different communities but they have remained friends, maybe, because I met them socially and not under the guise of a military midshipman. It was a nice summer for me. I could see the ice start to break between the men and women, because I started to meet many other people and realize, yes, there were some humans out there that saw that I was a girl with certain interests and not just an WUBA. You've heard that expression?

Sue Sweeney: Yes. Did you date much—either your classmates or upperclassmen?

Lieutenant Lewis: Yes.

Sue Sweeney: Was it difficult?

Lieutenant Lewis: I won't go into freshman year. That was pretty fun. Freshman year, you really don't have time to do anything. I did some illegal stuff. We all did.

Sue Sweeney: Any examples? They can't fry you now.

Lieutenant Lewis: I went over the wall a couple of times during the week and went out to dinner with some people. I'm telling you, we're talking risky.

Sue Sweeney: As a plebe you went over the wall with an upperclassman?

Lieutenant Lewis: Yes. This is funny now. My friend Nancy Burke, she's married now, we were in history class together. We sat next to each other freshman year, and kind of got talking to each other one day. She was dating somebody.

Sue Sweeney: An upperclassman?

Lieutenant Lewis: Yes. We'd tell each other funny things we'd heard about dating. One day—we had talked about this for several weeks, and we said, "Let's make a list. Between the two of us, we know all the girls here. Let's make a list of who we think is dating upperclassmen." We came up with five people who were not.

Sue Sweeney: How prevalent were first class–plebe relationships?

Lieutenant Lewis: Maybe a third of the girls dated first class, the rest of them, either second or third class.

Sue Sweeney: How awkward was it to date a firstie? How did it come about?

Lieutenant Lewis: Mine started on a bet. He made a bet with me. We made bets on football games. When you're a freshman, you have to make bets. "Yeah, Midshipman Lewis, I'll bet you a beer or something that Purdue wins by 10," or whatever.

"Yes, Sir." You always had to say, "Yes, Sir." And it turns out he won the bet, of course. They never made a bet they're going to lose.

So one night he passed me in the Hall and stopped and said, "Hey, you've got to buy me that beer sometime."

"Yes, Sir. The first chance I get, I'll buy you a beer."

But he was a nice guy and a real good athlete, and I knew who he was. So a couple of nights later, he came into my room and said, "Hey, let's go out and get that beer."

To tell you the truth, a lot of the guys had kind of—they called them "older brothers" in the old days—you know, a firstie who sneaks you out, he buys you a beer, kind of makes life a little more livable for you. It's illegal, but everybody did it. As a matter of fact, our whole plebe squad went out once with my first-class squad leader. We had the best time. We all brought civilian clothes along, we had a great time. What a morale builder. It made us a tight group because we'd all done something together that was bad.

I thought, "Well, shoot, I know that Pat Inglis and Charlie Kanewske go out over the wall with their squad leader. I can go out with this guy." He wasn't my squad leader. He wasn't in my chain of command, which I thought was even better. Okay, good, I'm not going to be hurting anybody here. Sure enough, I packed up my books like I was going to the library, and he met me in back of the library. I jumped in the backseat of his car, and he floored it out the gate. It just started with an innocent beer, and we met a couple of other times and ended up I'd just enjoy his company. He provided a little bit of—again, made me feel desirable and wanted and made me feel smart and attractive.

Sue Sweeney: How much trouble would you two have been in if someone found out?

Lieutenant Lewis: Oh, it would have been a really bad scene. So we really were careful. This went on for quite a while. I saw him for quite a long time that year. But pretty soon my roommate—who's one of my best friends, Sue Presto—she let me know that she knew I was doing something.

Sue Sweeney: You couldn't even tell your roommate?

Lieutenant Lewis: Heck no. I didn't want them to know, because the honor code would force them, if someone asked, "Where's Chris?" they'd have to say, "Well, she's dating a first class." I didn't even tell them. I carried my books out like I was going to the library, but I wouldn't say I was going to the library, because I didn't want to lie. You know what I mean—play the honor code.

So finally, she sat me down one night. "Chris, I'm worried about you. I know you're seeing this guy. I know when you look like you're going to the library, you're really not. To heck with the honor code. I want to know where you are and a phone number in case there's an emergency so I can reach you. I'm really worried. If something happened to you, I would be really worried, and I want to know. If anybody asks me where you are, I would lie and say I didn't know, okay? So just tell me from now on where you're going." Like Mom, you know.

"Okay, Sue." And we did. And later on, she dated a bit, and I did the same for her.

Sue Sweeney: Do you think your male classmates had an idea this was going on?

Lieutenant Lewis: They were all wrapped up in themselves. Of course, outside of the Hall, no one ever saw us together anywhere.

Sue Sweeney: Could you have openly been with male members of your own class?

Lieutenant Lewis: There were some gals freshman year who went out and had an ice cream cone downtown on Main Street with one of the other guys, just two of them. I had a couple of girlfriends get dumped on: "You're not allowed to be dating."

"It's my classmate."

But they'd say they were dating because there were only two of them. You couldn't win. It was a Catch-22. What—am I supposed to stay with the girls all the time? There are so many of them, you know [sarcasm]. Then in later years, when I was a first classman, I dated a youngster. He was only 11 months younger than I was, but he'd gone through prep school and other things, so he was a only a little bit behind me. He was the captain of the hockey team, a real good guy. We had a good relationship. I think whenever I dated somebody that was outside the company, my company mates would be kind of pissed and mad. I don't know why. "Oh, I saw you out with John Doe last night."

"Yeah?"

"What a jerk." You know, something like that. I don't know if it was jealousy or just a little bit—that it was not classmate loyalty.

"Why don't you date one of us?"

"You jerks never ask me out. Who'd want to go out with you anyway; I know you too well." I did. I tried dating one guy for a while. I think we just didn't get along. He was a little bit uncomfortable with me so close all the time. I mean, he was always there. I could never get away from him and he couldn't get away from me.

Sue Sweeney: In general, how awkward was it to date at the Academy? Was it uncomfortable to go to dances?

Lieutenant Lewis: The dances were awful until we became upperclassmen.

Sue Sweeney: I felt sorry for the girls in uniform when everyone else had fabulous dresses.

Lieutenant Lewis: Awful! It was just disgusting. I'm no big prom-goer. I did in high school, but it didn't excite me, really, to get all dolled up. But these dances were more just humiliating for me. I didn't feel like I was not glamorous next to these girls; I was just humiliated, because I was very proud in my uniform, and I felt like I was being thrown in with a bunch of gals who were there for completely different reasons than I was. I would have loved to have been there dancing with a tall, handsome man—even a midshipman—but I knew that nobody was going to want to dance with me. They were all going to give you that kind of look. "Oh God, a woman midshipman. I'm not going to dance with her." I knew it was going to be like that.

Sue Sweeney: You're talking about mixers, not the formals?

Lieutenant Lewis: Those were the formals. Mixers weren't mandatory.

Sue Sweeney: The formals were?

Lieutenant Lewis: Formals were mandatory, yes.

Sue Sweeney: Even dances like the Valentine Ball?

Lieutenant Lewis: I'm thinking of freshman year.

Sue Sweeney: I thought only mixers—tea fights—were mandatory for plebes.

Lieutenant Lewis: That's right. That's what it was. Your memory is better than mine.

Sue Sweeney: Did you ever date civilians?

Lieutenant Lewis: No. I never have, not since the Academy. I only date people I know pretty well.

Sue Sweeney: How about first-class year as the squad leader? Did you go on a cruise as well?

Lieutenant Lewis: Yes. That was great. I went out to San Diego on an amphibious assault ship, USS *New Orleans*, for five and a half, six weeks. We'd go out and cruise for five days and come in for the weekend. It was pretty nice—learned a lot. There were five first class and about 35 third class. No women third class; all men. Of the first class, three of us were women and two were guys. Of the two women—only Liz Durham and I—were from the Naval Academy. The other girl was from Vanderbilt. These two guys were from someplace. Good people. We got together for the introduction and they said, "Okay, we've got the engineering department, navigation department, air department, hangar deck. What division do you guys want to be with?"

I stuck my hand out first, "Air." So I got to be up in the air boss's place, got to ride the helicopter and all that stuff. It was a lot of fun.

Sue Sweeney: Were there female officers on the ship?

Lieutenant Lewis: There was one, and she was cross-decked for the purpose of this midshipmen's cruise. She was normally on the USS *Samuel Gompers*, and they put her on board the *New Orleans*. There were no Marines deployed aboard at this time; normally there would have been thousands of grunts running around. So we all had plenty of staterooms and a lot of privacy. It wasn't bad at all. We got a lot accomplished.

There was one thing that happened on that cruise that was kind of funny, again, along with what we discussed earlier, I was so naïve—we all were. I just did things without thinking about any implication or how it looked. With my dad, my sisters and I did whatever we wanted to do, pretty much, with regard to hobbies and chores like sons would. We had these general-quarters drills now and then. Everybody went to their battle stations and you lock all the doors to make the ship watertight, and you stay there for three hours while they do some drills. It's really boring especially for midshipmen who were not part of the crew. After a couple of these drills where I ended up sitting in some vacant dentist's office with the door locked for hours, I thought, "I'm not going to sit here for three hours with the lights off and a little red flashlight. This is ridiculous." So I started asking around the other mids, "Where do you go during GQ?"

A bunch of people said, "We go down to our bunkroom and play poker."

I said, "Great." It was a big bunkroom, a 30-man room, with a couple of big tables, not an intimate little room by any means. So the next GQ, where did I go? Down to the bunkroom. I was in there playing cards with everybody else, with the chips and my money. Then the phone rang. We'd been at it for about an hour. One of the guys looks up. "Chris, it's Commander for you"—who was the air boss, who is the guy who was training me.

"Yes, Sir. Midshipman Lewis. Can I help you, Sir."

"Chrystal, where are you?"

"Sir, I'm down here"—I gave the room number—"playing cards because there was nothing else to do." That was an acceptable thing at that time. He knew there was nothing for me to do during GQ.

"Chrystal, why are you in the men's bunkroom?"

"Sir, we're just playing cards."

"Listen, I want you up here right now."

"Yes, Sir."

" Good-bye, guys." So I went up through 18 million watertight doors to get to where he was. He sat me down and said, "I've got two daughters, Chrystal. You've got to watch appearances. You really have to be careful with what people will think when you're in there with all these guys."

I looked at him. "You must be out of your mind. What are you thinking, Sir? What do you think I'm doing down there?" This was finally just occurring to me. I wish I had remained blissfully ignorant, to tell you the truth. I learned the rules of life and impressions the hard way.

Sue Sweeney: Do you remember if he was Academy? You'd think he'd know you were used to holding your own around guys from Bancroft Hall.

Lieutenant Lewis: No he wasn't, but I think he liked me—Liz and me—and wanted to us to do well and to have a good reputation. He just thought that was bad for us. This situation just had never come up during my upbringing. I did everything the guys did.

Sue Sweeney: Was it easier at the Academy as each subsequent class of women came in?

Lieutenant Lewis: Oh, yes, because finally the focus was not just on us anymore. Like I said, we were guinea pigs—there were so many things we had to endure that freshman year before the next couple of classes came through. The guinea pig stuff included wearing experimental uniforms. I wore men's shoes my whole first year there. I have huge feet anyway, but they asked me if I'd wear them. Sure. So I wore these big old corfam shoes.

Sue Sweeney: They eventually got larger women's shoes at some point?

Lieutenant Lewis: Yes. These are the women's shoes now. This is a beat-up pair.

Sue Sweeney: How much competition was there within—or between—classes of women?

Lieutenant Lewis: We were a pretty tight bunch. I knew everybody's name and where everybody was from in my class. In subsequent classes, the gals couldn't do that. They were not that close. I think just that first year, we had so many meetings together, like I said, that we got to know everybody and know their problems and where they were from. Also our numbers were so few that it was easy to get acquainted with everyone.

Sue Sweeney: One of your classmates said she felt isolated, within her company, from the other little clusters of women.

Lieutenant Lewis: Yes. I agree with that absolutely. That was kind of a bad thing, because you'd almost be in adversarial relationships. Say as a freshman you went running through another company area and you saw some woman's name tag on her door. A couple of times I'd stop and knock and introduce myself. I'd like to meet somebody. There was always a little bit of, "Who are you? What are you doing here?"

Sue Sweeney: From the other women?

Lieutenant Lewis: Yes. Not a bad thing, just a subtle, "Is someone chasing you? Are you in trouble? Are you bringing trouble? Why are you here?" We just weren't allowed to socialize until finally in later years, we loosened up a little.

Sue Sweeney: Do you think the Academy was geographically keeping you from being perceived as this little clique?

Lieutenant Lewis: Yes. It was a good thing. The Air Force Academy—the first semester they had women there, they put all the gals in one wing, and they ordered in a bunch of Air Force captains to be role models. These gals hadn't gone to the Academy. How can you be a role model for something when you hadn't been there? They were role models performing as upperclassmen.

Well, they didn't know how to do that. You can't blame them. The senior cadets who were running the male plebes around back in the men's dorms were supposed to come over to the women's dorm and give them the same ration. It didn't work. They never came over there. These gals got completely cut out of the communications loop and the camaraderie loop. They weren't included. They just weren't a part of the plebe experience.

Well, at the Naval Academy, slam-dunk, we were assigned throughout all the companies, which was great. That's the one good thing that Navy did. West Point did the same thing, I think. Air Force saw that this separate dorm wasn't working too well, so the second semester of that year, maybe even sooner than that, they switched back and did it our way and it worked a lot better.

Sue Sweeney: While you were a midshipman, did you find unexpected pockets of support? Were you surprised by anybody's attitude toward you?

Lieutenant Lewis: I got a lot of mail, as I mentioned, freshman year. It was really neat, from all over the world—Korea, Thailand, all over the United States. Gals—"I'm a doctor and I've a private license. I'm 45 and think what you're doing is great."

And from men, too, older men who maybe had nothing to do with the Navy, but maybe saw a picture in the newspaper and would say, "Go for it. It's about time it started happening." I never, ever got any bad mail.

Sue Sweeney: Did you get strong reactions from alumni at homecoming?

Lieutenant Lewis: Yes. Some of my dad's contemporaries still didn't agree with it. And at tailgaters, some of them would bring it up with my parents. There was a general—he was a friend of my family. He was talking about women being admitted into missile silos in the Air Force and how appalled he was at this proposal. "Sir, being in a missile silo, what do you think they're going to do in a missile silo with all those cameras and everyone looking? There is no privacy in a missile silo, for God's sake. What do you think is going to happen?"

"They just won't be able to concentrate. Jobs won't get done. The security of the nation will be in jeopardy." Oh, wow. And he compared this with the academies, which also kind of disappointed me and Dad a little bit.

But I'll tell you something Mom found out, and this is something I mentioned at the beginning, how we weren't really in touch with the women's lib movement until it kind of hit you in the face there. Dad was part of the AV-8A Harrier program in D.C., and they went to a lot of embassy parties, Australian, British, really neat stuff. She had, probably on six or seven different occasions, ladies come up to her and say, "Your daughter took my son's place at the Naval Academy." He didn't get admitted, in other words.

"What's happening? I don't understand. Say that again. I beg your pardon?"

Officers' wives, of the 05 and 06 rank level, were downright derogatory about my presence there. They would make comments in front of Mom or within earshot of Mom saying, "Those little hussies in there, rubbing their boobs up against our husbands." Really wild stuff.

Sue Sweeney: What did your mom say to something like that?

Lieutenant Lewis: She was speechless the first few times it happened. Then she started getting mad and became more aware of women's articles in the newspaper, women this, women that, and on the news, you know. She'd listen instead of turning it off or changing the channel; she'd listen and became real aware of women's problem in general, the women's plight in the workforce and how women are treated. I didn't, by any means, call and complain to her. I did not do that. I don't believe in leaning on somebody like that. But she caught some of the stories, and it just burned her to a crisp, especially when these ladies, who were her contemporaries, were making comments about her daughter.

Sue Sweeney: That's pretty cold-blooded.

Lieutenant Lewis: Yes, it was. It was for her.

Sue Sweeney: That can lead us into the Webb article. As a Marine brat and a female midshipman, what was your reaction?

Lieutenant Lewis: It was such a disappointment. I was so disappointed that he wrote that, because all it did was give the guys at the Academy who were really bad more ammunition to flaunt in our face. Of course, the brigade got a hold of the article and it was reproduced en masse and pinned up everywhere so everybody could read it. It was just real disappointing.

Sue Sweeney: Was there any validity to it?

Lieutenant Lewis: It was all his opinion. I may be mistaken, but he was stationed at the Academy for just a very short period of time as associate professor. We had a lot of guest professors come in. He was there for a little bit, maybe a semester, maybe just a little more than that. And based on his experience—what experience? As a professor? He didn't live in the Hall and live our routine. He made all these judgments on how the women were getting along and how they had no place there, and it wasn't working at the Academy. I'd have to read the article again to be more specific.

He didn't see how it was working. It was. Yes, it was rocky, but we got tremendous educations. It worked. I got a great education out of it, and that's the whole mission of that place, to give me an education to be a good naval officer and be able to go out in the fleet and perform. They give you that 110 percent, even through those rocky years. So he's full of it.

Sue Sweeney: How about the argument that you can get a good education and be a good officer going through ROTC, but that the Academy's place is to graduate combat leaders?

Lieutenant Lewis: You get more of an opportunity to lead at the Academy, much more of an opportunity than you do at ROTC. You get the book learning at ROTC and you learn how to wear the uniform, and you get a little bit of leadership during the summers and maybe with your ROTC unit. It's in a collegiate environment. It can't be compared to the Academy's environment at all, I don't think, in my opinion.

I've never been to an ROTC group. If you tell a guy from the Citadel that it's not a good military institution, he'll slap you. The same goes for a guy from Texas A&M, where they have a real strong corps of cadets. It depends on where you are. You get a big picture at the Naval Academy and these other military institutions that I don't think you get in the ROTC program or civilian program. The big question is, "What am I really in this Navy for?"

You're not just conditioned to perform, but you learn to appreciate what you've learned. It becomes a part of your emotion, part of your heart and your soul, wearing the uniform, and why you have this uniform on. There's a lot of that kind of training at the Academy. You learn to know that you're in there for the defense of your country, and not just to get an education, and not just, "I want to go to flight school." You learn a deeper seated emotion, because you have bonds with people and you see people grow and mature over four years in a stressful environment. That's why you make friends there that will always be your friends. Of course, college grads have that, too. Guys that you will die for, friends that you learn to appreciate, "Yes, there is somebody that I trust so much that I would risk my life for them." I don't see how a bond like that could be made in a low-pressure program.

Sue Sweeney: But you don't have any ambivalence about women being at the service academies before the combat clause is changed?

Lieutenant Lewis: Oh, no. What a great education!

Sue Sweeney: That's good, but as far as the actual mission of preparing combat-ready officers?

Lieutenant Lewis: I anticipate the role is going to change someday, sooner or later. I really do. They need to have the people ready when this happens. You need to have the assets trained and ready to go. If they just up and decide to change the rules 10 years from now without any women graduates or women trained the way they want them, what a rocky transition that would be. You don't have the material to pick from.

Sue Sweeney: So in other words, you're very optimistic about your future in the Navy and the role of women?

Lieutenant Lewis: Maybe not my future; maybe the futures of the gals behind me. If it wasn't for the gals before me, I wouldn't have gotten to where I am, so I don't mind doing my part for later on down the line. It's important what we're doing.

Sue Sweeney: How about you personally? Do you see yourself as Captain Lewis 20 years from now?

Lieutenant Lewis: That's tough to say. I take my dad's attitude that I'll stay as long as I'm having fun and feel like I can make a contribution to the Navy. A lot of guys are getting out these days. My obligation will be up in a year and a half, and aviators, especially the jet aviators, are getting out left and right and going to the airlines, for the money, for the more time off, leisure life, it's really attractive. But I have never pictured myself doing anything else. This sounds kind of goofy. You're going to think I'm a little Hitler maybe, but after growing up in a military family and then going right into a military college, and then spending my life in naval aviation is just the happiest path for me. Naval aviation is the greatest. I just think we're the best and most open-minded people in the naval community; I still cannot see being in the civilian world. I'm a military person. I don't mean I have inspections in the morning. I'm a woman; I like to go out and have a good time, you know. But this is my life, really, not just a job.

Sue Sweeney: You said something off tape—that because women don't have the same career opportunities, they're not going to get the leadership positions or have the same potential for promotions. How does this affect your attitude towards the Navy or Navy air?

Lieutenant Lewis: It makes me disappointed, because I feel like I could be good at what aviation holds for me if given the chance. I've already shown so far that I'm pretty good at flying and contributing to the success of the squadron. I know that I can physically compete with my fellow aviators, so the only obstacles that hold me back are what kind of jets I can fly and where. I don't feel that badly, but still, professionally I'll never be able to be a part of that exciting operational front line. It's so exciting. I got a little taste of it out in WestPac, flying in the Philippines for two years, in Thailand, Korea, Japan, and Indonesia. I saw a lot of the Ivans up close—Russians. Exciting missions. I worked with the carrier groups and a lot of the missions they did, helped plan a few and flew with them. It was great!

After having a taste of that, it just made you want more and more, to be involved. I can see myself ending up, at the worst, probably in Washington somewhere, pushing a pencil. Hopefully I'd like to get into weapons testing, aircraft testing. It's not combat service, but it's still associated with the front of the line equipment and tactics that the guys are studying, learning, and using. At least I could stay abreast with what's really happening in the Navy. Maybe go for another overseas assignment.

Sue Sweeney: Do you feel you have much chance of changing things?

Lieutenant Lewis: We've got a couple of Navy gals who are senior women aviators. One of the gals is Rosemary Conatser Mariner, she's one of the first and the senior female jet pilot in the Navy. Another ground breaker in jets was Mary Lou Jorgensen. These are two really dynamic gals who are good role models for me, who have a real good handle on the career pattern for women jet pilots. They publish letters frequently and send them out to all of us junior pilots.

Sue Sweeney: Was Barb Rainey the senior woman aviator until she crashed?

Lieutenant Lewis: She was the senior woman aviator, period, in the military. The gals I mentioned were jet pilots, which is a smaller community within the realm of women in aviation.

Sue Sweeney: You obviously enjoyed the athletics aspect of the Academy. Do you think they put as much into the women's program as the men's—they tried for the best coaches, the best equipment, the best schedule?

Lieutenant Lewis: To be realistic, if you look at all the colleges in the country and rated Navy by the number of women they had to pick from in the student body to form into sports teams, we had it made. We had a lot of money and a lot of opportunity compared to other women in other schools. We had a really high female participation rate. Now, if you compared the number of women's sports to the men's program in our same school, we fell short in some areas. But at the time it was realistic. For heaven's sake, you can't appropriate money based [on] the number of people in your student body for whatever reason, and it's apportioned by law. We had so few women compared to men that women were able to compete in more than one sport over four years. This is not possible in many universities. Well, so what? That's all you have to go from. I never saw us lacking anything in any way, for heaven's sake. The limited number of sports offered those first few years was offset by the nice facilities and equipment and travel schedules that were provided. The volleyball team always had plenty of brand-new shoes every year and a beautiful locker room, a brand-new locker facility, our own gym to practice in.

Sue Sweeney: You sure had great records those first few years.

Lieutenant Lewis: You bet. Of course, we played some small schools and we got a little bit teased for that. We said, "Well, listen, buddy, you don't have a student body of 54 either, okay?" That first year the women's basketball team had everything we could have wanted. The first few years in women's crew, we used the old starting shells that the guys would will down to us. But towards my senior year and the year after I graduated, beautiful, brand-new fiberglass shells were purchased (or donated) for our use—gorgeous. We were outshining Georgetown University and all these other schools that have had women's crew for years. We had better equipment than they did. We had our own locker room, our own weight room. They'd come to our house and say, "Gee whiz. Where do you guys get the money?" Alumni, I guess.

Sue Sweeney: During your four years, did you ever play Army?

Lieutenant Lewis: We never raced them in crew. Of course, they didn't have a crew at that time, I don't think. We played them in basketball the year after I finished playing. I got away from volleyball and basketball and did crew full-time. That's when they started playing Army. I was mad, because I wanted to play them freshman year. That would have been great. We got a letter out of it. "Why can't we play Army? All the guys get to play Army." For some reason, they just didn't want that to happen. They just hadn't planned for it.

Sue Sweeney: Do you know why?

Lieutenant Lewis: To be fair, it might have had to do with the fact that we were plebes. I don't know if the plebe football team got to play the Army plebe football team. I don't know if that happens. It may not have. That might have been a perfectly good reason not to let us. I mean, why give us a chance to do something like that if the guys didn't get to? That was probably why—can't give the plebes too much rein, too many liberties.

Sue Sweeney: Another I Day question: You see pictures of the men getting their hair cut—the barbers madly shaving heads. Were they more judicious with the women's hair or did they just hack away?

Lieutenant Lewis: They hired a gal named Karen Zimmerman. She was there the first two years—what a great gal. Young—she was about 25—cute, just the nicest gal. Gosh, to this day I'll always remember her. She checked us in. She was very sympathetic to all of us. My roommate, Sue Presto, had long golden hair. She'd gotten it chopped to her chin for I Day, and the barbers continued to chop on it. It was such a quick day, and I think Karen was there but she had some male barbers in there helping and they did a real hack job on Sue. Her hair was straight and real thick. But we didn't have time to worry about it.

Sue Sweeney: Would they take any requests from you about style?

Lieutenant Lewis: That first day, not at all. They just cut it the way they wanted to. Frankly, after we had been established there for a few weeks, we all went back and had it finished a little bit. Sue and I did, anyway. I remember freshman year was kind of grotesque—you know how with guys, how they cut your hair and trim it around over the ears, and then they shave the guys' necks? Well, there was this rule at the Academy that you had to have your hair cut off the top of your collar. My hairline goes down below that, and so do almost all women's, especially gals who had short necks. So the guy would carefully measure. At first-class inspection, they'd look at you and go, "Your hair is too long. Go get it shaved."

"Oh, great." So you go down to Karen. "Karen, you've got to shave it so the hair is above my collar line, okay?"

She was horrified. Here she was a professional beautician. "You want me to do what?" So sure enough, she shaved it. It was itchy, like your legs feel after you shave, kind of nubby back here. Gross. So we put up with that for about half of that year, and finally somebody made it known to the administration that this was ridiculous. We finally went along with the Navy regulation, which was it had to be off the bottom of your collar, which made for a normal pixie haircut.

Sue Sweeney: Was she the only female beautician available to all 80 women? Did you have to make an appointment with her?

Lieutenant Lewis: She was the only hairdresser there for the first couple of years. But that first day, I believe, the men barbers were cutting hair also, because they were so fast. I can't remember if Karen was there that first day or not. I think she was. But I know a lot of the guys cut women's hair, too.

Sue Sweeney: By the time you graduated, could you pretty much have it done the way you wanted it?

Lieutenant Lewis: Sure. Oh yes, as long as it was within regulations—and Karen was good.

Sue Sweeney: After plebe year, you could have gone out in town to a salon?

Lieutenant Lewis: Sure. Absolutely. But she was good and she was free.

Sue Sweeney: How about conduct? Did you receive demerits? Did you give them?

Lieutenant Lewis: I got demerits a couple of times for weird things—maybe if my room was a mess, I'd get demerits for that. I never got any big-time demerits.

Sue Sweeney: As an upperclassman, did you give them?

Lieutenant Lewis: Just to my plebes for nickel-and-dime stuff. I'm not so sure I really enjoyed that demerit system. I don't think I really approved of it completely as an effective disciplinary action. I thought there were a lot more things we could have done discipline-wise to straighten people out, academic things. Rather than give a plebe demerits, have them do extra academic study and have to recite to you. That's what they did in the old days, or just good ol' PT them—"Give me 30 push-ups." They made that illegal when we came in there. You weren't allowed to haze people. Hazing is not allowed. You couldn't touch somebody, and you couldn't make them PT. I guess some guys got hurt. Of course, at Texas A&M they still do.

Sue Sweeney: Did you ever have an opportunity to let somebody know what you thought?

Lieutenant Lewis: Sure. I said that all the time. Even when I was a freshman, I would have much rather been PT'd than get demerits or have to recite these dumb poems. Being PT'd, it's good for you; it makes you stronger. You get the point across, and you can make the point instantly. It's a disciplinary procedure that can happen right now, a kind of conditioning. You screwed up, down now, and your punishment's done with; it's not lingering, it's not something you have to follow up on later, and there's no paperwork. Of course, there are always those people that will abuse it, but you can monitor that kind of thing.

Sue Sweeney: How was your first-class year?

Lieutenant Lewis: I enjoyed it. Crew was a blast. We traveled all over the East Coast and to Boston that fall. We rowed in the Head of the Charles Regatta with Harvard and Yale. We had a great time.

Sue Sweeney: Did you have your car?

Lieutenant Lewis: Oh, yes, I had my little Trans Am and just zipped back and forth all over the place and enjoyed wearing civilian clothes again. I had a real nice time. I really enjoyed that senior year—relaxing!

Sue Sweeney: What are your memories of graduation?

Lieutenant Lewis: June Week was fun. I had 30 relatives come up to Annapolis and rented a house. I'm the oldest of 13 grandkids, the first one to graduate from college, and it was a historical event. Everybody wanted to be there to see it.

Sue Sweeney: Good thing it was at the stadium and not in the field house.

Lieutenant Lewis: That's for sure. That was very exciting and emotional.

Sue Sweeney: Did the press coverage get in the way at all?

Lieutenant Lewis: A little bit. I kind of regret how I reacted to it. There were a couple of other gals in the class who were really sharp. Liz Belzer finished highest of the women and got all sorts of academic awards—a really neat person, smart. Too smart for the Navy, maybe. Her husband is an F-14 pilot. They were interviewed quite a lot. I think they enjoyed it, and they were very good on the interviews, real positive and outgoing at that time. We came into the stadium for graduation and threw our hats up in the air, yelling and screaming. We just couldn't believe that we'd actually finished, we were still alive after all that. Boy, I just couldn't even speak. I was surrounded by my classmates, we just couldn't even speak. Some lady shoved this microphone in my face with the camera rolling, "How are you feeling right now, Chrystal Lewis?"

And I just shook my head and didn't say anything, but I was inferring, "Not now, okay?" And I got away from them, which I regret, because it was such a special moment, and I would have liked to have shared that with anybody who was watching TV. Maybe some 10-year-old kid would have been watching and would have wanted to catch some of that emotion and seen the excitement. I regret that I did that.

Sue Sweeney: Would you be able to recommend the Academy to anybody—to a family member?

Lieutenant Lewis: Oh yes. Nowadays I would. The Academy is really a good experience nowadays.

Sue Sweeney: What changes have you seen since you left?

Lieutenant Lewis: The attitude toward women and their role in the Navy is much better. It's a healthy, healthy, positive modern attitude at the Naval Academy. They rebuilt a bunch of buildings which helped to change the face of things. Now old alumni come back and say, "This place doesn't even look the same." Well, good. The place was falling apart.

The new attitudes are established now. There are some traditions that have been established—even involving the women—like the class rings. There is a women's size class ring. Initially, women were going to have to buy the miniatures that guys got for their fiancées. Oh, that did not go over very well, so we made them change it. We wanted our own rings that only women midshipmen could have, and we got that.

Sue Sweeney: In time for your class?

Lieutenant Lewis: Yes. A lot of gals did buy the miniatures. Frankly, I fell into sway with my roommates and ordered a miniature, because my roommates said, logically, "When you're 35 years old, you're not going to want to wear this big hunk of a man's ring."

I thought, "Well, you know, you're probably right. When I'm 35, I won't." So I ordered a miniature. It came and I put it on, and, "Oh, my gosh, this is not what I wanted. It just doesn't make a statement." So I had it resized and gave it to my mother, and I bought this one.

Sue Sweeney: Are people conscious of it? Certainly you're dealing with many more non-Academy types now.

Lieutenant Lewis: Yes.

Sue Sweeney: Do people expect extraordinary things from you? Do you think you are watched more closely for being an Academy graduate?

Lieutenant Lewis: Maybe so. When they find out that I'm from the Academy, they go, "Oh, the Academy." But then the next question is, "Were you an '80?"—and that brings a surprise, which is kind of nice. It's one of the reasons I went there for that year, which was a real professional boost.

Sue Sweeney: Do you ever sense resentment from non-Academy graduates?

Lieutenant Lewis: No. There's kind of a joke among the aviation community for the ring-knockers. We're supposed to have a little bit of a cocky attitude, I suppose. It's true. The gals are great. There are so few women in naval aviation that we all stick together pretty well.

Sue Sweeney: Is there a lot of curiosity about the Academy?

Lieutenant Lewis: Yes, they want to swap places. They always ask, "What was it like?" So it depends. I say, "How long do you have? Two minutes? It was great. Two days? Okay, sit down."

Sue Sweeney: Do you think you're better prepared than your OCS counterparts?

Lieutenant Lewis: Initially, we definitely were. For the first two or three years, yes. The poor gals at OCS, the Newport 90-day wonder program, I feel sorry for those gals. They get chewed up and spit out. Eaten alive when they first check in to the squadrons, for example, in aviation, as outgoing as everybody is, anyway. The gals from ROTC are pretty salty—pretty well prepared.

Sue Sweeney: What did you do with your month's leave after graduation?

Lieutenant Lewis: I went home. I spent pretty much of the summer with my parents and my other relatives I hadn't seen for a while, it was relaxing. I came back for a terrible hardship summer teaching sailing lessons at the Naval Academy. That to date is the best summer of my life. That was just great.

Sue Sweeney: What kind of schedule did you keep?

Lieutenant Lewis: We wore shorts to work, for one thing, with our bathing suits underneath. I rented a house on the Severn River across the bridge, the little drawbridge. I rode my bicycle. I had a bike. I rode a bike to work in time for the 8:00 class, sailed all morning. The instructors got a break for lunch, and we went over to Riverside and have crabs and beer for lunch. Great! The lieutenant in charge of our program was really cool. He said, "Go out for lunch, do whatever you want to do. Have a couple of beers, but just chew some gum or something before you come back to work, okay?" It was great. So we'd come back and teach the entire afternoon, be out of there by 4:30 or 5:00, go home and play some tennis, then go out. It was just great.

Sue Sweeney: How many of you were there?

Lieutenant Lewis: I think a total of 60 instructors. Two of us were women. I was the only Naval Academy graduate, female type. Lieutenant (j.g.) Nancy Charles, who was a PAO assigned to the Academy and got interested in the sailing program was the other. We became good friends. It was kind of fun having a buddy who wasn't a Naval Academy graduate, the first officer I met who wasn't. She was a neat person out of Temple University, a beautiful girl. She'd done some modeling in Philly before she went in the Navy, a real pretty brunette. She's a pilot now. I wrote her a bunch of letters. We kept in contact. I think she got inspired to go to flight school from old friends of hers, hearing that it wasn't that tough. Now she's flying C-130s on skis in Antarctica.

Sue Sweeney: Did you specifically put in for the sailing program, or did you just put in for TAD at the Academy?

Lieutenant Lewis: No, I requested the sailing program. I had done some sailing in high school. I already knew how to sail pretty well, anyway. What a great time. The plebes that sailed with you were so uptight and a bag of nerves. Being an officer instructor instead of a firstie was much more fun and you could be a little more relaxed with them. You could be more candid with them on issues inside the Hall and maybe be a little more objective now that you're out in the real world. The kids were really neat. That sailing during the summer is the only time they got the chance to relax and get away from all the first-class harassment. You can sit back and tell them some funny stories, make them laugh; make them realize it wasn't all that bad. It's a little bit different role you play as an officer with midshipmen. It was lots of fun.

Sue Sweeney: I'm sure the plebe women enjoyed having a female graduate to look up to.

Lieutenant Lewis: It's funny. Out of all the students I had all summer, the only person I flunked was a girl. She was raised in the Midwest somewhere and couldn't swim or sail. She wasn't nautically oriented. It was ironic though. Her gifts were in other areas. I didn't big-deal it. I made her company mates swear that she would never check out a sailboat without one of them with her. They happily agreed.

Sue Sweeney: You all had to qualify to sail, didn't you?

Lieutenant Lewis: I think you just didn't get your sailing card. They're not going to refuse your graduation because you can't sail, but you just don't get a sailing card.

Sue Sweeney: That reminds me—we were talking about the 30-foot jump.

Lieutenant Lewis: The tower jump.

Sue Sweeney: There was a girl who balked at that.

Lieutenant Lewis: There sure was (and a couple of guys too), up until graduation. She was not going to do it but in the end she did.

Sue Sweeney: How scary was it?

Lieutenant Lewis: It's certainly an attention-getter. I didn't want to do it either. Once you stepped off and got it over with, you thought, "That was a piece of cake." While you're up on that high platform breathing in the ozone layer it's scary—and the water's always real cold.

Sue Sweeney: Now that the Reflecting Pool is gone, they jump off the tower after the Color Parade.

Lieutenant Lewis: I was lucky enough to be a jock, having swam for the high school team. Really, I think I ought to say something about the PT aspects the first year. They did a fine job recruiting women for our class. Like I said before, ours was the finest group of gals I'll ever hope to know—smart, with a lot of different personalities. I'll tell you that. We're probably a little strange in the psychologists' views, but we were all pretty strong. Strong people and determined.

Physically—gee, I don't know. They could have done a little bit better recruiting job in this area. I expected to go to college with a bunch of real physically active women, not a bunch of coeds—which I thought would be an added benefit for me at the Academy. If I went to the University of North Carolina [UNC], there would be a bunch of cheerleading homecoming queens, and I didn't want that; I wanted to go to school with a bunch of athletic jocks and get some real good competition going. It just wasn't the case.

Now, in isolated cases, we had some outstanding athletes, like Peggy Feldmann, All-American swimmer. What an athlete. C. J. Rayhill was a tremendous basketball player, and we had a couple of other really good basketball players. But on the whole, I'd say there were some gals there that were terribly underprivileged physically, and it wasn't really their fault. Can you blame a gal when she's been born and raised in a family and never had to know how to run or how to do an obstacle course or to swim? A lot of girls, even to this day, are not raised to have to learn how to do those things. I was horrified when we did the mile run the first time. Some girls literally didn't know how to run. Don't laugh; that's possible.

Sue Sweeney: You had been warned about the physical aspects, though, hadn't you?

Lieutenant Lewis: Yes.

Sue Sweeney: And told that you'd have to pass physical tests?

Lieutenant Lewis: Yes, we all knew that we were going to be athletically challenged. We all knew that.

Sue Sweeney: And told to prepare yourselves to run specific distances—like three miles?

Lieutenant Lewis: Yes. You bet.

Sue Sweeney: Some women just ignored that?

Lieutenant Lewis: Well, if you've gone 18 years never having to do it, you can't learn how to do it in a few months, which is the amount of warning they give you by the time you're accepted. Plus the physical demands were tough. Much of the conditioning you learn over a lifetime; it's not something you just up and do. But over the four years' time, I felt a tremendous admiration for these gals who, for whatever reason, in their growing-up years never learned how to run. In four years' time, by gosh, they could run a 7:30 mile. I'd like to see somebody take a coed prom queen out of UNC and let's see if she can do it. You know that? It used to piss me off, the guys would say, "These girls are on the weight tables and PT sub-squad because they can't run a mile in 7:30. My grandmother could do it in 7:30."

Bullshit. You take the average woman at any university and have her do what the minimum or easiest requirements are at the Naval Academy. No way. You just have to admire how these gals, over four years' time, extra time working out, dieting. Dieting is so hard anyway, but what about the gal who has never had to diet, it never even occurred to her that she had to, she always had the same build all her life? No reason to change it, and now she has to change it, or you can't graduate. Ugh! My roommate was in that situation. What a pressure. What a pressure. The place is bad enough without throwing that in, too.

Sue Sweeney: You said that many of the girls weren't as athletic as you'd thought they'd be. Did the Academy modify its standards or start recruiting tougher women?

Lieutenant Lewis: They didn't have standards. There weren't any standards when they recruited. There were no times. They didn't establish the times for the mile run until after we were there.

No, I think they changed the recruiting. I think in my class, they wanted to make sure that we were going to have a successful group graduate, and so they were more concerned about academics. They recruited an extremely smart bunch of women. If you check some of the high school backgrounds on these girls—they were amazing. I haven't seen the overall numbers, but I bet you, if you statistically compare our group of women against the guys in that class, we were academically superior in high school. I just bet you that was the case.

Well, it would be because of the numbers of female students that applied relative to the number of spots that were available that you could make that assumption. But I don't think the Academy put enough interest in athletic background for that first class. Like I said, they got themselves in shape and learned how to do something that no one else in this country expected them to do, which I really admired. Now, in subsequent classes, I think the Academy learned a little bit from that and either publicized the athletics a little more or maybe selectively looked a little more on the athletic side, because we got quite a few jocks in the next couple of classes. They are a tremendous group of people.

Sue Sweeney: You said that academics were okay, but not your strong suit. What was the hardest subject?

Lieutenant Lewis: I was inconsistent, depending on what I was interested in. I was a math major; the early math courses in calculus and differential equations—were very interesting to me because they were functional and you could solve problems and get an answer. Later on in the math degree, the math got spacier. I put my calculator away and used Greek letters, and it wasn't very interesting to me. I didn't do as well. On the other hand, in seamanship and navigation courses, I enjoyed the math and geometry. Practical application, that was really fun. Celestial navigation was kind of boring, but it was functional. It was very useful. I naturally did better in those kind of courses. Now, in history—I had to take two history courses. I love to read and am a passably good writer, but being able to read a chapter of history, sift the critical points out of it and write it down in a coherent manner wasn't my strong suit. My roommate, Sue, was a history major, so I managed to register for and get into her classes for the two courses I had to take, so we'd sit there and study together at night. She'd say, "Okay, read this paragraph." I'd read it. "Okay. What are three key points that you got out of that paragraph?" I'd tell her, and she'd say, "No. These are the key points of it." So with her leading me through the texts, I managed to get through history. I took Spanish for about two years, which was fun. I didn't get to use it at all. I wish I could have gone to Spain.

Sue Sweeney: Did you go right to flight school after teaching sailing?

Lieutenant Lewis: I taught sailing until September. The sailing season ended, and I wasn't supposed to report down here until October to flight school, so I stayed with the crew team, did a little coaching, painted oars and stuff like that around the boathouse, really rough. It was boring, and by that time I wanted to get the heck out of there. The days were dragging. I could not wait to get to Pensacola. I got here as early as I could, checked in, and went through the basic indoctrination training down there. Suzanne Grubbs and I went up to Whiting Field. We were roommates all the way through until we got our wings. We just had the greatest time. We both had Trans Ams and motorcycles and would chase each other all over the place.

Sue Sweeney: How many of your female classmates went to flight school?

Lieutenant Lewis: Four of us. That's another thing. Barbette Henry Lowndes sent out her survey of women grads, she said, "If you have any questions, please ask me. Maybe as a result of the survey, I can answer."

So I put at the bottom, "Hey, Barb, how come only four gals out of our class went air and only one went NFO? I just don't understand it, because there were five spots available in our case. In subsequent classes, they were snatched up. There are gals still wanting to go. We had billets left over. What was different about our class that made gals not want to jump at that?"

She wrote back and said that she got a variety of answers. Most of them said they were tired of the fight, and aviation was just another hurdle to have to climb, and they weren't interested. Actually, I knew that over half the class wore glasses, so that would have eliminated them anyway.

Sue Sweeney: Of the women?

Lieutenant Lewis: I'm not sure exactly. You can wear glasses as a line officer. You don't have to have 20-20 to get in to the Academy, but you have to have 20-20 to be a pilot.

Sue Sweeney: Even for the Academy, isn't it correctable to 20-20, but you've got to get a waiver?

Lieutenant Lewis: Right. I think everybody at school was correctable. You had to have uncorrected 20-20 vision to apply for flight training.

Sue Sweeney: So you got down here. Did you have a sense that this was another frontier you had to pioneer?

Lieutenant Lewis: Oh, no. This was going to be great. I was on cloud nine, just ready to eat up the world again. It was almost like being a freshman midshipman again. I was really happy to be here. The first thing I noticed, Suzanne and I—and I'm glad she was with me, too—the two of us really helped each other out emotionally, because we'd walk into our class with 36 other guys, the initial flight indoctrination classes, a lot of Naval Academy types, a lot of ROTCs, a bunch of AOCS [Aviation Officer Candidate School] guys. The Academy guys were the only ones who had attitudes toward us—not terrible but they were cool and derisive towards us a little bit, kind of a carry over from USNA.

But to the ROTC and the AOCS guys, hey, we were just another one of the group. They'd all gone to college with women. They had known women in AOCS, no big deal, and treated them completely equally. So that was just great. Suzanne and I felt, "Ah! We're finally accepted." We could finally sit back and relax and study and be like everybody else. Finally, that rubbed off on the Academy guys. I think they also matured a little bit, got out into the real world and realized everything was not just boat school, and all the silly little prejudices you have there. They opened up a lot. And like I said, a couple of years later I even had a couple of guys apologize for their behavior towards me. Wonders will never cease.

Sue Sweeney: Your two other classmates were in different flight classes?

Lieutenant Lewis: Yes, they were behind us. They were delayed a little bit.

Sue Sweeney: What other memories of flight school?

Lieutenant Lewis: Just the best. I'm an instructor now, and I can see some students really not having a good time. They're working hard and they're sweating it all. They're so worried that they are not enjoying themselves. I can never remember a day when Suzanne and I were not having the best time, even though we studied very hard. If I had studied at the Academy the way I studied at flight school, I would have been valedictorian. You know how it is when you find something you like.

Sue Sweeney: Did you find it challenging?

Lieutenant Lewis: It was hard. Very challenging. Wow, we just worked our butts off, sweated bullets. We had our own little individual crises, you know. We had run-ins with instructors and stuff. But like I said, it was so nice to be out of the Academy and into an environment where women were already accepted. Women had been in the fleet for years. In the real Navy, women had been through flight school five years before, so it was no big deal to see women in flight school. There was no hurdle here.

That's why I still don't understand why my female classmates didn't jump at the chance to jump into a warfare community like aviation. The most liberal men in the Navy are in naval aviation. The Navy is very conservative, but the most easygoing guys— outgoing, open-minded people, in my opinion, biased as it is—are in naval aviation.

Sue Sweeney: During second-class summer did you get a chance to go up?

Lieutenant Lewis: Yes, twice in a T-34 and a helicopter and a T-2.

Sue Sweeney: Did you ever experience fear during training?

Lieutenant Lewis: No, no. There's not much to be afraid of. The only time I ever felt any fear was in the helo dunker. The "Dilbert Dunker" was okay. The helo dunker is a huge can in which they blindfold you and strap you in. They submerge it in the pool and turn you upside down, and you're expected to get out of it after it's filled up with water to simulate escaping from a sinking helicopter. Still to this day, I haven't completely recovered from it.

Sue Sweeney: How many times have you done it?

Lieutenant Lewis: I've done it four different times now, because every time you PCS [Permanent Change of Station]—move, you have to do it. Four times. It does not get easier.

Sue Sweeney: What else sticks out about your training?

Lieutenant Lewis: Carrier qualification was thrilling. Of the physical things I've done in my life, racing crew was one of the best. But CQ, carrier qualification, was the most exciting physical thing I've ever done in my life.

Sue Sweeney: Can you describe it?

Lieutenant Lewis: Coming aboard a carrier, your whole mind is just scanning two different instruments. You're looking at the lens, the optical landing system, and you're looking at your angle of attack, which tells you what air speed and attitude your plane is at. You just glance back and forth and at the line up of the ship. You touch down, and you just hope the hook grabs, and you pretty much know it will if the ball is reasonably near the center, and you come to a stop in a short distance. You're at 130 knots of air speed, and you come to a stop at a distance of 100 feet or less. It's like hitting a telephone pole in a car, or something like that. I got bruises on my collarbones and my hip bones from the jolt. But what a thrill!

Sue Sweeney: Have you ever been scared?

Lieutenant Lewis: You don't have time to be scared. You're concentrating very hard. It's a precision thing. That's what's so rewarding about it, because you do it yourself, with no instructor. You go out there solo the first time to the ship. Can you think of an instructor who would want to go with you? Not me! It's a very rewarding feeling to do that.

Sue Sweeney: Is this off the *Lexington*?

Lieutenant Lewis: Off the USS *Lexington* right out here in the Gulf of Mexico is where I qualified. Well, I was in Texas out of Beeville. *Lex* was operating out of Corpus Christi. After doing a preflight inspection of the jet on the carrier deck, I climbed in and started engines. I taxied out and followed the hand signals of the plane captain toward the catapult. He hooked me up, took up tension, told me to run the power up to military and hold it. The only thing holding you back, keeping you from going anywhere, is this little hold-back fitting. When you're ready to go, you wiped out your controls to make sure they're not jammed and scan your instruments to make sure everything's okay. And if everything is all set and you're ready to go, the catapult officer is standing there, and you salute him. That means, "I'm ready to go. Catapult me." So you put your head back against the chair so your head doesn't go *SMACK!* which has happened, and you lock your throttle hand forward, which kept your hand from being thrown back and pulling your power to idle. He looks down, clears you back and fore, makes sure nobody is in the way, and then he goes down and touches the deck. You've seen that in the movies, right? Then the guy over here reaches down and presses the button, and off you go.

Sue Sweeney: Is there anything like it?

Lieutenant Lewis: Oh, I just go, "Ahhhh!" screaming the whole way down, because that's probably the only time that you're really not in control of your destiny, during the cat stroke. You're just along for the ride. It's amazing.

Sue Sweeney: How many times have you taken off?

Lieutenant Lewis: Just in training command, eight times. Well, eight traps, about 15 touch-and-goes. It's exciting—what a thrill! It's an E ticket at Disneyland!

Sue Sweeney: Has that been the highlight of your aviation career?

Lieutenant Lewis: So far in the Navy. Except for some isolated things, like seeing some Russian airplanes up close and some ships. That's exciting. That's what makes us different from our zoomie-puke counterparts.

Sue Sweeney: Did your parents come down when you got your wings?

Lieutenant Lewis: Oh yes. Actually, back then women could not go directly into jets like men could. You'd go through primary, and if you got real good grades, you could go jets. Other than that, there were helos and props left over. Women weren't allowed to go directly into jets at that time. You had to prove yourself. You had to go through props, get great grades, and get winged, then submit your request. Two women a year were allowed into the jet community. If you finished at the right time, when a slot was ready, and you had the grades, then maybe you'd get a slot.

Suzanne and I finished the same week. Her primary grades were excellent. I think she was number two in her class or something out of 60 guys. Amazing. She had some private time and was a really good stick. She was dying to go jets but women could not go directly into that training. We both took maritime props. She was just sick about it. She was a real go-getter. She was three years older than I was. She just thought it was asinine that these pukes behind her were getting jet slots, and she had super grades and had to go prove herself again flying props. It just made her so mad. It was the same feeling she had experienced back in training for parachute school.

So we went down to Corpus Christi, and her attitude wasn't really good. She was just mad and frustrated. Her boyfriend, who was, I think, a few classes ahead of her, was already in jets. He'd come over and leave his jet manual lying around the house, and that just made her green—I've never seen anybody just practically physically ill for months over the fact that it was so unfair. I mean, she had gone through all this BS at the Academy with flying colors, and then had the one big opportunity she needed taken from her. It meant a great deal to her.

Over the years, I've realized more and more how much it meant to her. So prop training came along. Her grades were good in maritime, but maybe a little bit declining, instead of increasing, and mine were increasing, though she had had better grades out of primary. We both had the jet cutoff grades. I ended up getting the slot based on that. That's what the detailer told me. Suz and I were good friends, and I can't say it came between us, but it took her a long time to accept the fact that maybe it was her own fault that she didn't get it, and yet it was the Navy's fault for making her do this the hard way.

It was stupid and a waste of time and money because I was the last girl to go jets that way. Trish Lasell in '81 did it with the men in the normal pipeline without having to earn wings first. I went through Beeville and transitioned into jets. I already had my wings going through, so I received different handling than I might have if I'd only been a student. That's a nice way to go through it too, a very nice way to go through. So I kept a low profile.

Sue Sweeney: Did she ever get jets?

Lieutenant Lewis: As a matter of fact, she did. She went from there, she got assigned to C-1s, which is carrier onboard delivery, multi-engine, rotary piston aircraft. She got stationed at Sigonella, Sicily, and was flying out there for, I think, a year and a half when she was killed. I called her folks from the Philippines to offer my condolences as soon as I found out it happened.[5]

Sue Sweeney: Where were you when you heard about it?

Lieutenant Lewis: At NAS Cubi Point, Philippines. I read about it in the Sunday paper. I was reading an article that said, "Two C-1s, Midair in Sigonella, Sicily." I thought, "Oh, my God." They didn't have any names. How many C-1 pilots in Sig can there be? For the first time in my life, I was able to get through on the Autovon line, halfway around the world in about two minutes, I was talking to their duty officer. I said, "Listen. I don't

---

[5] Suzanne Grubbs was one of seven lost on 24 November 1983 in what is thought to have been a midair collision.

know if you can release this on the telephone to a stranger, but Lieutenant Grubbs is a good buddy of mine. I just want to know if she's okay."

The guy paused and said, "Ma'am, she's not okay." He didn't have to say anything else. I tried to get some details, and they didn't know anything. They never did find any debris, nothing. There were two of them; they both went down. They figure it must have been a midair collision.

So when I called her mom, she sounded really good. I was really impressed. Her mom was a real strong gal, anyway. But she told me, "Suzanne, after this year of heartache over the jet thing, was finally happy. She was engaged." Unfortunately, her fiancé was in the other COD that went down, so they were both killed. "But she was very happy. We got a couple of letters from her recently. She's in love, she finally found a man that she wants to be happy with, and she got her jet transition, she's got orders to NAS Meridian, she's leaving next year." Of course, she died happy. Old Mrs. Grubbs, you know.

Sue Sweeney: How long after the fact was it when you saw it in the paper?

Lieutenant Lewis: It was four days after it happened. I finally read it in the paper. It was very tough. That's the kind of stuff that doesn't happen to my cousin who works in a bank. I don't mean to feel sorry for me, because it happens to everyone in the service . . . the loss of a good friend in the line of duty. It's just the job.

Sue Sweeney: Do you think about that aspect much?

Lieutenant Lewis: Yes. I don't think it's going to happen to me. If I did, I wouldn't do it.

Sue Sweeney: As a training pilot now, how do you feel about the quality of your students?

Lieutenant Lewis: We're real careful and diligent with these guys. They get good training—and I'm not just patting myself on the back. The Navy set up an excellent program. The guys who can't make it don't get through. You don't let them finish if they can't make it. Who wants to be responsible for a guy dying? I don't let a guy go out and drop bombs in a weapons pattern if I don't think he can handle the airplane. Forget it.

Sue Sweeney: Have you trained women yet?

Lieutenant Lewis: I have not had any women students yet. I've had foreign students. I've had some students from Singapore. My Spanish student just got his wings a few weeks ago.

Sue Sweeney: You got to use your Spanish!

Lieutenant Lewis: A little bit. There are a couple of really funny stories with this Spanish guy, because he had a crash course in English, poor guy. Smart, but could barely speak the language. The controller in English would tell him to turn right, and he'd turn left. In instruments, it was just killing him. He was all over the sky. He was getting flight violations, or would have, anyway.

"Why are you doing this?" I asked him.

"I memorized it backwards."

"You did what?"

"When I translate—when he told me—I translate into Spanish and I memorized left and right backwards. I'm still trying to remember." So these are the kinds of troubles he had.

I had to find out whether he's stupid or whether there was a communication problem, and obviously it turned out to be a language problem. He was not a dummy.

Sue Sweeney: He'd have to be the cream of the cream to be sent here to learn.

Lieutenant Lewis: He sure was.

Sue Sweeney: Back to your transition into the jets. You were down in Texas.

Lieutenant Lewis: I went to Beeville and earned my wings. I went through a bunch of schools, went through the survival, escape, resistance, evasion [SERE] school. The Navy one is not coed. I think the one in Maine is, but it's not like the one at Warner Springs, the Southern California one that the pilots go through.

Sue Sweeney: What was SERE like?

Lieutenant Lewis: Women couldn't go through there. I went through the Air Force one, which is coed, up in Spokane, Washington. Three weeks—wow, what a course. I'll never do that again. I spent a week up in the mountains—first a week of classes, to teach you, "Don't eat this, you can't eat that," how to build tents out of parachutes, how to use your survival equipment, Morse code, how to use a signal mirror, flares, basic principles of survival, first aid, hypothermia, all that kind of stuff. Then you go out in the mountains and you spend the first couple of days camping and learning how to do these things. The only thing you have is your flight suit and a parachute. There is no other gear or food. You end up being starved by the end. We all lost all sorts of weight that week.

Sue Sweeney: Is it similar to the survival training during flight school?

Lieutenant Lewis: That's a Girl Scout camping trip compared to what you do in SERE. I spent the first couple of days doing that. Then the rest of the week is spent doing orienteering, which is a sport that a lot of people do for fun, and they do it the right way with the proper shoes and beer cans in the backpack. But we were doing it for real, hiking 10 to 15 miles a day in the mountains, practicing using a compass, maps, being able to read terrain maps. It was interesting, a lot of fun. You had to be in good shape. They put me in charge of a squad; as a lieutenant j.g. I turned out to be one of the senior people, because they were mostly enlisted going through, or second lieutenants. Lucky me.

Sue Sweeney: How many of you were there?

Lieutenant Lewis: There were over 250 people there and, I think, about six women. I was one of the senior ones, and a jet pilot, which the Air Force found fascinating, going to a VC squadron, where we flew A-4 E's in the Pacific, which was a big taboo for them. The Air Force women can only teach in jets. I was put in charge of all these guys and hiked all over creation, all over the Cascades. Then the last few days was more toward the evasion side, where you cammied yourself up, we were in cammie for two days. Oh, man. A cammie stick, it's like crayons on your face. It was so grotesque. You're starving to death by this time, just starving, chewing on pine needles for the vitamin C, drinking a lot of water to keep you from getting dehydrated.

So finally, on the last day we finished evading, they captured us and then they put us in this POW camp. Well, you're already starving to death. In the camp they'd usually work in two phases over about two, two and a half days. Initially you're in solitary confinement the whole time for the first day and a half. Then after that, they put you in a work camp to simulate working with people and setting up the covert communications chain and other stuff. This was what was learned from Vietnam: resistance principles, survival and how to combat propaganda. There was a lot on that; I was surprised. It was interesting.

Sue Sweeney: Was the training modified for the women?

Lieutenant Lewis: No. If anything, I was so impressed with these guys. Unlike the Navy, they were finally addressing the issue of women in combat. I mean, the Air Force is talking like it's happening now, which it is. There are lots of gals in the Middle East and the Orient that could possibly get in trouble. For instance, the POW scenario, your C-141 crew goes down in North Vietnam or wherever, North Korea, and they've all got you, and there's one woman and eight men. They want you to tell the characteristics of the radar, and you won't give, and you won't give, and we all discussed this afterwards in our talk groups—seminars afterwards—to discuss this subject.

"Bob, if they're threatening you with your life to tell the characteristics of this top-secret radar—they're abusing you and slapping you—are you going to tell?"

"No, no, of course not. Of course not."

"What if they say, 'If you don't tell, we're going to abuse her?' Then what are you going to do?"

"Oh, I'll tell. I'll tell."

You'd look at him and go, "Bob, don't tell! I can take it. Don't do that."

"What if they say they're going to rape you? What if he rapes you right in front of Bob? Bob, what are you going to do?"

"Oh, I'll kill the bastard."

"No, Bob. If you do that, then he'll shoot everybody else."

"Bob, it's okay. Let the guy rape me. Let the guy rape me, Bob, because he's not raping my mind; he's raping my body. I'll heal. Don't tell. Don't give top secrets away, because if you do that, it will happen again and again and again."

See what I mean? These points are finally coming out, able to be discussed, because this situation is going to happen someday. The Navy ignores that. They don't address the male-female relationship bit in a POW situation. I guess they don't think it exists. Good ol' Air Force, they're finally waking up. It's interesting.

Sue Sweeney: It seems as likely a scenario for a female naval officer as for an Air Force officer.

Lieutenant Lewis: It may be. Just as I was finishing survival training, a group of six Navy SEALs, a chief, an officer, and some other enlisted guys were coming through the program, were going to go through the entire program to observe. They were from Warner Springs. Maybe they learned something from that. Someday I probably ought to write a letter about that. It made an impression on me, it really did. I was really happy. I felt like we were making some progress in a man's world, that this was already happening.

So then after I finished all that, I went through a couple more flight prep courses in San Diego and flew out to the Philippines for a two-year tour of duty. I flew in a single-seat A-4E Skyhawk, which is the same airframe the Blue Angels fly, with a little bit smaller engine, but still a bigger one than the one we teach in. Great mission. I had some interesting situations as a woman with the foreign air forces, foreign navies.

The Japanese and the Koreans, especially, are a little leery about dealing with a woman, especially when I got more senior in the last year—I was officer in charge of a detachment and would fly up to and represent the squadron at several conferences and meetings. They just weren't real hot about telling a woman what their requirements were going to be for the exercises next month. "We'll need eight sorties here, we'll need some target services on this date," blah, blah, blah. But, not talking to me because they don't deal with women in the Orient. They just don't. You're a second-class citizen. It's interesting.

Sue Sweeney: How did it work out?

Lieutenant Lewis: I was tall, so that helped. Isn't that funny? I was very polite, trying to be professional and businesslike. As long as you gave those guys a comfortable medium to work with, act like a man, maybe sort of act like a man, keeping your voice neutral, not smiling a lot, be very serious, don't try to flirt at all, not even a smile, be very serious, you might get the meeting completed successfully. The Japanese and the Koreans would relax a little bit, still be very, very stiff and formal, but then at least they'd listen to you. I'd get interrupted many times.

I'd be in the middle of the brief, "Sir, I'm from VC-5. These are our assets available. On this day we're deploying here and will be going there," and some navy captain, Japanese, will just stand up and interrupt me and talk to my lieutenant j.g. assistant I brought with me, and say, "Lieutenant j.g. Smith, do you have any D-704 buddy stores?"

And I'm a senior lieutenant up here giving the brief. I didn't get upset; just let him answer the question. The j.g. just looked at me, because he didn't know the answer. "Yes, we do." He was content to ask the questions through my male assistant and receive answers the same way even though I was speaking to him at the same table. It was their culture. I wasn't going to try to beat that, you know. The point is to set up the exercise, not to make a statement.

Sue Sweeney: That never happens with American officers much, does it?

Lieutenant Lewis: No. Maybe in different ways, in some ways. Gee, I had to brief a lot of guys off the carriers when we planned flybys, or we'd take turns doing multiple strikes out on the battle groups. We'd get together with the detachment on the beach. The carrier, when it goes to the Indian Ocean doesn't have room for all its airplanes, so it leaves some behind at NAS Cubi Point, and those pilots enjoy a six-week vacation in the Philippines, so they fly with us in our strikes. I had been stationed there about a year and a half, knew the ropes around PI, and would give some of the briefs before the exercises.

It was my own fault. I hadn't been exposed to ship tactics, as far as knowing how to fly around the carrier, they do what's called m-conn, where there are no radio transmissions when operating near the carrier. You don't use a radio; you just do everything by hand signals or timing. I hadn't been exposed to that very much. I knew some of it. Sometimes I'd get going in the brief, and someone would interrupt and say, "Excuse me, Lieutenant. Why don't we do it this way."

I'd say, "Roger that, Sir. We'll do it that way." I didn't mind the corrections or suggestions. What the heck? They were pretty nice.

Sue Sweeney: Out in the fleet, do you ever get negative feedback about being a woman jet pilot?

Lieutenant Lewis: No. I'm not a threat. I've had a couple of moments of glory. I've shot down a couple of guys. [*Action simulated.*] That's kind of fun. I've had a chance to do people favors, which is kind of fun, like there were a couple of planes in situations that needed gas really bad, and I went and just jumped in a tanker. We have a tanker store. I flew off and risked my life over the Sea of Japan in the winter, in bad weather, to give a guy gas who really needed it. Months later, he'd see me in the club and buy me a beer and say thank you. It was kind of neat, that kind of stuff.

Sue Sweeney: It was while you were in the Philippines that you were seeing the Russian planes?

Lieutenant Lewis: Yes. I had a couple of chances. We were deploying out of Guam. They had a couple of big TU-95 Bear bombers come down and take a look at the battle group. We rendezvoused with those guys, got a whole bunch of pictures. I have a beautiful picture on my living room wall of me flying next to this Bear, a beautiful airplane. What a thrill! To my knowledge no other women aviators have had that opportunity.

Sue Sweeney: The Soviets spy on us all the time, but still your adrenaline must have been going.

Lieutenant Lewis: Yes. The guys were close enough that I could see their faces. They were taking pictures of us with those little cameras, making finger motions, like Navy a hand signals for a number. They were doing that with both hands. I wish I knew what they were saying. Maybe it was a radio frequency.

Sue Sweeney: "Woman!"

Lieutenant Lewis: The pilots would lean out, they had their shades on, like naval aviators, waving at us. They did, I swear. We were just comrades in the air. Of course, back at the station at Guam, they were intercepting all the transmissions that these guys were making back to Vladivostok, or wherever. I think they were real surprised to see us, because they hadn't seen our A-4s since Vietnam. "Where did these A-4s come from?" Because we were deployed there; we weren't permanently based. That was funny.

Sue Sweeney: Any other highlights from that tour?

Lieutenant Lewis: Just flying in Thailand, teaching the Thai Air Force close air support procedures with their F-1s (Albatross) which is a light, great fighter. We helped teach these guys how to use the Marine tactical manual. Close air support is going in and dropping bombs to protect your troops. You've got guys on the ground saying, "Hey, we're getting enemy fire from Round Top Hill. We need some close air support to come in and wipe those guys out because they're bothering us."

So then the A-4s come in. You use some timing. The Thai marines gave vectors from the ground. It's a ground-air coordination deal. So we were practicing with Thai Marines. Do you know how hard it is to understand a Thai Marine on the radio? We'd simulate dropping bombs on a designated spot, and they'd vector us around, and we'd practice being vectored. If they gave us a bad vector, we'd follow it so they'd have to correct. We would teach them the basics of forward air controlling and basic radio comm.

Sue Sweeney: Did you ever feel that you were hazarding yourself with less competent pilots?

Lieutenant Lewis: It was good practice. To tell you the truth, we were the instructors in the whole thing. By then I was a real senior lieutenant in the squadron. I had gone to a bunch of classes and was kind of not the expert, but had all the info on close air support. So I ended up giving all the lectures to these pilots on the facts that came in, not just a JO, but a woman JO giving lectures to foreign air force types with their group commander standing in the back. Yeah. How many other women in the world get to do this? I was on cloud nine.

Sue Sweeney: How cooperative were the foreign pilots?

Lieutenant Lewis: The Thais were great. The Thais were just super. Of course, Thailand is unlike any other country in WestPac, in that they've never been overrun. They've always been their own country. They've never been occupied by a Western power. They're independent. They're a cocky group of people—happy, cocky. Of course, they've got trouble up in the northeast.

Sue Sweeney: Were they quick studies?

Lieutenant Lewis: Very smart, yes, and aggressive, too. But they didn't like flying low over water or low at all. Fighters are used to flying high, and we'd get down there in the dirt and they didn't like to do that. I can't blame them, I guess, when you're not used to it.

Sue Sweeney: So how long was that tour?

Lieutenant Lewis: Two years altogether, then I got orders back to the training command. This was not even on my preference card at all.

Sue Sweeney: Where did you hope to go?

Lieutenant Lewis: I wanted to go to VAQ-34, which is an electric A-7 outfit on the West Coast—it's just standing up now, a brand-new squadron—to fly missile pods around. You're flying missile profiles and shore installations and ships practice tracking you. But it's a new airplane; it's an A-7, a tactical airplane. Maybe if I got NATOPS [Naval Air Training and Operation Procedures Standardization] qualified in that, maybe I could get into some other area that's a little more tactical.

Sue Sweeney: Is this the first time you didn't get what you wanted?

Lieutenant Lewis: Well, so far, yes, I guess it is. But Pensacola is a beautiful area, great squadron. I lucked out. I'm very happy to be here. I bought a house on the beach—hurt me! But the detailer was a woman aviator, and she just lied through her teeth. That's the first time I felt really betrayed. I wasn't real happy with that. Now, of course, every person you'll ever meet in the Navy will always have a moan-bitch story to tell about their detailer.

I don't know if you're familiar with a warfare specialty. You have to have that in the Navy to be promotable. In jet aviation, that means flying in an aircraft that deploys on a carrier—A-7, S-3, F-14, F-18, F-4, E-2—that's a warfare specialty. In my job—A-4 Echos in VC-5—is a composite squadron. It's a support squadron; it's not a warfare specialty. So for any of the guys—and me included—to get promoted or be eligible for command in a tactical environment, you have to fly one of those other airplanes in another community. So she tried telling me, and I said, "Hey, I can't go to a training command. I want to get VAQ, because that's a warfare specialty. It's the only place I can get it as a woman. The only place in jets."

"Well, VC is a warfare specialty."

"Come on, Wendy. No, it's not."

"Well, it is for women."

"Wendy, don't bullshit me. No, it's not."

Second lie. Her third one was, "Well, Congress is changing it."

"Third bullshit flag, Wendy. You know, I don't think I want to talk to you anymore." That's what I got out of her.

Then they came back and said, "VAQ-34, no, they're not letting any women into that squadron. It's going to be all men."

That month McDermott was detailed in there, so she's there now. It was just a real blow—I guess I was mostly bummed because it was a woman aviator who wouldn't be straight with me. "Chris, you're going to training command. That's where they want you. That's the bottom line, okay?"

If she had said that, I would have shut up and gone. But she didn't.

Sue Sweeney: How long have you been here?

Lieutenant Lewis: About a year. Teaching is a riot. There's a lot of reward in it, a lot of flying. You learn a lot about flying yourself, because you're teaching precision and you learn to see things a lot faster than you did before.

Sue Sweeney: Do you teach both classroom and practical?

Lieutenant Lewis: Yes, mostly flying, an incidental classroom lecture. We have to do that once in a while. The flying is great. I was a weapons instructor for the course, teaching everything from basic instruments to familiarization, how to land, formation, how to do multi-plane formations, airways navigation, cross-countries flights. You either specialize in air combat maneuvering or in weapons, which is bombs, strafe, and rockets. So I went weapons. I don't have a background in ACM [air combat maneuvering], so I went to bombing, and though my background in bombing is fairly limited, at least I could teach that.

Sue Sweeney: What has been the highlight so far?

Lieutenant Lewis: As I said, teaching students has been a highlight. I think when Luis Belazon (Spain) got his wings, I was so proud and felt like he was my kid brother. He was a good student, but he had a few minor problems coming through. I gave him some breaks here and there . . . extra training. Of course, he earned the wings. I didn't give him anything; he earned them. But I gave him the benefit of the doubt in certain cases—and I'm glad I did. He proved himself. It's a real good feeling.

Sue Sweeney: Considering what you've gone through to get here—if you had to do it all again, would you?

Lieutenant Lewis: Canoe U, now that one—you know what? You know what I think about that? I'd do it again. Having done it, I'd do it again because the rewards of having gone there are so great. But if that situation was offered to one of my sisters, I'd tell them not to do it.

Sue Sweeney: Really?

Lieutenant Lewis: Not for that first class. Nowadays, yes. But for that particular situation, knowing what I knew about it now, I wouldn't want to wish that on any of my sisters. I had a real good backing from my mom and dad. I think that me, in particular, being the oldest, had conditioning to prepare myself for that situation. My two sisters are strong and smart, but I don't think they would have been emotionally prepared for all that stuff, and I wouldn't want to wish that on them. But I'm glad I did it.

Sue Sweeney: What's been your greatest satisfaction?

Lieutenant Lewis: The time I've been happiest or most proud of? I'm most proud to be a naval aviator tail-hooker. That's the thing I'm most proud about myself. I feel like I'm on top of the world. The happiest I've ever been at any one time has been in WestPac, flying with the fleet, flying at night doing dangerous stuff, being right there in the front lines, you know, where the action really is happening. That's when I've been the happiest.

Sue Sweeney: Where do you see yourself going from here?

Lieutenant Lewis: I have an application in for test pilot school. My average grades may not do anything for that, but I hope so. If not that, then pursuing my master's degree in aeronautical engineering or some type of engineering.

Sue Sweeney: Will you be the first female Blue Angel?

Lieutenant Lewis: Are you kidding? They wouldn't let a girl in—they just admitted their first Black guy. The first Black guy got selected. Isn't that great? It's goddamn time!

Sue Sweeney: What are your long-range goals?

Lieutenant Lewis: Stay in the Navy. I am semi-engaged to a guy who I met in WestPac. We were in the same squadron. He's got orders to F-14s in Miramar. Maybe I can get to Monterey to PG School and we can be in the same state. He's been on the other side of the world for a year. We've been communicating for a year, a long-distance relationship. He's the one for me. I found the man I really want. He's worth waiting for. I just hope that someday we can get together.

Sue Sweeney: How hard will it be to coordinate your careers? How cooperative do you expect the Navy to be?

Lieutenant Lewis: It's not the Navy's concern. It's not the Navy's purpose to make my marriage work. So if it works. I'll make it work.

Sue Sweeney: Good luck—and thanks very much for an interesting interview.

***

Interview with Lieutenant Barbette Henry Lowndes, Supply Corps, U.S. Navy

Place: Edison, New Jersey

Date: 17 November 1985

Sue Sweeney: Good morning, Barb. Would you start by telling me about your early years and family background?

Lieutenant Lowndes: I come from San Diego. I was born, actually, in Illinois. My dad was in the service—the Navy—and was transferred to California when I was three. We stayed the rest of the time right in San Diego. Both my mother and father had been in the service. My mother was an ET [electronics technician], one of the first female ETs. She got out when my parents got married. My dad stayed in for 24 years and retired as an E-6 [petty officer, first class]. They're both very proud of my going into the Navy and continuing their lifestyle, although it's totally different being an officer growing up in an enlisted family. I have three sisters, all of whom are still at home in the San Diego area. They're all married, but at least in the San Diego area. I'm kind of a renegade in the family, disappearing off into the Navy and seeing and doing things that some of the others aren't doing.

Sue Sweeney: Were your parents your big influence in coming to the Academy?

Lieutenant Lowndes: A good part of it. I really wanted to go to college. My parents couldn't afford to send any of us to college. It was a choice between going to a parochial school and becoming a parochial schoolteacher—where I had a partial scholarship, but I'd need to work a couple more years—or going into the service. At the time I wanted to go into the Coast Guard, because at that time women were allowed to go on ships, and the Navy wasn't allowing women on ships. I said, "I'm going to go Coast Guard."

And I tried, but for medical reasons they kept disapproving me. My dad had influenced me to at least put in the application to the Navy. I kind of fought on that one a little bit, and I said, "I really want the Coast Guard."

He said, "Put in an application to the Naval Academy just in case." And it was a good thing I did. The Coast Guard turned me down for medical reasons. I told the Navy about it, and the Navy said, "Well, let us do a little more testing." They did a little more testing and said, "No, you don't have a problem. We'll take you." And I continued with the rest of the application process, got an appointment through my congressman, and managed to get in.

Sue Sweeney: But it was a choice between the Academy and being a parochial schoolteacher? Did you ever consider just enlisting in the Navy or Coast Guard?

Lieutenant Lowndes: No, I probably wouldn't have immediately after high school. Waiting to get into parochial school, just trying to get up enough money, I might have eventually given up hope of saving that kind of money, and gone into the Navy or done something else. But at that point in time immediately after high school, it was a choice, really, of the Naval Academy or waiting and saving up enough money for parochial school.

Sue Sweeney: Was your mom particularly excited—reliving her career through you?

Lieutenant Lowndes: Her career and her college. She was the only other person in the family who had ever gone to college. None of my other sisters have ever gone to college. My mom had done about two and a half years at college in Nebraska. Her family needed her to quit college and go back to work. I think she was also very excited that I wanted to go to college.

Sue Sweeney: When did you first see the Naval Academy?

Lieutenant Lowndes: The day I arrived, two days before induction. I really knew nothing at all about the Naval Academy, hadn't even seen pictures of it. I didn't even know what an officer was. I really didn't know what I was getting myself into. I just knew it was college and it was in the Navy, and that was good enough for me.

Sue Sweeney: Did your parents come out with you?

Lieutenant Lowndes: No they didn't. They never came to the Academy until graduation. It was tough going that far away. I'd never really been away from home before. I guess the California attitude is that things are too far away, and you usually have to go by plane or something. I had no reason to go anyplace else. We really don't have much family anyplace else. So I had never traveled. I found a friend at one of the Alumni Association dinners for the new candidates, met up with him at the airport and flew out. I think that if he hadn't been there, I might have turned around, chickened out, and gone back. I was scared to death that first day.

Sue Sweeney: How much before induction did you come?

Lieutenant Lowndes: We came two days early. Because of the distance, we wanted to have a little time to adjust to the time and temperature.

Sue Sweeney: Did you tour the Academy ahead of time?

Lieutenant Lowndes: Mostly we stayed away from the Academy. We knew we'd have to go there eventually. We toured Annapolis but stayed outside the Academy grounds. I guess we figured that if we went in too soon, they'd grab us and never let us go. So we waited.

Sue Sweeney: What was I Day like for you?

Lieutenant Lowndes: Induction Day was—gosh, a harried experience, just so many things that were going on, and never really having time to think about what you're doing, meeting so many new people, your new roommates, worrying about if you're doing everything right. I guess I'm a little more nervous or was more nervous back then to make sure I did everything just right. I didn't want to get in trouble. I hated getting in trouble, and I made sure I paid attention even when they taught us how to roll our socks. I paid very close attention. I was never going to have them yell at me about how to roll my socks, I was never going to let them catch me putting my shoes in the wrong place. I wanted to make sure I did everything just right so they couldn't yell.

We got through the usual training during the day in learning how to march, got to the induction ceremony, and it was a little tough because I didn't have my parents, and everybody else, my newfound friends had parents there. I made it through the ceremony. Our big worry was if we could make it back up the stairs and get back into formation by dinner, we were going to stay. That was the decision my roommates and I had made; if we could make it all the way back up, we were going to stay. We were staying on the fourth floor. That means a lot when you're a plebe. This is the first time they're going to start yelling at you. They were nice to you all day, but when you come back into the Hall, you have to start chopping and squaring corners, sounding off, saluting. Everything had to be done then, and it had to be done right. It was a little tough getting up all those flights of stairs and getting into my room, getting ready for formation. Once we made it, we looked at each other and said, "We made it this far; we can do the rest." And it was a nice feeling to end that first day that way.

Sue Sweeney: Your roommates had their parents looking on?

Lieutenant Lowndes: Yes, they did.

Sue Sweeney: Was the media already in your way from the very first day?

Lieutenant Lowndes: It sure was. It was kind of surprising that my picture ended up in one of the local newspapers, a fairly big picture. A couple days later when it had actually hit the press, my squad leader called me in and said, "What do you think of this?" I was totally surprised. He said, "Do you know who that is?"

I said, "Yeah."

And he said, "Yes what?"

I said, "Yeah, that's me."

He said, "How about 'Yes, that's me, Sir.'"

I said okay, I'm really here.

The media was a big surprise, but it didn't really hit until further into plebe summer, how much interference the media really was—how often they were really around. The first day you expect it. I guess I just expected they were taking pictures of everybody. I didn't realize then that this happens every year, and I guess in the Annapolis paper it's no big deal, but our group was special, so they really did us up. By the end of the summer, we got to noticing the media constantly. We were always aware of the tourists also. Anytime you happened to be walking or marching anyplace, they'd always say, "Oh, there's one. There's one." And I remember one time some tourists stopped and said, "I think that's a girl. Do you think that's a girl? I'm not sure." They were also not sure if they should take pictures of us or not, because they couldn't really tell. You could see the way it was going to go.

Once school started, especially, you only have 10 minutes to get between classes. Sometimes that's a long walk between, say, the gym and your next chemistry class. You really have to keep moving, but you've got to be nice to the tourists. They'll stop you and ask simple things, "Can I take a picture with you?" You know, that's nice, but all the other guys are standing around watching, and you know you're going to hear about it tonight. Somebody will get back and say, "We saw Barbette getting her picture taken."

The media wasn't really allowed to stop and ask us questions unless they had formal requests for interviews put in. That was pretty good. They tried more towards the end to keep us segregated when we were doing that, instead of just stopping us in the yard or walking around with movie cameras. That was getting obvious, and we were getting in trouble from the guys on things we would say. The media would twist some of the things you would say, or just take a partial statement, without understanding what you were trying to tell them. It got to a point where we started saying, "No comment," every time they would ask for one of us specifically. They'd know who gave them good answers and who wouldn't talk. Towards the end we all started saying, "No comment," all the time and they'd never ask for us again. That didn't break my heart.

Sue Sweeney: What else sticks out from plebe summer?

Lieutenant Lowndes: Oh, gosh, so many things from plebe summer, just being that first group of females to get through. The guys were just as scared of us as we were of them. They didn't know what to expect, they didn't know how much they could ask from us, they didn't know a lot of things about our uniforms and how we would survive that first year. When we arrived the Academy made us send everything we brought with us back home. We had to get all new underclothes, all new uniforms. Everything had to go back.

So they tried issuing us the pantyhose, slips, bras, and underwear, the whole bit, but they didn't have enough in stock ahead of time. They couldn't guess what size every female was going to be. They figured everybody would be in one size range. One funny thing was that they didn't order anything special for Jane Mines, who was the only black female. She had to wear the same beige or nude-colored pantyhose as the rest of us until the new things came in. The bras were a really funny story. The guys didn't understand why we had to keep running back down to the uniform shop to check on the bras we had ordered. We were a little embarrassed and had to tell just one squad leader what was going on, none of the others knew. We were always running to him saying, "We have to go down and check on them. We have to go see if they're in."

It became a little private joke. We'd call them "over-the-shoulder boulder-holders," and "gun slings," and "Did you check on your gun slings today?" All the rest of the guys wouldn't understand, and we'd be just giggling away. It was kind of fun for a little while, getting the guys used to us and us used to the guys, trying to make sure that we all got along.

There were no problems, really, with our rooms side by side next to the guys. During the summer they kept one room of women right next to another room of women, from two separate companies. You'd be on the edge of your company boundaries and you would have at least another female to go to. We roomed right beside the guys and it helped in company unity. That really helped a lot just getting along with the guys.

Sue Sweeney: Did you ever feel that your privacy was infringed upon?

Lieutenant Lowndes: No, not really, no problems with privacy; just the usual getting used to your new roommate. With the guys, no problem at all. We were allowed to have the doors closed only at specific times. They had to knock on our doors; we had to knock on theirs. I guess at the end of my four years, I started to feel that that closed door was more of a barrier from my classmates, because I had to have an excuse to go knock on their door. I just couldn't bebop in and sit down and chat with them for a little while; I had to have kind of an excuse. Especially if their door was closed during study hour. It kind of was a barrier, but not during plebe summer, because they were so strict on keeping the door open unless you were changing clothes.

Sue Sweeney: One of your classmates suggested you were too isolated from one another. Would you agree?

Lieutenant Lowndes: Very, very important. We weren't allowed, really, to see any of the other gals. Because you're a plebe, you don't want to go wandering around looking for the other gals. You can't really stop and look. We had different-colored nametags on the door, white for females, black for males, but you can't, as a plebe, just stop and look around, "Where's a white nametag? I wanted to see so-and-so, I knew she was in this company. I think they're on this floor in this wing," and go looking around for the females. So you really just got to know the other gals right in your immediate area. We did try once to get all the gals together. I believe the gal that organized it was kind of put up for mutiny charges, you know, someone felt there's no reason all the women had to get together.

Sue Sweeney: A female mid tried to organize you all?

Lieutenant Lowndes: It was a female mid, and she was working with one of the female instructors. There were a lot of problems with it. Someone got in trouble, and it was just never done again.

Sue Sweeney: Do you remember who the classmate and the officer were?

Lieutenant Lowndes: It was either Patty Taylor or Janice Buxbaum organizing us. The officer, I don't remember. But it did give a serious impact to our feelings about trying to reach out to each other. We wanted to be there to talk to each other and we really couldn't. I'd know something about every single female there, I had some exposure to every other female at the Academy in my class, I'd know something about each one of them, but I wasn't really allowed to associate with them and make friends with anyone else other than those in my immediate area or in my classes or on my sports team.

Sue Sweeney: Do you think camaraderie suffered?

Lieutenant Lowndes: I think we have a stronger bond, really, than the males, because we couldn't talk about it while we were going through it; it was a very isolated feeling. I felt I was being picked on by the guys, they were always laughing at me, barking like dogs when we walked down the Hall, "You're fat, you're dumb, you're ugly," they'd always say. I thought it was just me. I didn't feel very comfortable with me as a person. I started believing what they were saying. When you're hearing it from so many different people 24 hours a day, seven days a week, it starts to wear down on you. I didn't care what my hair looked like. I didn't wear it in a feminine style, I never wore makeup. I started eating more and really put on a lot of weight. It was all because of their attitude to me, and I couldn't go to the other gals and say, "Hey, are you getting this same type of treatment?"

I didn't realize that some of the prettiest gals at the Academy were getting that kind of talk, too. "She's gorgeous. Why are they saying that to her, too?" I'd ask myself. It was just the guys' way of lashing back. If I had known that they were saying the same derogatory comments to, say, Sandee Irwin or Lynn Rampp or some of the others—that they were being picked on for the same thing—I think it might have made it easier for me to kind of laugh off what the guys were saying. We didn't really find out what was going on until after the Academy, when we'd get together.

During the first two years after graduation, anytime you'd see another female, you'd sit down and talk, and it would always end in tears, and you'd say, "That's exactly how I felt. I hated the place. I felt that I couldn't go to any of the other females. I felt I lost a lot of personal contact with my own classmates and I was shut out from my own classmates, male and female." That's when we first realized that we were missing something, not being able to talk to each other at the Academy.

Sue Sweeney: What prompted you to write the *Shipmate* article ["First Alumnae." July–August 1985]?

Lieutenant Lowndes: I wanted to know how the other women felt about the Academy, how they felt about the adjustment, and I knew somebody would be writing an article. I didn't want somebody from the Naval Academy or some local newspaper to go and ask one female, like Maureen Foley, who was stationed at the Naval Academy, and ask her for her opinion, which perhaps wouldn't represent all 55 of us. It would just say what Maureen Foley was like. If Maureen was very up on the Navy or very down on the Navy, it would reflect on all the rest of us. I didn't want something like that, and I didn't want the kind of questions we were getting while we were at the Academy.

While we were at the Academy, we filled out so many questionnaires from everyplace you can imagine, all kinds of wonderful studies, very good study groups, but all the questions were all biased so that you felt that if you answered negatively about the Academy, it would reflect on your career. It was always a very positive, "How much do you like the Academy? Do you still like the Academy?" It never gave you any room for alternate answers. So when I wrote the questions, I wanted to be able to ask the questions the way I wanted the gals to be able to answer. I asked for the negative. If they felt positive, there was room for that.

I'd ask, "Did you ever feel any resentment from the guys?" I didn't say, "Did you always get along with the guys?" "Did you feel the resentment?" I asked in the negative.

"How much? Do you still feel that resentment? Do you feel a difference between yourself and other females in the service who didn't go to the Naval Academy?" Instead of just asking some simple question, "Do you feel you are equal with everybody else?" Well, yes, I'm equal with everybody else, but, yes, I feel a difference between myself and the females who didn't go to the Academy.

So I wanted them to be able to answer those kinds of questions and be able to understand the answers. A lot of times if the surveyor didn't know what we had gone through, he wouldn't understand the answers. I wanted to be able to do that for myself and for the other gals.

Sue Sweeney: Were there surprises?

Lieutenant Lowndes: There were some surprises in career choice. Some of the gals that I thought were so gung-ho were getting out, and some of the gals that I expected would be getting out were staying in. So it was a surprise in that respect. The rest of it was what I had expected. I expected the negative answers, that they felt resentment, that they still didn't get along with the guys, they weren't making that many friends, they didn't keep in touch with many of the males. Very few of the women said they kept in touch with their male classmates. Those were all expected answers. There were a couple of individuals I didn't expect to get out or stay in.

Sue Sweeney: What kinds of answers did you get about their relationships with non-Academy female officers?

Lieutenant Lowndes: I got what I expected. I got most of the women saying, yes, they felt they were different, that we were more dedicated, we had more leadership background. I still get a feeling when I meet another woman in the service that she's some dumb female in the service, who knows how she got here, why she's here.[6] She's doing a desk type of job—admin officer, public affairs officer. You very rarely see women coming from places other than the Academy who are doing the difficult jobs, doing the flying, the ship driving, really making a career out of the whole effort. Some are just in for something to do. I still feel that, and that's the gals' answers, that they do feel a difference between themselves.

Sue Sweeney: Your husband is not an Academy graduate. Do you feel the same about other male officers?

_____

[6] Interviewee's note, 2016: I meant no disrespect to the other women officers, but at the time they were predominantly general unrestricted line officers with little or no exposure to the warfare communities. Career opportunities have changed significantly since this interview.

Lieutenant Lowndes: No problem. No, no. Most of the other women don't feel that either—that you really don't segregate Academy males from others; you don't usually ask. If anything, there's almost something against the Academy guys because if it's too close to your time frame when they were there, you still kind of feel that "you were part of it against me," even though a lot of the women did end up marrying Academy graduates. I think 67 percent of those that married military, married Academy graduates. Academy graduates are predominant in the fleet. It really doesn't make a difference when I meet other guys, whether they went to the Academy or not. It usually comes up in conversation. If somebody is new to our command and he went to an academy—I currently work for a Joint Service Command, where we have Army, Navy, Air Force—and if anybody went to any academy, they always make sure when they introduce me, "She went to the Naval Academy too," as if that's supposed to be a bond, and that's nice. It's a point of conversation, but it really doesn't matter to me.[7]

Sue Sweeney: Were you surprised that three of your classmates married civilians?

Lieutenant Lowndes: No. I thought the figure was low, and that's the way it should be, because we really don't have much opportunity to mix with civilians. We also don't have

---

[7] Interviewee's note, 2016: I have since changed my opinion drastically. There is a special bond with all Academy grads, particularly with your own classmates. Time and distance make a difference in your perspective.

much choice. When you're a female in service, you're going to have a choice of either marry a military person, marry a civilian who's dumb enough to follow you or rich enough to be able to follow you, or marry a civilian and get out.[8] I think it's a tough choice. At first I thought I'd never get married, because you have to find someone in the military but only one career can guide the duty station choices. It's very difficult to have both careers strong and driving in the family. If you marry a civilian, he really has to be in a job where you can pick up and move. Even somebody who is in real estate or a traveling salesman type of operation, it's still not easy for him to pick up every three years and follow you. So it's a very tough choice. I didn't find any surprises in the low figure.

Sue Sweeney: Whose career takes precedence in your marriage?

Lieutenant Lowndes: It's a nice balance. My husband is eight years senior to me, we're both in the Supply Corps, which has a very positive effect. At least all the supply detailers are sitting side by side talking to each other. One of my classmates is married to a submariner and she's a pilot. If their detailers happen to pass each other in the hall and happen to say, "Do you remember the Ozimeks? What have you thought about a next move for them?"

---

[8] Interviewee's note, 2016: I was referring to the husband's need to change jobs and locations with the military wife, which at the time was not a common practice in society.

My husband's and my detailers sit side by side. When I call up, I say, "What have you found out? Why don't you ask Captain Stone?" He can put me on hold and walk right over and ask Captain Stone what's happening. So it's a nice aspect of being in the same community. The eight year difference is good. My husband is a lieutenant commander; there is a difference in trying to find jobs. It's hard to find two jobs open in the same community at the same grade level; it just doesn't happen, especially in the Supply Corps. We have very few billets in any one command to begin with, and to find two at the exact same grade level, you just wouldn't have much luck.

With the difference in rank, I think we have a lot better luck. He should be retiring in about seven and a half years. He's decided that he doesn't want to make more of the Navy than his 20 years, and that's his own personal choice; he would have done that whether he married me or not. That leaves me with the opportunity to do what I want. That gives me the freedom to say, "Okay, this next career move is important to me. I need it so it will look good for the lieutenant commander board." Next we'll go where I need to go, and he'll follow along.

Sue Sweeney: Back to the Academy. What else sticks out about plebe year?

Lieutenant Lowndes: Plebe year. A lot of things were unusual and hard to deal with as females, I guess because we were in this sterile environment, where we all looked like the guys and tried to act like the guys. I remember one time—well, I guess that first whole year—we had a barber doing our hair. Sometimes we'd come out looking like a guy. They eventually got us a female beautician, but that was almost the opposite extreme. This gal felt that if she couldn't use a curling iron and make you all beautiful when you walked out the door, then something was wrong with her work.

You could always tell the females who had just been to get a haircut from the beautician, which you needed about once a month; they all had the curls. Nobody else had curls. We just didn't have time to put in curls every day. It got to the point where I just couldn't stand those curls and standing out—"Aha! She's just been to the beauty shop. Look at her. She's trying to look good. She's trying to curl her hair." I started scheduling my appointments just before physical education class, especially before swimming, or if I had a free period and I knew I could go over to the gym and go swimming immediately afterwards.

It wasn't like just going back to take a shower to wash out this curl nonsense she put in my hair. I'd let her curl it. I'd always try and persuade her, "Don't do it. I really don't want it. I'm just going to go jump in the pool." She'd always curl my hair, and I'd go jump in the pool afterwards. But they still had kind of that attitude of needing a beauty shop/salon for the females. We really didn't need that; we just needed somebody to cut our hair in a somewhat feminine fashion.

Sue Sweeney: Were girls discouraged from fingernail polish or makeup? Were the girls who used makeup kidded about it?

Lieutenant Lowndes: It's hard to say. There were some gals that had been very used to doing that type of thing, very used to putting on a lot of makeup and doing their nails before the Academy. We didn't have the time at the Academy, which was a driving factor. We weren't allowed to wear nail polish other than clear, and it just didn't pay to take the time to put on clear nail polish. The makeup—there were only a couple of gals who used makeup. You didn't do much more than put on a little foundation and mascara. You also had to keep running to PE classes, where it would all wash off, and you wouldn't have time to redo it. I don't think too many of the women really worried about makeup. Then again it comes back to me, especially, where they kept saying, "You're fat, you're dumb, you're ugly," so I wouldn't even try to look good. It didn't matter to me. I never even tried to wear any makeup at all while I was there. But a lot of the limited makeup was driven by the lack of time.

Sue Sweeney: How homesick were you while you were at the Academy?

Lieutenant Lowndes: Very homesick. My folks never came to visit. They really couldn't afford it. I had three sisters at home that they still had to take care of—they couldn't take the time to come all the way to visit me. A lot of things were tough to try and explain to them what I was going through.

There was a retired Navy captain, he was in the Supply Corps, working with my mom in her business. He worked in a different department, but he knew I had gone to the Academy. Even though he didn't like the idea of women at the Academy, he was very proud that somebody at the office had a relative at the Academy and always kept in touch with my mom. I could write letters home. If she didn't understand what I meant, he could always translate the Navy slang for her, which was nice, but it was still difficult to try and tell my parents about what it was like. How you have to chop and square the corners, and how I'd get frustrated if someone waxed the corners, which made it very slippery, and would spin you off—trying to explain some of the silly things. The end of plebe year when we climbed Herndon was so emotional to me. I wanted to go back immediately to call my folks and say, "Guess what? I'm not a plebe anymore." They wouldn't understand. I just couldn't finish the telephone conversation and started crying. "You don't understand. This is very important to me." They couldn't understand what it felt like because they were so far away.

Sue Sweeney: Was it tainted for you by the move to keep the girls away from Herndon?

Lieutenant Lowndes: You bet. That was a very strong part of it. I saw what was happening, and I got out of the crowd, I just stood on the outer edge. There were a lot of jeers from the crowd, because there were a lot of the gals just standing around. "Why are you just standing around? You're not a part of it." But if you got caught in the middle, they were going to try to kill you, just about, try to elbow you a little too hard or knock you around a little bit, or push you down or something.

When some of the gals started climbing Herndon—they'd start to get up toward the top—there would be a hand that would all of a sudden come up and pull them down. Why should I get in there and get myself hurt? I didn't like any type of gatherings of large groups. I never went to the pep rallies; I'd hide. I always hid in my closet. They didn't understand why I was scared to death to go out in the big mob. I always felt that somebody would be out there trying to hurt me. It's innocent fun, but they were always trying to get rough and I didn't want to put myself in that situation. So when plebe year was over, I thought that would be the end of all the troubles; it wasn't.

Sue Sweeney: Did you ever see it get better?

Lieutenant Lowndes: Yes and no. I think that the Academy has adjusted better. I still hear horror stories of some of the things the guys are doing to undermine the women.

Sue Sweeney: Any examples?

Lieutenant Lowndes: For example, I still hear that the guys go in and plant stories about the gals and trash their rooms on purpose. You do that to somebody you really hate. Or maybe they'll set up a gal, have one guy pretend he likes her so that they can go out on a date in town and have all the other guys come along and laugh at her. It still goes on, but not like it was when we were there that first year.

A lot of it was driven by the media. I could understand my classmates getting jealous. Every time I'd turn around, there was a camera in my face. No one wanted to take pictures of the men. In their minds I was fat, dumb, ugly, and they were the cream of the crop, they were good-looking and had wonderful girlfriends, and why wasn't anybody taking their picture? It was sort of driving a wedge between my classmates and myself within the company. It never really got better within our little group.

There was a time when somebody purposely told the plebes to walk out on my roommate and me. As a youngster, you had to take the plebes down to breakfast. At that time it was still mandatory for plebes to go to breakfast. We'd take turns. A week at a time, a roomful of youngsters would have to get up early to take the plebes. I don't know who put the plebes up to it, but the plebes all walked out on us one day, totally embarrassing my roommate. They went down to the breakfast table. As soon as the anchor rang and they were allowed to sit down, everybody just walked out. They had to have placed their hats already underneath the chair, so my roommate and I were totally embarrassed. We finished our breakfast, because we didn't know what else to do, we went back upstairs, talked about it with the midshipman company commander, with the company officer, and ended up putting every one of the plebes on report.

The only reason we could put them on report was because not a one of them had asked for permission to leave the table. It was hard, it was fighting back the wrong way to say, "Okay, you're all now on report," and it drove a further wedge. We never found out who put them up to it, or why they really did that to us, but it was our only way of fighting back so they wouldn't do it again. That meant all of the plebes in our company had to march for two weekends.

Sue Sweeney: How much sympathy did you get from the company commander?

Lieutenant Lowndes: Very little from the company commander. The company officer was somewhat sympathetic. He thought, "You're blowing it out of proportion. That wasn't all that bad." They weren't there, and they don't know how often little things like that go on. When you're an upper class, chewing out a plebe in the Hall, you've got him braced up against the wall because he isn't remembering his rates, he doesn't remember what's for evening meal, he can't recite the newspapers, which was just something that any upperclassman would start chewing on a plebe for. If he had come around and didn't know what he was supposed to know, that's what you're supposed to do, chew into him. Then you'd have a second class or somebody even lower than you say, "Ah, don't listen to her, she's only a girl."

"Excuse me. I'm still a first class. I don't care if I'm a girl or not." You know? And there was a lot of that. The guys in '80 would just stay away from us. It just got to a point where we basically didn't talk. The guys in '81 were always throwing the digs; they were always getting back at us somehow, some way. It bothered me, because I was there before they even applied. They knew I was there. You can't tell me I'm ruining "your" Academy as an underclassman. I was there already. That bothered me a lot. We didn't get a lot of support.

There was one person in particular that thought he was being funny. He was the big man in the group, he was prior enlisted. I was selected for battalion staff. I didn't live with the company anymore so I didn't really have an assigned place to eat anymore. As battalion staff, you are roaming at meals, you find a seat wherever you can. I usually sat with my roommate at her table, which meant that somebody from her table had to find another table. That was acceptable. I was upper class; the plebe has to go on, instead of me having to go find a seat to sit down. I only did this a couple of times, but one of the second classmen, in particular, every time I'd come to the dinner table, he'd say in a very loud voice for everybody else to hear, "Oh, you're coming. You're taking one of our places so some poor plebe can't eat. You eat more than anybody else." Just things that he thought were joking. To me, in the tone of voice he was saying it, in front of plebes, this second class was saying to me as a first class, there was something nasty about why I was there, and I didn't like it. I took him aside after dinner and said, "I don't like what you're doing."

He said, "But we're just joking."

"You and I know that we're joking, but you're all the way across on the other side of the table. Nobody else in the whole dining hall within hearing range knows that you're joking with me." And he continued. It only took eight times. I only went to dinner eight times that entire semester; I physically could not go back without getting sick, because he was there.

I talked to my company commander about it. I talked to my company officer about it too. They both said, "Yeah, we hear you. Talk to the offender about it." I'd already talked to the offender about it, and I put him on report for insubordination. What else could I do? I talked to him about it, and I could not physically go down to eat dinner because of this jerk, and he was a second class. It ended up that he was the company commander the next year, and that's the kind of support we were getting for the women. It just doesn't pay, because people weren't listening. But I did have a good battalion officer who listened. When he found out that I was not eating dinner, he was so hurt that this was going on.

Sue Sweeney: Who was that?

Lieutenant Lowndes: That was Commander Paul Galanti. I think he understood because he was a former POW; he knew what it was like to be set aside, to be picked on, to be persecuted. It helped a lot that he was there.

Sue Sweeney: In general, what was the attitude of male officers?

Lieutenant Lowndes: Most of them were encouraging. They were just as curious as anybody else. They hadn't been there very long, but they wanted to see us succeed. There were occasional officers who didn't care for women, who would make it very obvious. If you were walking in single file, and the guy ahead of you would salute and the guy ahead of him would salute, the officer would return the salutes, and then I would come up in line and I'd salute, and the officer would just turn his back to me. You'd find instances of that.

I don't think that I had many instances of problems with the officers. If anything, my company officer toward the end was more sympathetic to what I was going through. In some of the other areas, there were times when he would understand and times when he didn't. He would always be there to listen, though, if I had a problem. We started getting surprises in the night, surprise visits. It's a game—the guys go around and throw shaving cream bombs in your room at night, and that's always fun. Everybody gets that once in a while. It scares you when the shaving cream goes off. It makes a mess, but it's easy to clean up.

But then it started getting worse and worse in the attacks on our room during the night. We weren't allowed to lock the door, so they could do just about anything they wanted. We started getting red tempera paint thrown in, and it splashed all over our uniforms. We were going to march in a parade the next day, so we had little pink dots all over our white uniforms. We had manicotti thrown in at us; I think that was the absolute worst. They brought some manicotti up from the table. It was pre-planned. They just hurled the manicotti in there in the middle of the night. It really bothered us. We didn't know what it was. It smelled horrible, and it was just something evil coming at you in the night.

Each time something like that would happen, I'd call up my company officer at home. I didn't care if it was 3:00 in the morning. I'd call him up and I'd tell him. I'd say, "You've got to come. We just can't take it." And the last time, when the manicotti came, his wife answered the phone in the middle of the night. I said, "This is Midshipman Henry. Is the lieutenant there?"

And she said, "Oh, Midshipman Henry, how are you?"

I said, "It's 3:00 in the morning, Mrs. Hayworth. I'm not doing well. I need to talk to the lieutenant." He was very good. He immediately got dressed and came to our room to see what was going on. He knew what had happened in the past, so he was able to help us. The officer of the day obviously had been called. The officer of the day came up and was just hysterical that we were up making a disturbance, that I was running around without my bathrobe on. I was too hysterical to care about putting on a stupid bathrobe. But my company officer came over and basically told the officer of the day, "We'll take care of this."

The officer of the day was a company officer from some other company, but he didn't know what had happened to us in the past either. He didn't know why I was so hysterical about manicotti in the night. It's easy to clean up, big deal, no permanent damage. Fine, except we couldn't sleep for weeks after that. Every night at 3:15 we'd wake up, scared to death. We got permission to lock our door, and we'd sleep with the covers pulled completely over our heads, but you know at 3:15 all three of us still woke up. "God, is it going to happen again? When is it going to happen again?"

It just kept happening. The manicotti was second class year, and it was still going on. Naval Investigative Services got involved on that occasion because of all the past problems we had. My company officer at last called NIS [Naval Investigative Service] in. I guess baby powder had also been thrown around too, and there were footprints leading to one of the bathrooms up on the upper floor. They found the top to the sawed-off milk carton that the manicotti had been stored in. It ended up that 10 guys were caught by NIS for doing this to us. They were all put on probation.

Sue Sweeney: What class were they?

Lieutenant Lowndes: They were my classmates. I was disappointed in that I don't think they got a hard enough punishment for what they were doing to us, but to me it was also more emotional than rational, "Yeah, it was just a nice prank."

Sue Sweeney: Were they from your company?

Lieutenant Lowndes: No, they weren't in my company, thank God. They were guys I didn't even know—that bothered us. They were usually guys we didn't even know, but because we were females, it could have been just about anything we did or said that would trigger them to have to come all the way across, sneak all the way over and do something like this to us. All 10 of them were given some disciplinary report; they had to march time, they got punished in some respect and put on probation. "If you do anything wrong in the next year, anything at all, guys, unshined shoes, anything, you're out." It ended up two guys did get kicked out. I think part of it was having that in their record, because they did it to us. So I'm glad for that point.

Sue Sweeney: By the time you were a second classman, were there underclass girls in your company?

Lieutenant Lowndes: Yes.

Sue Sweeney: Were you still singled because your class had been first to break the barrier?

Lieutenant Lowndes: Yes, we were the first class of women, and we always would be, but we did have gals in the class behind us ['81], then there was a gap of one year ['82], and then there was another group with females ['83]. I never felt close at all to any of the other gals in my company in any other class. In the clubs I belonged to I knew and understood the gals in the glee club that were junior to me, but any other females in the classes of '81, '82, I just barely knew their names. If you told me they were in that class, I'd pretty much say, "Oh, really? I didn't know," unless they were directly in my company.

I didn't even get along very well with the underclass gals in my company. I guess I was jealous of the fact that they could get away with a little bit more than we could, that they didn't have to go through what I had to go through. I wanted to make sure they understood what I had to go through. I don't think '81 understood as much as, say, '83. By the time '83 was in, everything was pretty much calmed down, and they could start to see some of the problems, the difference in the males and females in the upper class, and they could feel some of the resentment. They said, on a couple of occasions, in interviews with the media, that they understood what we went through, and I appreciated that. Some of the other gals didn't understand it, what we had done for them.

Sue Sweeney: You have compared notes with your classmates. Were they going through similar harassments?

Lieutenant Lowndes: Not within our immediate area, and if it was happening in any other parts of the Academy, I would never know, because I couldn't talk to those other gals. It was something that was so personal that you didn't want to talk about, because some of the other guys might overhear and start doing it, too. Once I had made battalion staff first-class year, I got moved downstairs. I got a room to myself and thought, "Here I'm really going to be in trouble." It was on a main corridor, big hallway, a lot of people passing through. I knew I'd be in trouble. I knew I'd be too easy to pick on. Nobody else was really around; maybe three other people living down in that area. I thought, "Gosh, this is it. I'm really going to have problems."

I talked to Commander Galanti, the battalion officer, about it. I had a phone in my room, and he said, "Try and call the other guys on staff if you have problems, or if it really gets bad, go ahead and lock the door." I never had a single problem, not one visit in my whole last semester. That gave me a good feeling. I sometimes wonder, was it because they didn't like my roommate more than they didn't like me, were they picking on her? Or was it that they just didn't realize how easy it was to get down there? I never got visited while I was on battalion staff.

Sue Sweeney: Did you room alone because you were the only girl on the battalion staff?

Lieutenant Lowndes: I roomed alone. What frightened me at first was that I would be totally by myself.

Sue Sweeney: Did you ever get advice on how to deal with men when you were in such a minority?

Lieutenant Lowndes: No, not really. I don't remember anything they told us on how to get along with the guys. I remember in plebe summer they were going through an awareness of minorities and EEO [equal-employment opportunity], trying to get us up into the Navy's thinking on EEO. We had one black guy in our company, and the three of us gals. The instructor pointed his finger and said, "You, you, you, and you, do you realize you're all minorities?"

I thought, "I guess I am." And I kind of felt that way for the rest of my time, because he singled us out as a minority. But I don't remember them teaching us enough about how to get along with the guys, or especially how to get along with other gals junior to you when you get out in the fleet. I was scared to death, because I didn't know how to deal with other females. I just knew how to fight, to survive, to get along with the guys. That was all survival instincts.

Sue Sweeney: Was there much competition among your female classmates?

Lieutenant Lowndes: Yes and no. There was some rivalry because there were a couple of gals way at the top and some of the more popular gals. And if anything, I was trying to figure out why were they popular, why did they like one of the cheerleaders, but they didn't like me? So there was some animosity. "Some guys get along with them. Why can't I get along with the guys? I'm trying. I'm trying to do everything I can, and I can't get along with the guys." So there were some feelings of resentment and animosity that way, but for the most part, we were all pretty much hoping everybody would make it.

There were very few gals that you really wanted to see get thrown out. Anybody that embarrassed the rest of the group, we'd all kind of wish they'd get thrown out. A couple of them did get kicked out, but a couple of them graduated anyway. There was a very strong feeling that you've got to make sure that what you're doing doesn't embarrass the other gals either and doesn't have any repercussions on any of them. We didn't feel that way about '81. I didn't care if what I did messed up '81's life. I just cared if it would hurt someone else in my own class.

Sue Sweeney: Were there many opportunities to embarrass the group?

Lieutenant Lowndes: Sure. There were a lot of ways of getting in trouble and getting by. Sometimes to get along with the guys, you had to kind of date them. Most of the guys didn't want to date a female midshipman, but some of the gals would date the guys, and there would be stories flying around, and you'd be embarrassed, but you'd say, "At least she's trying to get along with the guys, I guess."

Helping out with studies also helped. My roommate was very strong in aerospace engineering, and she was always helping the guys. There would always be guys in the room that she was trying to help with their studies. It was nice to see somebody trying to get along and you'd try to encourage something like that. There were ways of getting along with the guys, it was just very difficult.

Sue Sweeney: How hard was it to date?

Lieutenant Lowndes: Very difficult. I think I had two or three dates in my four years there. Even that was so sterile, because there were so many rules on what was allowed in dating. Where could you go that he wouldn't be embarrassed being seen with you? There were a lot of problems with that. The Academy had a special board that I got to sit on. I don't know why I was chosen, but it was a board to decide what was allowed for dating. We decided important issues like how long were you allowed to kiss goodnight and could you hold hands. Were you allowed to link arms? Were you allowed to put your arms around each other? It was a silly kind of a thing.

Sue Sweeney: What was the makeup of the board?

Lieutenant Lowndes: I was the only female. I think I was either a plebe or third class. I was fairly new at the Academy. There were first-class midshipmen. It was mostly midshipmen, several officers involved. But it was just a kind of general guideline of going over, I guess, existing policies, that they were just now unsure what do you classify as dating and what don't you classify as dating. It is a kind of gray area when you're living next door to each other. Maybe you have a close friend who is one of the guys, and you can go off to the library every night together and study. Is that dating? In uniform, the big rules were on public display of affection, do they apply equally to males and females in uniform at the same time, versus a male in uniform and a civilian? The civilian gal would do some things that we couldn't do in uniform. I believe it really came to a head at the Ring Dance for us second-class year, when we said, "Hey look, we want to be just like all the other gals."

The Academy came back and said, "No, you're not allowed to wear corsages, you're not allowed to wear the ring around your neck." That's what the other gals do. We weren't allowed to do it because we were in uniform. There were a lot of things we weren't allowed to do in uniform. Kind of as a group, one by one, you'd see a gal pinning a corsage on or putting the ring around her neck. One by one we all started doing it and thinking, "Now you tell me to take it off. I'm going to do it anyway; I don't care. This is my Ring Dance, this is what's supposed to happen, and I'm going to do it."

Sue Sweeney: You got away with it?

Lieutenant Lowndes: We got away with it. I think maybe that helped the other gals. Any time there was a formal dance of any kind, we always had a lot of problems with what were we allowed to do. I heard the story once that one of my female classmates came in civilian clothes with a wig of long hair, and nobody knew she was at the dance. I don't know if it was true or not, and I hope it was. There were some things you had to do, to be able to break the ice and say, "We're allowed to have fun, too," because we never had fun at the dances.

Sue Sweeney: When you had a small group—like the board that discussed dating—were you treated better than when you were at large? Did you feel you were listened to as an equal?

Lieutenant Lowndes: Yes. That has proved out from the time I first went into the Academy and still today, if I deal with a large group of people, they automatically say, "There's something wrong with her. She went to the Naval Academy; there's something wrong with her. She's one of them." It was hard to fit in comfortably, because we did stand out just a little bit with our different kind of hats and whatnot. When we were in a smaller group, like a small discussion group or a club, when you were with the choir or something, everyone was very good to you, because they got to know you as a person. Once they got to know you as a person, they could accept you. But in a large group, you're just one of "them."

And it still holds true. I still don't feel comfortable in large groups of alumni. I probably never will. I hate homecoming, because I know it's a large group of people, and they don't know me; they just know that I'm one of "them," I'm one of the class of '80, or I'm just a female who went to the Naval Academy.

Sue Sweeney: Do you take a lot of personal pride in having survived the Academy?

Lieutenant Lowndes: Yes. Now especially I can finally say to other people that I went to the Academy. I don't wear my class ring. I don't tell anybody when I first meet them, "Hi. I'm Barbette Lowndes. I went to the Naval Academy." I just don't do that. Especially after graduation, most of the gals didn't want to be picked out anymore. We were tired of being singled out. We tended to not tell anybody else.

There were some that wore their rings, and there were some that were very open and honest about it. If anybody asked if I had been at the Academy, I never denied it, but I never volunteered the information. I think somehow they could always tell—just by our attitudes and the way we conducted our business—that there was something different about us. Now I guess I'm getting more used to the fact that nobody's laughing anymore when I tell them I went to the Naval Academy. They're not laughing, they're not holding crosses up and saying, "Oh, God, stay away." It is a more proud feeling. If somebody does ask if I went to the Naval Academy, I'll volunteer right away, "Yes, I was one of the first women to have gone through." I'm proud of that fact now.

Sue Sweeney: Are you conscious of ring-knockers among your classmates?

Lieutenant Lowndes: There are some within the gals that are a little more open about it, that will tell everybody right away. That's their personality. Just by wearing the ring, I think, it says more than what I'm saying. I don't give them even that much notice.

Sue Sweeney: What were your summer cruises like?

Lieutenant Lowndes: Summer cruises were good. They were a chance to meet with people you hadn't met during the school year, to mix in with real world people. The first year we went on a YP [yard patrol] craft, which was a little difficult, because it was something the women had to do. It was forced on us, and they had to select one male for every female that went. It was almost a lottery: "Guess what? You lose. You have to go with the girls on the YPs this summer."

Oh, God. So they were giving the guys that kind of an attitude to start with. YPs just aren't exciting, as opposed to going out on a ship and being an enlisted man. You're not getting that same kind of training. As it turned out, we had probably more fun than anybody else. We went up and down the East Coast. We had a good time. We partied together, everybody had fun. We learned a lot about the YPs, about navigation, about different cities in the U.S., and it turned out to be a good experience.

The second year we went with the guys to Pensacola, Quantico, and Norfolk, to do what the guys were doing. We got to go on the plane rides. When we were in Pensacola, some of the pilots didn't like the idea of females being up with them, and they'd do everything they could to make us sick. I figured if I could get by without getting sick, you know, I scored another point on the guys. That's one up for me. But we at least got to go with the guys that year, and that helped a little bit in getting along with our classmates.

But we did spend one week separate while the guys were on submarines for a week. We had to get assigned to a running mate somewhere in the Norfolk-Washington, D.C., area. They'd ship us out individually to hang around a female officer. She obviously wasn't from the Academy, so she didn't really know what we were going through. She probably didn't even understand what a midshipman was. It was a week of seeing what the real world was like for a little while, and then getting back in with the rest of the crowd.

Sue Sweeney: What was your experience?

Lieutenant Lowndes: I had a Supply Corps officer. It was, I guess, destiny for me, and I enjoyed it. I'd never been around an older person. To me she was an older person. She probably was in her mid- to late 20s. She was a lieutenant in the Supply Corps. I was still with the Naval Academy mentality of, "She's still a lieutenant," and lieutenants were gods at that time. But she let me see a lot of what she was doing. In a week I can't be expected to do anything, but she would go out of her way to show me around. She and her boyfriend would take me with them at night. It was a very pleasant experience.

Sue Sweeney: Were you already leaning toward Supply Corps by that time?

Lieutenant Lowndes: I think that I had the leaning with the retired Navy captain that my mom worked with, and then meeting the female officer. I was kind of leaning that way. Let me tell you about first-class summer, and then I'll get back to why I went to the Supply Corps. That's something I think you need to know.

First-class summer I got very lucky; I got to go on a cruiser, which was heaven to me. There weren't too many women allowed to go on the combatant vessels, but I was one of them, and I went with one of my very best friends right there to my hometown of San Diego. That was the most perfect thing in the world. It was great. We were out about five weeks, Monday through Friday for five weeks, we'd come in on the weekend.

They always managed to get duty for me on the weekend, just a tough break, being right there at home. I did get to go home once in a while, and it was a good experience to see what the real Navy was like, to really mix with the enlisteds for the first time, and to get used to the shipboard life. I really enjoyed it. I think that's when I decided that if I was going to go to sea, I wanted to go on a real Navy ship; I wanted to go on a ship that did something. No tenders for me. So that was a big deciding factor.

Up until about February of our first-class year, they had absolutely no idea what career fields a woman could go into. Second-class summer is the kind of make-or-break point. You're either coming back or you can quit, no obligations. They sat us down the weekend before we had to start our classes, and they said, "Look, gals, we really don't know. Congress hasn't decided if women can go on ships at this point. We don't know if you can fly. We don't know if you can go restricted line and the staff corps, because you have to be not physically qualified for ships and planes."

Well, I'm not physically qualified because I'm not male; but I'm still a physically qualified person. I don't have bad knees or motion sickness or anything crazy. So it was, "We have no idea where you girls are going to go." Why should I commit myself to two more years at the Academy, plus five years in the fleet, and not know where I'm going to go or what kind of job they can give me? It was a very tough choice.

I don't think any of the gals opted to quit at that point. Once you start second-class year, that's it, you've made your decision. And I think every one of us still went ahead to class, scared to death, but we went ahead. First-class year, still no decision came out, they already had the Marine Corps service selection. If you wanted to go to the Marine Corps, you could do that. They still hadn't come out with any kind of a list with what jobs were available to the females. It was February, just a week or two before service selection night. At that point they had been asking, all four years, "If you could do anything in the Navy, what would you do?"

Well, when you first come in, you always think, "Gosh, I'd drive ships, I'd fly planes, I'd do anything. I want to be an astronaut. I want to do everything."

And by the end of the four years, you're tired. "I've already answered those questions. I told you, I want to go to sea. I've told you I want to fly a plane. And you're telling me that it doesn't look like there's going to be a very good chance of it. I'm tired of dreaming. What have you really got for me?"

I was looking into the Supply Corps, because I realized women had been in the Supply Corps for a number of years, and there would be no more icebreaking for me, I'd fit right on in, and it was a definite career pattern. I still don't like the 1100 designator code, because it's too much jumping around within the career field. One time you could be the BOQ [bachelor officers' quarters] manager, next time public affairs, next time admiral's aide, next time word processing. You know, what does it add up to? It's worthless to me. That's the kind of job for some dumb female, in my mind, who didn't go to the Academy, who just wants to come in to do something for a little while and get out, that's something she can do. That's not something you put someone through the Naval Academy to do. So I chose a career progression over everything else. I still think that's one of the smartest moves. Of the gals I interviewed, the most satisfied with their careers were those in the restricted line and the staff corps.

Sue Sweeney: About how many are in those areas?

Lieutenant Lowndes: Probably about 15, 20 at most, restricted line and staff corps. The rest are the general line, the unrestricted general line, those doing the basic 1100 work, those flying planes, those driving ships. But those flying planes, I think, are still pretty much satisfied, because you do have hands-on work. Maybe down the road when the billets start filtering out and there's no place else for them to go they won't be satisfied, because at that point there aren't any more career progressions without having to go into combat planes or combat missions. I think they'll probably hit a wall at about the lieutenant commander level. They'll say, "I can't go any further in my career."

The gals on ships are all dissatisfied because they're all on tenders. If I'm going to go to sea, I want to go on a combatant ship; I don't want a tender as a ship driver. As a Supply Corps officer on a tender, that's fine. There's a big need for a supply officer. I'm not the one driving the ship. I'm not trying to make my career out of driving a ship. You can't get qualified as a ship driver on a tender that doesn't go anywhere. That's what the other gals are starting to feel that are actually out on ships now.

Sue Sweeney: You mentioned second-class year and the deadline for dropping out. Did you think often about quitting?

Lieutenant Lowndes: I only thought once of quitting—during plebe summer. The physical fitness part was getting to me. I couldn't do a man's push-up and that bothered me a lot. I think they didn't know what they were looking for in the women coming in, that first group. We weren't physically oriented at all, and that has a lot to do with my high school. I had gym all three years during high school, but the kind of classes I took were dancing, badminton, archery—nothing that gave me any kind of strength or physical coordination. Then to get to the Academy, where they say, "Okay, do push-ups," I just couldn't do it. I can't run. To me, running a mile was just about death, and to have to run a mile in seven and a half minutes—or during plebe summer to have to go on a two and a half mile run around the Academy—was very difficult. I just felt that I couldn't do it. I went in to see my squad leader during the summer and told him I wanted to quit and I couldn't take it anymore. I was not the kind of person they were looking for, and I wanted out.

He said, "Henry, go back to your room. You don't know what you're talking about. You're just not thinking straight today. Go back to your room. I don't want to talk to you about it. If you still feel that way next week, then see me again."

In the meantime, he talked to the midshipman company officer for the summer, and I guess he had also had problems physically, trying to do push-ups. He came to see me and told me, "I had troubles, too. I couldn't do a push-up if I had to." He came back a little while later with the company officer who said the same thing. "I couldn't do it either." He said, "Why don't you show me how much of a man's push-up you can do."

I got down and did about half of a push-up, and he said, "Well, that's a half more than you could do when you first got here. It's not that tough. You can do it."

Because they told me that they had the same problem and they were still there, I said, "I guess I can." I never thought again about quitting, even with all the pressures put on us.

Two thoughts went through my mind: One, I was too stubborn to quit. I guess I was too dumb to know when to say, "I've had enough. This is no fun. I'm going home."

Too dumb to know it. And two, I didn't have anything to go home to. If I went home, I was going to go back to working at McDonald's, Jack in the Box, wherever, to try to save up a few pennies, and try to go on to another school, and I knew I'd never be able to do that. I said, "This is my only chance to do something with myself." So I stuck it out.

Sue Sweeney: Have you talked with any of the girls who left? Were there ever cases when a firstie made it a little too easy for a girl to leave?

Lieutenant Lowndes: I've only met three of the gals that have gotten out. One got out because she had found some guy that she was really interested in. She was very religious, and she decided, after a lot of praying, that this was God's answer to her, to get out, get married to this person, and to start her family and family life. Another gal—I'm not sure why she got out. She wasn't exactly encouraged, but, yes, they let her. They didn't fight as much to help her stay in. She ended up marrying her squad leader two or three years later. She wasn't dating him while she was there, but she ended up marrying him anyway. She wasn't really encouraged either.

The only other gal I knew that I've talked to since getting out was kicked out for an honor violation. She was my roommate. She didn't want to leave. That was a tough one, because it was an honor violation. She had done something wrong. She went through the honor board process, the board found her guilty, the board decided that she would have to leave. That's a clear-cut rule; they would have done it with a guy. It went all the way up to the superintendent. She had her exit interview. She was good friends with the superintendent's daughter through church. To have been over to the superintendent's house on kind of a personal basis with the daughter and to now sit in front of him and have to explain yourself in a situation like that was difficult. He told her that she'd have to leave the Academy.

Some time between the time he told her that and the time she was actually supposed to leave, some women's group out in town stood up and said, "You're chasing the women out. You can't do this. You did this on purpose. You're railroading her." It took five months for them to process her out. That was a very hard time for her. She was resigned in her mind to say, "I'm out. Why bother going to classes and trying to study? I'm out of here." To have to keep going along with the routine day after day was a very tough time. Being with her in that same room, I know it was hard.

Sue Sweeney: Did she get more grief from the guys because they knew that if it had been them, they'd be out?

Lieutenant Lowndes: Yes and no. I guess she just kind of relaxed and opened her mouth more, because she knew she was out, she didn't care. She could tell people what she thought, and she could, I guess, relate better to the guys because she could talk about it. She was out and she could start planning other things, what she was going to do. She could just go in and sit down with the upperclassmen. Who cares? She followed the basic rules, but she could just go in and sit down and talk, say, to a first class. "Hey, Brad, this is the way I feel." She could do that.

Sue Sweeney: How well known are honor violations? Did everybody know her situation?

Lieutenant Lowndes: They heard about it. Everybody heard about it. Also, in plebe year, another one of my roommates was brought up before the honor board. It looked bad. Everybody was pointing their finger, saying, "God, I don't want to be anywhere near Henry. That's bad news. She's turning in her roommates." Yes, I had something to do with it. I was called in as a witness in both of their cases—two totally separate incidents. They didn't like the second roommate at all, and they tried to get to her. They really wanted to get her on an honor offense—she was a chronic liar. If they really wanted to get her, I probably could have given them some things. "Don't go for that charge, go for this other one. This other case is a stronger case if you want to get rid of her." I didn't do that, though.

But it was tough. Everybody knew that there were some honor problems. They knew who was getting processed for academic boards. There were a couple of gals who were extremely overweight or had medical problems, the "crutch corps," they were always on crutches. It had a bad effect for the other gals—we're all weak, we try to wimp out on everything. There was some pressure in those areas whether to keep the gals. One of the gals was extremely heavy and couldn't pass the PE test. We all have to pass. If she doesn't pass, it's not fair to the rest of us. We were just as glad that they eventually got rid of her.

Sue Sweeney: How about that second roommate?

Lieutenant Lowndes: Yes, she got out of the honor offense. It was a hokey charge. She was supposed to be in some particular place at some particular time, and her normal habit was knocking very loudly. You could hear her up and down the Hall, knocking very loudly and asking permission to come in. I don't remember hearing her that day. They tried to say that she did not go to a particular person's room, and she said that she had. She knocked very loudly. If she was knocking, I think anybody would hear. But I know she left our room at the right time so that she could go down the hall to the person's room. Now whether she made it there or not, I don't know, but I know she wasn't in our room. I know she left with the intent of going to that room, but I didn't hear her knock.

So it was kind of—was she there or was she not? I don't know. There was no real evidence, and it was no big deal that she wasn't there at that particular point in time. So it was a strange charge that they tried to get her on. I ended up switching roommates after awhile.

That was an interesting point too, how they got the women to get along with their roommates. Most of us didn't get along with our roommates. You're forced to room with some person, you've been through a lot of stress with this person, and there are just personality conflicts. I did not get along with the roommate I was left with. I got along with the roommate that was kicked out. The women in our battalion got together kind of as a group, in little groups of women. We obviously could never all be in the same room at the same time or we would possibly be in trouble, but we'd get together in groups and start talking. We came up with our own grand plan of who would go where, within the battalion, keeping everybody within the battalion. We presented it to the battalion officer, who immediately said, "No way. We don't switch guys outside the company. You can't do it."

But if a guy doesn't get along with his roommate, the next year he can room with somebody else in the company. Big deal. But we couldn't do that because there weren't any other gals in the company to swap with. We fought and fought and fought. They finally said, "Okay." They sat down with us and said, "Here are the problems with your plan." We got pretty much what we wanted out of it. We were all fairly happy. There were one or two gals that I don't think could have gotten along anyplace within the battalion. It made it easier, because we kind of had a choice in roommates.

They've changed the whole policy now, which I'm very happy to hear. They have a whole group of women in one company, maybe six in one company, instead of putting two or three in every single company. The whole group can decide among yourselves who you want to live with. If after a year you're not getting along, you get together in that little group and say, "Okay, let's switch," and you could do it within the company. For us, how do you say which one of the two of you have to go to another company and meet all new people, try to get along with all new people. How do you decide which one has to go? It was a real problem. I think they've pretty much gotten it straightened out now.

Sue Sweeney: Have you seen other improvements since you've been gone?

Lieutenant Lowndes: Sure. There were a lot of things. I said to Captain Busik, the executive director of the USNA Alumni Association, "Gosh, if we had this while I was there, it would have been a lot better."[9]

And he'd say, "They do that now."

"And if we had such and such . . ."

"Oh, they do that, too." A lot of it was the little things like getting the clothing. They are allowed to bring their own undergarments, which makes life a lot easier because they have it all to begin with. It is something you are comfortable with. As long as it was wash and wear, white, cotton, basically some plain underwear that you could mark and throw in the laundry. As long as it could go though the industrialized laundry system and still come back, fine. I didn't need to have the Naval Academy buy a particular Playtex bra for me that just does not fit my size or my style. So little things like that helped.

---

[9] Captain William Busik was appointed executive director of the Naval Academy Alumni Association in 1971 and remained in the position until 1994. *Shipmate* is the Academy's alumni magazine.

Female role models—we had no female role models. They have female role models now. They have more of my classmates drifting through the Academy, if not actually stationed at the Academy. They have increased the number of women company officers and officers that you would have more direct interaction with. At first their theory was the same percentage in female company officers as in the fleet. That meant one out of 36 company officers was female, and most of the time it was a female Marine. How many of the women go into the Marine Corps? That's not a role model for you. Ours was a very stereotypical Marine, very straitlaced and creased. That wasn't what the women in the fleet were really all about. The other women we saw or were exposed to were all in the academic fields, and they were all in the wishy-washy subjects—political science and English—nobody in a good, solid course like the male officers were teaching. They now have some of those at the Academy, which is good. We need a role model who is more than just some dumb blonde, with a good attitude about her. She's got to be professional, intelligent, and show that she's just like one of the guys. That's very important to me.

Sue Sweeney: What else would you like to see changed?

Lieutenant Lowndes: I also felt that we didn't know how to dress or act or look feminine in any way. We were never taught those kinds of things. Coming out of high school, these are four very important years in a young gal's life, learning how to adjust to her changing body, to becoming an adult, how to dress, how to carry herself, how to act. It was very important, and we didn't have anything at all like that. Now they do have some classes in how to pick clothes. You go through the institutional four years of wearing black and white, and it was all tailored for you. How to go shopping—where do you start buying? We never had any guidance. Now they have some optional guidance. I think they should make it mandatory, not just a one-hour sit-down, saying, "This is how to do it, gals." Have somebody show me how to put on makeup. I never knew. I went a long time before I ever learned how to put on makeup.

I only really learned last year how to take care of myself. I missed those kind of important years. I think they need to do a little bit more to help the women in the last year. Sure, you don't need to do it as a plebe—but as a first classman, you've got to adjust, make them look like women, teach them how to dress, how to look and act like a female. They need to have more of an awareness of how to wear the uniform, too. There was a big difference, especially for my group, between what we wore at the Academy and what we wore in the fleet. The only uniforms that were the same were the service dress blue and the mess dress, which you wear maybe once a year. Other than that, I didn't know how to wear any of the uniforms. I walked out of the Academy being a know-it-all compared to OCS graduates or ROTC graduates—and I would look sillier than all the rest, because I was still putting my belt on like a man. All the others said, "How come the belt clip is on the other side?"

"That's the way we wear it."

"No, here's the rule books on how to wear it." They never taught us. They never taught us what uniform hats go with what uniforms. I don't know that they teach that now. I know that they need to teach that. If they're doing anything at all, they really need to.

Sue Sweeney: That's quite an oversight.

Lieutenant Lowndes: Yes. Here's the order book; go order them. But nobody told you how to wear it.

Sue Sweeney: How much feedback were you asked to provide?

Lieutenant Lowndes: That pretty much was more informal. They had some of the gals wear-testing some clothes during different time periods. I wear-tested a lot of different types of shoes while I was at the Academy, and I could give my formal feedback there. Most of the time it was while you were down at the tailor's while he's fitting you for some particular outfit, you'd say, "Gosh, this doesn't feel very comfortable. It's designed nice if you're standing up, but I can't sit in this stupid outfit. How do you sit in this thing?"

The extra seam in the long formal skirt we wore was a big wow to us. "Wow, they finally caught on that we need another one." When we tried to walk in formation with the guys, when we wore the mess dress, we had one slit on the long slim skirt. You can't go very far hobbling down the hall. They put in that extra slit and gave us two advantages: one, we could walk, and two, when the wind came through that opening, it can go out the other end—otherwise it made a kind of balloon effect and off you'd get pushed.

Other areas, we had some say. I don't think they asked us enough about the uniforms we were wearing. We were wear-testing the tropical whites that were going into the fleet. The gals in the fleet really didn't have them yet. The tropical whites that we were wearing, we heard after a while that they decided that the women didn't like it. We said, "Who ever asked?" We were wearing it more than anybody else, and I could have told them what I liked or didn't like about the uniform.

Sue Sweeney: You had the over-blouse.

Lieutenant Lowndes: Right. We had the over-blouse, which was a big change from what actually came into the fleet. But nobody ever asked me if I liked it or if I liked the material.

Sue Sweeney: Did you?

Lieutenant Lowndes: I liked the uniform, I liked the material. It was a little see-through, but with the over-blouse, we didn't have a problem. The problem they still have in the fleet is with the white slacks. For some reason, you can still see through them. With just a tucked-in shirt, you see the whole outline of your shirt being tucked in, and I don't think that presents a very good-looking uniform. It may in pictures or in actual design, but when you're actually wearing it, it isn't worthwhile at all. I don't know how come we can't have the same material the guys have. You don't see through the guys' pants. It doesn't seem to make any sense. I don't know who sits on the uniform boards. Maybe they should have some of the younger gals on the uniform boards who are experiencing the uniforms for the first time, instead of saying, "I've been wearing this thing for 15 years, and I guess I'm used to it now." Somebody putting it on for the first time will say, "I like it" or "I don't like it."

Sue Sweeney: Were you ever asked to complete questionnaires or surveys?

Lieutenant Lowndes: We had a lot of panel meetings, where they would select a large group of females. We would sit down with female commanders and lieutenant commanders. We rarely saw females above the rank of lieutenant—and that was even rare. We'd usually see ensigns and j.g.'s. A female commander was a big inspiration, just to have her sitting there in front of you asking questions. But we did fill out a lot of surveys. Most of it was, "Is the Academy being good to you? Has the administration helped you?" That's nice, it's all a very bland kind of a question, but it didn't really ask me anything that I could help them decide on. We were pulled in for a lot of study groups, brainwave testing. We never found out any of what happened to the tests we were involved in. I kind of think we would have liked to have had some feedback.

Sue Sweeney: Did you feel like a guinea pig?

Lieutenant Lowndes: Sure. We got called to do some tests. They'd ask the exact same questions over and over, just in a different order with a different person asking the questions. "I already told you what I want to do. I've already told you how I feel about this place. I don't see a change, and I don't get any feedback. Don't ask me these questions anymore." It got to be more of a nuisance than any feeling of any good coming of it. There were some studies by some, I guess, fairly renowned groups, but still we didn't get any feedback. Who cares? They were all the same.

Sue Sweeney: Tell me more about academics. What did you major in?

Lieutenant Lowndes: I majored in oceanography, really had no idea what I wanted to major in. I liked mathematics in high school, and I kind of thought about it, but they just gave you one day, pretty much, to decide what you wanted to major in. You could wander around through the academic building, talk with each group of instructors. Instead of giving us a full presentation or documents to read ahead of time, it was pretty much go in, meet the board, or, I guess, the academic staff, the teachers in each of the particular majors. Considering how many different majors are offered, that's a lot to try and soak in in one day and try and decide which one you want. I'm not sure why I chose oceanography; I guess it sounded fun, sounded like something about the Navy. I liked it and I am glad I made the choice. It was a good major, I enjoyed it, and now I realize it didn't really matter what I majored in, as long as I was interested in it. It was something I enjoyed.

Sue Sweeney: Were academics difficult for you?

Lieutenant Lowndes: Yes. Having come just from high school, with nobody else around, not knowing what the college course is supposed to be, I didn't know what I was expected to know. I had no idea what my own potential was. After going through enough of the plebe summer, I started to understand that I was separating myself top and bottom of the class, I just mentally put myself in the bottom. I was female, I was being picked on during plebe summer. In my own mind I wasn't all that good. I was having trouble in physical fitness, and I was having trouble in everything else, so my mind thought, "Well, if a 2.0 grade is passing, as long as I get 2.0 or better, I'm great. I'm happy." I guess I didn't push myself hard enough that first year.

My two roommates at that time had grades lower than mine, and they said, "Oh, you're the genius in the room?"

What did I know? I couldn't talk to anybody else. I thought, "I guess I am doing pretty good. I must really be doing well." I didn't realize that it was possible to do a lot better, to study harder. They gave us classes on how to study, but that really didn't help. How do you get around the other pressures and problems of being at the Academy? How do you get over the fears of walking out the door? Every time I walked out the door, I was scared to death. How do you get over that and still study? So I didn't know I could do better the first couple of years. That set my pace for education.

There were certain subjects that I just didn't care for, naval history especially. I just didn't have the time to read. I didn't know enough about speed reading, so that was one of my big failings. I did not do well; I got a D in the course. I figured, well, I had enough other good grades, and it would pull the whole average up. I think I must have gotten a B or something else to balance it out. I always came up above a 2.0, not much, but I did. Now I can look back. My father-in-law is very big on naval history. He's just shocked that I wasn't more interested in it. At the time it wasn't interest or anything else stopping me; it was time. I wish I knew how to study.

My grades were low, lower than most almost everybody else in the company, but still above passing. They put me on a study program where I'd have to be in at night, turn in a little slip to my squad leader saying what courses I studied, how much time I put in, and which of those classes did I have the following day. You didn't always have the same class every day. My squad leader realized my grade was a D in history, and I always got zero for study time on history. "You're just barely staying alive. How come you're not studying it?"

This was kind of sealed in fate here; I was paying attention in class, but why waste time on a class I know I wasn't going to do well in, when there are other classes I was having trouble in? He didn't understand my theory of how to study. All he could tell me was, "You ought to read the book." At that point I was just too far behind.

There was no real guidance, no one sitting down, saying, "Here's how to do it." There were people who said, "If you have problems, come see me." I'd come to see them, and unless they were absolute geniuses themselves, they'd forgotten how to do logarithms and the basic things in life with some of their own strange courses. So it was always a challenge to just stay above the passing mark for me.

In my third year I got a new roommate—the aero-engineer major—she was smart. All of a sudden I saw somebody who was getting good grades, and I said, "God, it is possible to get a good grade at the Naval Academy." I had no idea you could do that. She helped me, encouraged me, and I started to do better. I think I got an A for the first time in class, and I loved it. I still had low grades because they averaged the whole thing in, they averaged in your PE grade, which I still was having problems with, but I felt better about the whole situation. Because of my sports and my involvement with the glee club, the commandant knew who I was.

Sue Sweeney: Was that Admiral McCauley?

Lieutenant Lowndes: That was Rear Admiral Winnefeld at the time. He knew who I was. He was a very big supporting element for the women. He and the superintendent knew who I was from the choir and sports. Both, at one time or another, said to me—to me personally—"You know, you're going to have a lot of trouble in electrical engineering coming up. Electrical engineering takes out almost all of the second class. You're not going to do well, because your grades are showing us you haven't got much chance. You're really going to have to study that one."

To have them at that level say to me, some little midshipman, "You personally are going to have problems with it," I took it as a challenge almost, and I did my best. The first semester and second semester was the best I had ever studied for a course. I really tried. I think I had the best grades I'd ever had. It wasn't because it was any easier, but because I had confidence in myself that I wasn't going to get the lowest grade, so I really applied myself to try to get the higher grade. I didn't come out too high on the list of overall grades, but it was worth it.

Sue Sweeney: Did you have a feel for how the civilian profs viewed the women?

Lieutenant Lowndes: Not really how they, as a group, viewed us. I think they were more accepting of the fact that they used to have just men in their classes, and now they had men and women in their classes. I don't think it affected them. They don't know what really happens when we got out to the fleet, where the military instructors at least knew we were going out to the fleet. To the civilian instructors, you were just people in the class. And yes, there were some things that women tend to know more than men—areas in English that women typically understand more or study more—and they could draw on that, but not really saying, "You're going to do good because you're a girl, and you're not because you're a guy," or, "You're a girl and this is chemistry, so automatically women just don't know anything about chemistry and can't understand it."

Sue Sweeney: Did the military profs treat you differently than the civilians?

Lieutenant Lowndes: Yes, I think they could almost get along better with us, because they didn't have to worry about the rules. Their only rule, I think, was they stood back a little bit, because they were afraid of fraternization. Everybody was scared to death of fraternization. What are the final guidelines on it? If they had you in for extra instruction, they were a little more nervous, I guess, about it, but they could see through the problems of the Academy. Many would say if you had an academic problem, you could talk about the academic problem. I don't care if it's 2:00 in the morning. If you have a question that's academic, I don't care if the rules say you're supposed to be sleeping. If you have a problem and need to talk to me, give me a call and we'll talk about the academic problem.

Sue Sweeney: Were there cases of fraternization with profs?

Lieutenant Lowndes: With profs, no. No. There were rumors of fraternization with company officers on the administrative side, because we were more directly involved, but never with the profs.

Sue Sweeney: What were your extracurricular activities?

Lieutenant Lowndes: I started off on the fencing team. I was not up on sports at all. The first summer, we had to sit down in the gym and have them present all the sports you could possibly play. Then you had to pick one because you had to play it every afternoon, I said, "Oh gosh, don't you have anything for the women?" At that time they didn't have anything for the women to get together and play except softball. There weren't regular women varsity teams set up.

So I said, "What's a safe sport? What won't I get hurt in with a guy? I'll take fencing. That sounds easy." I learned to enjoy fencing. It's not an exactly safe sport. I saw one guy get stabbed in competition. A blade had broken, and he just about lost his spleen from the accident.

We got together as a group. We all had to learn, basically from ground zero. There weren't any women who had been fencing all along. The coach helped all of us, but the biggest advantage was we had to use the same loft as the men. We had to practice with the men, which gave us a big competitive advantage when we were out playing with women from other schools. We had somebody a little more forceful, a little more aggressive to play against during practice instead of women who tend to just put in 50 percent, 70 percent; the guys put in 100 percent, they're going to win every time. We had a little advantage that way.

It was also fun being on a sport that I could try to work up in the levels. I could go away on a sporting trip. They were usually just one-day trips. We only played teams in the local area. Once we went to Princeton and stayed overnight. That was where the commandant really took notice of me as a person, because he was a fencer at the Academy. He was already our "friend." He came in and he told us during plebe summer that he was starting with us, with the class of '80 the whole way—and you felt he was with everybody. He was at one of the matches. It was a very tough match. We had six or seven people fencing. For each person that wins, that's one point for the team. The team with the most points takes the entire match.

The top gal in our group ended up being a rated fencer. None of the other gals really panned out in that first year to be much good, but we were up there, we were trying. Robin Druce proved to be a very good fencer. She won her match. None of the other gals won that day. Somehow, against this very, very tough school, I won my match. I got a call that night from the front office. They asked what my home phone number was. I was scared to death—"What did I do wrong? They want my home phone number."

They said, "Never mind. We just need to know your home phone number."

They got my home phone number. I thought, "I'll let them call first, and then I'll call home and find out what happened." So I waited a little while and called home. It was the commandant who called my parents to tell them how proud he was that I had won. So it was very encouraging, in a sport that I knew nothing about, in a tough match, that he would take the time for something like that, to call my folks. My folks didn't understand. They didn't know who he was.

They said, "Admiral Winnefeld called."

I panicked. "Admiral Winnefeld called you?"

They said, "Yes."

"What did I do wrong?" It was just an immediate guilt complex.

They said, "Well, what did you do wrong? Why are you worried?" But it was nice to know that he had called, that he was proud of me that day.

I got tired of fencing after a little while and wanted to try something different. I had just switched roommates. My new roommate was very good in academics; she was also an excellent singer. She got me started singing with the choir. That wasn't something to take the place of sports in the afternoon. I think I really had to give up the fencing because I was still failing swimming, and I had to spend so much time in the pool every day. I couldn't go on in fencing. I was losing that edge and just losing interest. Carol Thompson, my roommate, gave me an out. I started singing with the choir. She had been in a musical performance, and I got to help her backstage. I watched every single show she did. The musical was usually just the choir coming in and doing the show. She had the lead in *HMS Pinafore*. I was so proud of her. I got so wrapped up in helping her backstage that I said, "This is what I want to do." So I started singing with the choir in church. I tried out for the musical the following year and got to be a part of it. This was my calling in life. I enjoyed doing musicals for two years. That took me out of the sports program for a little while.

But I still had to find a sport to do in between musicals. That only lasted one of the sports periods. You go through three or four sports periods a year. They still didn't have enough women playing general kinds of sports. There were women in the varsity volleyball, varsity crew, varsity this, varsity that, and just a handful of those left over that weren't in varsity. They were trying to make up games for us. I remember once they put us on a tennis court, took down the tennis nets, and gave us a ball for kickball. At 18, 19, 20, I don't need to play that kind of stupid game. Give me a sport that's worthwhile.

So then they gave us badminton, which was okay, but it was women, and it was a sissy sport, and we were taking a lot of ribbing from the guys. Then they made it mandatory in PE class that everybody go through one or two lessons of badminton and volleyball. The guys found that it wasn't such a sissy sport. They kind of liked it. One year they opened it for women and men to play volleyball one season and one season to play badminton. It was kind of neat. They finally got something that was kind of fun, not overly contact sport related, and we got to play with the guys. I don't know what they do now, but they needed an organized program where they can get the gals together to play softball or play field hockey, or something where they can get the girls aside. They'll be very competitive, they're all athletically inclined.

At the Academy, after going through plebe summer get them out there, get them together. You can't play on company soccer teams or football; the guys would kill you. I know one of the gals tried. She insisted that she be allowed to play on the company football team, and by the rules, every team was allowed x number of people. Every person had to be allowed to play. When it was her turn, they put her on the end as God knows what, a wide receiver or something, and said, "Run down the end of the field or just stand there. We're going to fake out to you." Sure.

Then she'd just basically stand on the field for the right amount of time. Nobody would ever come near her, nobody would try and touch her to knock her over because they didn't want to be accused of doing anything wrong. She just basically stood there. That's not for me. If I have to play a sport in the afternoon, that's not it.

Sue Sweeney: When you were in the glee club, how did you feel about doing *The Messiah* with Hood College?

Lieutenant Lowndes: You ask a good question there. The choir and the glee club were separate. Choir was a mixed organization. We were used to being with the guys and they were used to us. There were two choirs in the Protestant group: the Protestant choir was the group that was in the forward part of the church; they were all male. The only reason they were all male was the marching. They marched up the aisle during the church service. We'd do that only when they were on vacation. In the old days, I guess, the Protestant choir was the good choir, the antiphonal was the weaker of the voices. They didn't want to have the women march up the aisle and back down every Sunday, so we always sat in the back in the antiphonal choir. The guys were used to us. They had no problems singing with us. We went to Hood College for *The Messiah*, and it surprised me when we went to rehearsal, all the Hood gals were in their curlers, and they had on mudpacks and all that. I thought, "Gosh, these guys are looking at you now. I don't care if they see you tonight all dolled up, but they're looking at you right now." I thought, "I'm being picked on for being fat, dumb, and ugly; here these girls wear curlers to a rehearsal!"

There was also the whole difference in professionalism. We were there. We wanted to sing *The Messiah*. We got started practicing late, and they'd never had a chance to practice women in their alto-soprano parts before. All of a sudden they've got to have special rehearsals just for us and for Mr. Talley to get used to leading the gals in those parts. My roommate insisted on being able to sing one of the solos, but they said, "No, we were always going to go professional." I think that maybe they should consider having one of the midshipmen sing if she has a good voice.

But we got there, and the Hood College girls were all excited. They had pre-arranged with the orchestra that where they break in *The Messiah* for the instruments to retune, the orchestra was going to break into "Rudolph the Red-Nosed Reindeer." So the gals were all giggly just before the break because they knew, ooh, Rudolph was coming up next. Boy, they were all excited. We had heard whispers of it. Of course, the baton dropped and the orchestra starts playing "Rudolph the Red-Nosed Reindeer," and all the girls are singing it, and their director doesn't know what to do.

I guess he was used to this kind of silliness, but to us it was totally silly. These women were giggling and disturbing the practice. We only had so much time to practice *The Messiah*, and they were doing this kind of nonsense. It started driving in the wedge between us—who's professional and who's not. After we sang "Rudolph the Red-Nosed Reindeer," the other gals from Hood College basically started to fall asleep. They didn't care about practicing the rest of it.

We were still worried because we'd never sung this part before and we needed the practice. We kept on and they mouthed along with us. The performance went well, no problems. They came over to the Naval Academy to do the performance the following weekend. At our school, again we had the practice—Mr. Talley was leading the practice, he's very professional. He's not used to the girls giggling. The girls were sitting beside us, and one of them turned to me and said, "You're only here to steal my boyfriend. I know you're trying to steal my boyfriend."

"Honey, I don't even know who your boyfriend is."

That was her whole attitude to us as females at the Academy. They didn't realize that we weren't dating anybody because nobody would date us, and here she was very jealous of us. We never got along with the Hood College girls. It was always there from the very start, when they'd busload in all the gals for the tea fights, for the dances. All the girls would come in their buses, all looking so pretty in their wonderful, nice, long, sexy dresses, and we stood there in this wonderful long uniform and couldn't kick off our shoes and have a good time like they could. We were always jealous of them in that respect.

We had asked once, "If you're going to busload in girls for the guys, you should busload in guys for us at these dances. The guys don't like dancing with midshipmen. Neither do I. Why should I have to dance with some crummy mid?" They never would go for that, because I guess they were afraid the civilian guys and civilian girls would hit it off and we'd all be left out in the cold. There was always that animosity.

Sue Sweeney: Did you or your friends ever date civilians?

Lieutenant Lowndes: There were only a couple that really dated civilian guys. I had a very good friend who was a civilian out in town. I met him through a local church. I guess he wanted to date. I just didn't have the time and was still going through all the other problems at the Academy, and I didn't think anybody would want to date me.

I was at one point engaged to a civilian, a guy who wasn't at the Academy, but he was enlisted in the Navy. During second-class year, almost every girl came back from vacation with a diamond on her hand. It was just unbelievable. You were left out in the cold if you weren't engaged to somebody someplace, usually some guy at home. I joined that crowd of people after enough of this, "You're fat, you're dumb, you're ugly." I said any guy dumb enough to ask me to get married, I'm going for it, it sounds good to me.

This guy I was engaged to was in the Navy, he was enlisted, he was my best friend's brother from home. Whenever I went home, he always drove my friend and I around, the two of us, he'd drive us to the movies, drive us wherever we wanted to go, because she and I didn't have cars. I never dated him. I never really went out with him alone, because it was always the three of us. He dropped me off first and then took his sister home. That was fine. Somewhere along the line, I don't know why, he decided that he wanted to marry me. We'd never dated, really.

He was so shy, he wrote a letter to me and asked me to get married. I was in that mood, "This is some dumb guy who's dumb enough to say yes so, okay, let's get married." So we got engaged just like everybody else, and after a year of that kind of nonsense of long-distance letters, I finally said, "What am I doing? I'm finally to the point where I like me a little bit, and I've got to take control of my life." I liked me a little bit then. I told him, "I can't go through with this. This is nuts. I just can't do it." About that same time, everybody else started throwing away all their diamonds, too.

All of a sudden, everybody who got them in second-class year got rid of them— got rid of them in first-class year. There were a lot of gals in first-class year that were scheduled to get married June Week and I think only five of the gals actually did graduate and get married June Week. We just went through this major swing in moods about ourselves and about the Academy.

Sue Sweeney: What was your company officer's reaction to your engagement?

Lieutenant Lowndes: He told me the company line that officers and enlisted don't get married, that's not a good idea. He was questioning why I was getting married to this guy, how I knew him, where he came from, how this was going to work, did I really know what I was doing.

Sue Sweeney: Did you tell him that you'd never really dated him?

Lieutenant Lowndes: Yes, and that he was my best friend's brother, so that was okay, and I knew his folks and I knew his sister, so that was okay. But he couldn't come up with a rule—that it's against the rules for a midshipman to date an enlisted. He couldn't come up with that one, so he kind of let it slide and never really said anything about it. I guess he knew I'd wise up eventually.

I'd like to tell you what happened in my life at the Academy, why I finally liked me. I was just thinking of that. For almost the entire four years, I didn't like me at all. I mean, I liked me as a person less and less. "You're fat, you're dumb, you're ugly. And now to add to that, you're stupid." I couldn't get the grades, I couldn't do anything else right. I didn't like me as a person at all. I started to put on a lot of weight, no longer took care of myself.

In my first-class year, coming back from Christmas leave, one of the plebes—I don't know why—he decided he liked me. We were kind of dating, first class and a plebe, and that was so against anything I'd ever done—I've never jeopardized anything. But he encouraged me so much: "Why do you have to eat so much? If you combed your hair once in a while, you wouldn't look so bad. If you'd use a little makeup you'd look good." He had been prior enlisted, so he was my own age, and he saw something in me— that I could be pretty good if I really tried. I had also had braces on, and the braces were changing the shape of my face; I had cheekbones for the first time, my buck teeth were being pulled in.

I looked at myself and said, "Yes, I guess I could."

He really encouraged me to lose 15 to 20 pounds and start dressing a little bit better, and take care of myself. He was a big encouragement in my life, mostly to convince me that I was okay. Because of the braces I wore headgear around, this massive piece of metal all over my head. I heard all kinds of hoots and hollers from all the guys at the Academy. Finally I could turn around and say, "I may be ugly, but I'm doing something about it. What are you doing about your face?" I could finally say it to the guys and believe it myself—that I was doing something to improve myself.

I see a difference in looking at pictures of me then and what I look like now, and how I feel about myself now. My husband has continued that whole encouragement. He's the one who convinced me to take classes on how to dress, how to pick out colors that will go well with me, how to put on makeup.

Sue Sweeney: You're so attractive—it's hard to believe what you're describing as a midshipman.

Lieutenant Lowndes: If you could go back and see those pictures, my attitude at that time, even up to a couple of years ago, was I was okay. I don't think I am gorgeous, but I think I do look good now. I can look in a mirror and say, "Yes, that face isn't horrible to have to look at every day." I couldn't do that five years ago, I couldn't do that nine years ago.

Sue Sweeney: Much trepidation about dating a plebe—the fear of being caught?

Lieutenant Lowndes: Sure. Oh, sure. To me at the time, though, he was more my mental strength. I needed him to get me through, to make that transition, to be so encouraging, that I really didn't think of it as dating as much as I needed him as a person. I needed someone—and it was him. I didn't care what class he was. We kept things very cool.

Sue Sweeney: How did you find time? Under what circumstances did you see each other?

Lieutenant Lowndes: He was in the choir with me, so we could sit at choir and talk a lot. I didn't need the physical contact. I didn't need to go hold his hand or kiss him; it was more that I needed him to be there, to talk to me. I could write letters to him—they'd go out through the post office and come back through the post office. I had a phone in my room the last semester, so he could go down the hall to the pay phone and call me. There are ways to get around the whole system if you really have to.

Sue Sweeney: He wasn't in your company?

Lieutenant Lowndes: He wasn't. He was completely on the other side of the Hall. No one ever really knew about it. I guess when I graduated, we still had grand plans that we could date, because now I was a no longer a midshipman, but the distance was a problem. He found some other plebe he started dating, which was fine. It was fine. I was finally encouraged through my experience out in the real world at Supply School that some of the guys were interested in dating me, which shocked me. I was so excited about it. I didn't feel I needed the plebe anymore, didn't need him to be there to help me.

Sue Sweeney: A valuable experience.

Lieutenant Lowndes: Sure.

Sue Sweeney: What did you do after graduation?

Lieutenant Lowndes: Immediately afterwards I went home and just relaxed, to get away and try to think about what was going to happen next. There's no way of preparing you for that big cutoff from the Academy—that total dependency. I went to Athens, Georgia, for Supply School. I got down there, and my first big fear was checking in. They'd say, "Sorry, we don't have any more room at the BOQ." What am I supposed to do now? I had no idea. I had never lived in an apartment by myself. I had no idea how to find an apartment; I didn't know what to do.

It ended up that same day, a couple of the guys who were living at the BOQ decided they'd move out and get an apartment together. So that freed up a room that very same day, and I never had to experience living in a hotel. I think I would have fallen apart. I think I probably would have jumped on a plane and gone home and said, "It's too much, and there's nobody there to help me at all for the transition."

Sue Sweeney: Do you consider that a shortcoming of the Naval Academy—that they encourage too much dependence?

Lieutenant Lowndes: You bet. They give you a one-and-a-half-, two-hour class on how to budget, how to pick out a new car, how to get an apartment. But one and a half hours isn't much. The guys, most of them, I think, get married because they still need that dependency, they need somebody else to ask if they're doing the right thing. I didn't have any family anywhere near Athens, Georgia, so I couldn't turn to somebody else and say,

"What do I do now, coach? Where do I go for the night? What's a reasonable rate to pay at a hotel?" How would I know after four years locked up in the Naval Academy? I sure didn't know what a reasonable rate was.

How would I know what I was signing myself into when renting? Do I need to buy? Do I need to put myself in hock to buy furniture, or do I rent it? Is that cost-advantageous? What do I need? I got into the BOQ, which was a good transition for me. I needed that. I was so scared to death of the world. There were other gals from the Academy, there were guys that I met. We formed a little family within the BOQ. We were close together, but we had our separate lives and I started going out with the other couples. I was put in charge of social functions—me, who knows nothing about socializing at all. I was designated the social coordinator for the singles.

The guy sitting next to me in class was the social coordinator for the married couples. I got to talking and said, "What's the difference? We're all about the same age. Why should we have to have separate functions?" I didn't understand and he agreed. We talked it over as a class and decided there was no distinction between those who were married and those who were not. We all partied together all the time. We'd plan things in advance, or maybe on Friday night say, "Let's all go to the O Club tonight and see what's going on over there." So it got me out, meeting new people.

But I was very scared of the guys. When the guys who had not gone to the Academy started trying to hit on me, I didn't know what it was because I'd never had that happen in four years. I thought they were trying to set me up for something again. I thought they were somehow going to end up humiliating me. Or I thought maybe they wanted to use me to get better grades, because I was positive about myself and doing very well grade-wise. I thought they were trying to use me somehow. It ended up that they didn't; they were all good, honest guys, and they said, "What's your problem, kid? What are you scared of? Why do you have to ask these kinds of questions?"

I told them what it was like. "Why are you using me, guys?"

They'd come back and say, "Hey, you're a girl, and there aren't too many girls around here, and you're better-looking than So-and-So, so we'll go out with you."

"Oh! Really? Okay. Fine." It was a gradual change to get used to something. I thoroughly enjoyed Athens, Georgia, and I would go back there in a heartbeat. But that to me was a big transition in my life; it was a security point. I felt confident, for a change, about me.

After that I got orders to Bermuda. That was a stroke of luck. The two gals who had been rated above me grade-wise at Athens were engaged. One wanted a one-year unaccompanied [tour] anyplace—so she got Alaska. The other wanted a one-year unaccompanied tour anywhere in the world—so she got Cuba. I said, "Gosh, what's left on the list?"

"Bermuda."

"Okay, sure! I'll take Bermuda." I couldn't believe they were passing up Bermuda, but it was a two-year tour and they didn't want to have to go two years anyplace. As it ends up, the one gal who went to Alaska never got married. She is now married to somebody else. That defeated the whole purpose of going to Alaska. The gal who went to Cuba got married, eventually moved up to be with her husband, and they're now divorced. I got the good end of the deal. That's where I met my husband, in Bermuda.

Sue Sweeney: What was your job?

Lieutenant Lowndes: In Bermuda I was the disbursing officer and the assistant officer in charge of the Personnel Support Activity Detachment. It was good. I wasn't thrown in with a whole bunch of other ensigns. It was a small command. I was basically in charge of the office. I had a lieutenant above me, but he was worried about the personnel matters. I was worried about the disbursing, which I'd just been taught how to do. I had 27 women and three men working for me. I was scared to death of the women, because I hadn't been taught what to do with them. I went through all kinds of problems with them.

We decided—the lieutenant and myself—that what we were going to do was use my Academy background as kind of a threat against them. I'd say, "I'm used to formal inspections, so we're going to tighten up this whole organization this way. We're going to cut down on the fingernails and the fingernail polishing." The gals, at first, didn't understand why I was doing it, but a couple of times they'd see a gal come in in uniform and have on dark blue or black fingernail polish, and they'd say, "That doesn't look good in uniform, Lieutenant."

I'd say, "Yeah, I told you that. There is a method to my madness." They were used to personnel inspections every single Monday. I had the best bunch of people on the entire island in the military—I know I did, the best-looking girls—because they took care of themselves. I made them wear dress uniforms every day. They had to wear a tie, they had to be polite. We would function as customer service. "When you go to the bank, you don't like the teller to be nasty to you. You don't like the teller to blow smoke in your face. So we're not going to do that to anyone who walks in the door. They're always right. They get preferential treatment."

The people at first, of course, didn't like the change. But I think they're a better bunch of people for it. When I see other personnel detachments around, I just get sick that I have to wait around for somebody to decide it's important enough to bother to come up and see what I want. I don't care if I'm an officer or not; I'm a person standing there. But also, "Yeah, what do you want?" Well, this is the military? I want Sir, Ma'am. We are officers.

I had some strange things happen in Bermuda. The first time a gal came up and needed an abortion—what did I know about abortions? I know as much as a male officer about abortions. I had absolutely no idea. I know it's not legal in Bermuda, so I had to find out for her what to do, where to go, how to have it done, how much time she was allowed off, if any. I had to learn it all just like the male officers. It was a very good experience for me.

I met my husband there. We weren't married there. We weren't sure at that time if we wanted to get married or not. I didn't want the Navy telling me how to run my life, telling me I had to get married so we could be stationed together. We weren't quite sure that's what we wanted to do. He had to go to Philadelphia for a career move, and I said, "I'll take anything near Philadelphia."

They said, "There's nothing there, but we've got something in San Diego." Tough choice: go home or stay near him. We talked a long time about it, and the detailers kept saying, "No, nothing anywhere near Philadelphia." There are a lot of supply areas in Philadelphia, and they couldn't find anything for me? They finally said, "We've got this great job at DCASMA [Defense Contract Administration Services Management Area] New York." Okay. I looked on the map and didn't see DCASMA listed any place. They didn't tell me DCASMA was the abbreviation for the command or that it was in New York City. They told me it was only an hour and a half away from Philadelphia. My husband and I eventually got married. Two months after we got married, the Navy moved him up to New York, which was a surprise. The Navy could have very easily taken the attitude that, "Well, you can see each other on weekends or split the difference and each take an hour commute."

Sue Sweeney: He was shifted solely because you two had married?

Lieutenant Lowndes: Yes, two months after the marriage. That was the reason he transferred up to the New York City area, so we could be together. That was very encouraging. We're happy and we can see a lot of good coming out of this. We're expecting our first child in April. I can see how our whole lives can still fit in with the Navy and with my original intentions of joining the Navy to do 20 years and to do the best I can. I can still do that.

Sue Sweeney: What is your personal opinion of women in the military—what they can and can't do?

Lieutenant Lowndes: I still think that they need to lift the combat restrictions. We're finding society is changing. I don't think it's the Naval Academy as much as society that won't let the women go in combat roles. I can see not having women in hand-to-hand combat like in the Army and Marine Corps, but we're on ships. My goodness, what does it take to drive a ship, stand up there, especially as an officer, and say, "Five degrees left rudder"? It doesn't matter whether I'm male or female; I've got a job to do. If there's a missile coming in, there's not much a guy can do about it and not much a girl can do about it either. I don't think that there's any reason why we can't do those kinds of things. There are some areas where physically a particular female cannot do a job. There are a lot of guys that are tiny and can't pull an anchor chain. If there's a big amazon female and she wants to pull an anchor chain, fine, let her do it. I think that's what we should be allowed to do instead of being forced into typical female roles such as secretaries and office managers.

Sue Sweeney: What was your reaction to James Webb's article "Women Can't Fight" in *Washingtonian* magazine?

Lieutenant Lowndes: Oh, gosh, that was horrible. We all hated it.

Sue Sweeney: Did he have any valid points?

Lieutenant Lowndes: I don't remember enough of the specifics now, but I know at the time we were very much against it. He wrote another book later that I didn't want to even bother reading, because I didn't want to endorse him in any way. I didn't want him to get any more money by my reading his books. It just hurt very much, what he had to say. He didn't have enough hard facts, too much generalization, and he wasn't fair. He wasn't at the Academy when we were there. If he was one of the company officers and could see the difference in women at the Academy versus women not at the Academy, yes, he might have had an argument. But he wasn't there. He never saw us or talked to us. He never found out what was inside our minds.

We're a different breed from any women who have ever been in the service before. Yes, you'll find a few, like Commodore Grace Hopper and Admiral Fran McKee and all the women who have really been very dedicated to the Navy—yes, there are a few like that. But prior to our group coming in, there hasn't been anybody with as much drive and determination as this group. James Webb never talked to any of us, and I think that's what bothered us and got all the guys so excited: "Yeah, yeah, here's what we were looking for. Here's a chance to throw 'em out."

What a lot of guys didn't realize was that while we were there, it was still not a fact that women have to be at the Naval Academy. It was still kind of a testing program, that if they could get enough facts to show why women should not be there, they could have canceled and said, "That's enough. After '83, we're not allowing any more women in. It's just not proving out. We're losing way too much money. They're not doing the right kinds of things. They're getting married, they're pregnant, they're getting out, whatever."

If they could have had those kinds of facts. The guys didn't realize that there was a possibility there would never be women at the Naval Academy again. They didn't realize that. It was a possibility. I don't know what the rules are now, I don't know if it's just been proven that women do belong there, they stayed in, or whatever. I don't know if they would ever consider it. Very personally, I don't think that women belong at the Academy while combat restrictions still apply, because I'm over-trained for the types of things that I'm allowed to do in the Navy. I personally appreciate the entire education; I think I am a better person, a better officer for it, but I don't think the Navy's going to get their full money's worth out of me.

Sue Sweeney: Do you see the combat restrictions lifting within your career?

Lieutenant Lowndes: Within my career, yes. Not within my time frame to do anything about it. We were surprised that the Women at Sea program has grown as much as it has. Once you get your foot in the door, they'll start letting you go.

I think they need to encourage more women on temporary duty on combatant vessels. That's one of the loopholes in the whole deal. You can't be permanently assigned to a combatant vessel, but you can be assigned for up to six months on a combatant vessel, as long as it is not on a combat mission. So you can go out on its training run.

You can go out on a UNITAS [United International Antisubmarine Warfare] cruise, which is not a combatant mission on a combatant ship, for up to six months. Granted, the COs don't like it, because if they were ever called to Grenada or wherever in a combat role, here's this extra officer or here's the person they've been using as their communications officer all of a sudden taken off the ship. Then what do you do? You're missing one vital part of the whole system. If they'd force the issue and take more women off and force them to go for six months, pull them off for a little while, force them on again a little later—onto a combatant vessel for a long period of time, I think you'd have proof that women can do it.

If a particular ship has always had a female on it—there's never been a female on for any longer than a month or two at a time, but fine, they've had women constantly on the ship and they've survived. I think that's what we need, our foot in the door. That's a start. Once you get the Women at Sea program going, then they can start getting the women in the flight program. That's always going to be a little harder to do, because you do have to fly more. I guess a combat mission is a little more dangerous in a plane than in a ship that's farther out to sea. You need to just start little by little. But I think it can be done, and I think it can be done in my lifetime, but never in enough time for any of my classmates to do anything about it.

Sue Sweeney: Do you have any ambivalence about raising a child while staying in the military?

Lieutenant Lowndes: No. Right now it's just the feeling that I know I want to stay in, I know it can be done. I don't want to stick my child into daycare centers where he goes through different people taking care of the child. If it's just one particular woman—say a live-in nanny—or my sister or somebody, the same person, it doesn't have to be Mom; it just has to be a person instilling some constant set of standards for the child. I can see that now. Maybe when I have the child, more maternal instincts will pop up and I'll rethink that, but I don't see it as a problem. The Navy is very supportive of all of our efforts. We think that in seven and a half years, my husband will retire. The child will be seven years old. If there are any problems or future children, my husband can take care of them.

Sue Sweeney: What is your current job?

Lieutenant Lowndes: I am currently an officer-in-charge of a residency office of the Defense Contract Administrative Services Management Area–New York. DCASMA is a joint service command, where we administer government contracts. We don't write the contracts, but we oversee them for the military offices that do write the contracts. Any company that has a government contract for anything in the New York City area, we're in charge. We're responsible for making sure that the product is being delivered when it's supposed to be delivered, how it's supposed to be delivered, and that it is doing what it's supposed to do. It may be a food contractor, a clothing contractor, anything in the New York City area. I've been here at this command for three years. I've gone from one spectrum, being a production control clerk, to actually doing contract administration, which is a higher level of work, more detail overall, knowledgeable with contracts and the contractors.

We started a residency office at a particular contract which has $150 million in government contracts. I had to set up a brand-new office in a brand-new building, hire all the people, bring in all the supplies. We are now kind of functioning on our own. Twenty people work for me. I'm just managing an office now, which is nice. I'm ready to move on to another job. I think I've learned all I can at this command about government contracting. I'd like to move on now to maybe the buying side. In buying, you have to decide which parts and which company will supply, and then give the contract over to DCASMA to administer. I'd like to move to the other side.

Sue Sweeney: The $7 million ashtrays.

Lieutenant Lowndes: Right.

Sue Sweeney: Tell me about the Batchelder Award, Federal Government Employee of the Year.

Lieutenant Lowndes: Vice Admiral Batchelder.[10] It's a fairly new award. It's only been given out two years now. It's not for the best supply officer in the Navy, but to supply officers who have done the most for the Navy. This year there were 94 people nominated and four selected. So I was one of those nominated. My boss decided, when he saw the criteria, that the work I had been doing on one particular contract was very supportive of the Supply Corps and the Navy. It's a very big Navy program. I don't know the exact criteria and how they decide who did the most for the Navy, but it isn't something that's

---

[10] The Vice Admiral Robert F. Batchelder Awards, named for the former inspector general of the Bureau of Supplies and Accounts (today the Naval Supply Systems Command), were initiated in 1984 to recognize operational contributions in supply readiness.

only for commanders or ensigns—it covers the whole range. It was very nice for me to have received a nomination. I received a commendation letter from the Chief of the Supply Corps for being nominated, which is a nice little touch instead of the usual letter saying you were nominated and you weren't selected.

The other award is the New York Federal Executive Supervisor of the Year Award—that's the actual title. It's more of a New York City government award for those who have done something to help the federal government in the New York City area. I don't know how I did in that; I didn't receive the award. I never heard anything except that I was nominated for it. It was nice to be nominated. Again, my boss thought I had done so much more than any other officer at DCASMA New York. Out of 32 officers, they decided to nominate me for the award.

Sue Sweeney: What type of contract contributed to your being nominated?

Lieutenant Lowndes: It's a Navy contract for causeway sections. Currently the contract is $76 million, which is half of the work that this one company is doing. The Navy's buying a whole bunch of pontoons and causeways that are used with the amphibious forces. It's a complex type of an item, not as complex as a ship, but more complex than anything else going in our office currently. It's a real struggle to work in the extra requirements to make sure that this thing works, make sure the horn is the right pitch . . . things you don't ordinarily have to worry about, but when you see it as a naval vessel—small as it is, it's still a naval vessel—and I know that it has to help the guys out in the fleet. It's a very time-critical contract, very high level. The Assistant Secretary of the Navy is briefed on a weekly basis on this particular contract, so it does have a lot of high interest, not just at management level.

Sue Sweeney: What do you consider the greatest satisfaction of your career to date?

Lieutenant Lowndes: A couple of high points. One was graduating—just to have gone that far—and to have my parents come out for the graduation was a very important point in my life, to know that I could do something. It gave me the confidence in myself to say, "I can do just about anything." I have since earned a master's degree, I've gotten very high grades in my master's degree, I've gotten very high grades at the Navy Supply Corps School in Athens, Georgia, because I know now that I can do it.

Sue Sweeney: What is your master's in?

Lieutenant Lowndes: My master's is in business and management. I got that in Bermuda during night school. If I had had that confidence going through the Academy, I don't know how good my grades could have been. I wouldn't have been a 4.0 student, but I think I would have been a lot better than the 2.5 I was.

Another important point was deciding to get married and deciding how to work that in with my career goals. I'm finally able to deal with the Academy as a school, as an institution. I think the *Shipmate* article helped me get over a lot of my fears and kind of calmed what was going on inside of me just to reassure what I was feeling. I wasn't the only one; I wasn't alone out there. I called one of the gals because of some of the comments she made, and I asked her, "What did you mean?"

She said, "Well, I know there are several women who had nervous breakdowns." She was one of them. She had gotten out of the service because she had a nervous breakdown. I thought she was one of the most well-adjusted people at school, very well-liked, and here she had a nervous breakdown coming out. It could have been me, too, because I went through the same things, and I just didn't know that she felt the same way that I did. This study confirmed everything I believed in. We're trying to arrange a meeting of the gals and our own separate homecoming, so to speak, totally away from the Academy, so that we can get together, cry on each other's shoulders for a night and say, "I'm doing better now. I can adjust now. I feel good about myself. It's over, completely over. No one's picking on me anymore."

It's going to be very important for us. I don't know how the plans are coming. I'm one of the key figures in keeping the interest going, and there are a lot of gals interested. I hope we can make this happen. We really need it, I think, listening to their answers.

Sue Sweeney: Have you been back to the Academy since graduation?

Lieutenant Lowndes: Yes. I went once to homecoming from Athens, Georgia, and there were too many people who still knew me, even though I was in civilian clothes. I was prepared to take in the whole fun of homecoming, but I got there and people started using the same derogatory names that they'd always called to us—"WUBA"—which is the working uniform blue alpha. That's what they called the females. "You're dating a WUBA." Or just yelling out, "WUBA." That meant you were one of them. They wouldn't let it go. I really had a hard time. I sat next to one of the guys in my company at the football game. He didn't know who I was until towards the end. I could see once he figured out who I was, he moved over just a little bit and eventually moved on and found another seat, where had he not known who I was, I would have just been some female sitting next to him.

I could feel this kind of thing and I hated it. I hated the whole place. I left early without finishing the football game, I didn't go to the tailgater. I immediately got back in my car and drove away. I was staying at a friend's house, and I was too embarrassed to have to go back there and tell them how I felt, so I just went away someplace and had dinner outside of town, by myself. I didn't go to the dance that night. I was going to go, but I just couldn't bring myself to do it. I was so afraid of what somebody would say or do. I went to church the next morning and it just tore my heart to hear the songs. I missed that part of the closeness. I knew that there were probably eyes looking at me, saying,

"There's one of them, too." So I avoided the Academy. I was lucky, since I was in Bermuda for the next two years, I really didn't have a chance to go back.

When I got up to the New York area, I had some friends from other service academies who were down in the Washington, D.C., area for training. They said, "How about coming down and showing us around?" I went down with them. I flew down to Washington, got a hotel room for myself, and drove over with them the next day. We got to the edge of town and I said, "Stop the car. I can't do it. I just can't go in. I can't go inside the gate." It hurt too much and brought up too many of the bad feelings. We went away. One of my friends understood. He let me go. He went to another academy and didn't know what I was going through. He had gone way before women had been there, so he couldn't understand at all what I was feeling. But he knew, "Don't push. Let her go back." So it was a wasted trip, and I felt sorry about it, but I just could not face the Academy at that time.

My husband and I went down another time, passing through, staying with a friend who was a supply officer at the Naval Academy. We stayed with his wife and him at their house on Perry Circle, which is just outside the gate, so that was okay. We looked at the Academy, that was okay. My husband and I drove through the Academy, but I could not stop the car, I could not get out. I was scared to death of the place, and it still brought back too many of the bad feelings.

Then when I was doing the article, we had about an hour to kill before my appointment with Captain Busik, the executive director of the Alumni Association, so I told my husband, "I want to go back and try one more time," because I was starting to feel really good about myself after the survey. We started away from the main part of the Academy, down by the marching field, where there are no mids. It was just a pretty place—I could look at it as a very lovely place. I could point out to my husband, trying to remember, "Gosh, what classes were held in Rickover Hall? What's the name of that building? I don't remember." I could remember Mitscher and Chauvenet, but I couldn't remember which classes I had in which one. I couldn't remember the names of most of the buildings or the names of the walks or the statues. Gosh, I used to know that stuff. It's because I was so afraid of the place, I forgot all this.

I took my husband and walked all the way around. It was when I went into Bancroft Hall, walked up to Memorial Hall, and on the way back out, I saw a midshipman looking at me. He didn't have hatred in his eye at all. That's when I said to myself, "He doesn't even know I went here. He doesn't even know me. He doesn't care, probably, either." That's when I thought, "I should have worn something nicer and looked pretty to give him something to look at," because they do like the distraction. I can now accept it. I felt very good about it, I had every intention of going to homecoming this year and told Captain Busik, "I'll see you at homecoming. I can't wait. I'm going to do it." I encouraged all the gals in my letters. I sent them copies of the article. I sent them separate letters to explain some of the things to them that you can't explain in an article. I said, "I think that we all ought to try to go to homecoming this year. It's important."

But I personally could not do it. I have never been to an Army-Navy football game since graduation. Philadelphia is not that far away. If my father-in-law had come out, he would have forced the issue, because he's also an Academy grad. If my father-in-law had wanted to, but he didn't want to. But I just can't face the large crowds yet.

Next weekend I am a guest speaker of the Alumni Association chapter meeting in New Jersey. It's a small group, it's a group of totally new people to me. I'm speaking on women at the Naval Academy and in the Navy, how we adjust. They don't know me, I don't know them. Most of them have never met females who have gone to the Naval Academy. It will be an important time for me to try to get my feelings out, try and convince them that one-on-one, we're good people, we mean well, we didn't try to do anything to the Academy that the Academy wouldn't let us do. We didn't ruin the Academy by being there. I want to be able to share that with these people. I think a fun part of it is going in uniform—they normally have their meetings at the officers' club in civilian clothes in the evening. I asked the personnel coordinator, "Can I wear my uniform?" I told him that I am pregnant. "Please don't tell anybody else. I'm going to give them an interesting surprise and also reinforce to these people, 'Hey, not only can we do our job, but we can have a private life, too. Here I am, I am pregnant. This is the maternity uniform. This is how the Navy deals with it. This is what I am personally going to do with my life and how I can still give 100 percent of me to the Navy and have a family.'" I'm very excited about being able to do that next week.

Sue Sweeney: Good for you! Thanks so much for your time—it's been most interesting.

Lieutenant Lowndes: Thank you.

**

Interview with Lieutenant Pamela Wacek Svendsen, U.S. Navy

Place: U.S. Naval Institute, Annapolis, Maryland

Date: 8 November 1984

Sue Sweeney: Can I get a little of your background—where are you from?

Lieutenant Svendsen: I was born in 1958 in Chicago. I lived in Chicago until I was about 12 years old, when my parents moved to the suburbs. That's where they still are, so most of the family is still in the Chicago area. I remained in the Chicago area until I was 18 and came here to the Naval Academy.

Sue Sweeney: Had you been interested in the Naval Academy long before women were allowed? Is this been something you always wanted to do?

Lieutenant Svendsen: I have a funny story about that. I didn't even know what the service academies were, and my congressman sent out his regular newsletter to us. He said that the Congress was kicking around the idea of admitting women into the service academies in the class of '80, and anyone who was interested should submit their name to him. And so my father said, "Well, why don't you give him a call?" And I said okay. I had heard of West Point, but I didn't know that the other services had similar academies. So I called up my congressman, I guess his secretary, and spoke with her.

Sue Sweeney: Who was the congressman?

Lieutenant Svendsen: Edward Derwinski. She said, "Well, what is your first preference for a service academy?"

I said, "Well, which ones do you have?" I knew so little about them. And she explained that there were four of them because they also took appointments at the Coast Guard Academy. I said, "The Naval Academy is my first choice because I really like the water."

Sue Sweeney: Makes sense!

Lieutenant Svendsen: So that's how little I knew about the whole thing beforehand. That was in the fall of my senior year in high school, and then as the year went by, they finally announced that they would, in fact, admit women into the class of '80. I started reading about all of the academies, and I never really had an interest in the Air Force Academy for one reason or another, and I can't even recall why. But as I read and read, I almost wanted to go to West Point more than I wanted to come here.

Sue Sweeney: Why was that?

Lieutenant Svendsen: I don't know. It was just something—I think the foot soldier in me sort of was drawn to West Point.

Sue Sweeney: Had you given thought to military service?

Lieutenant Svendsen: As a matter of fact, yes. I really felt—and this sounds really cornball—but I really felt the strong sense of "Duty, Honor, Country."

Sue Sweeney: You did go to the wrong academy!

Lieutenant Svendsen: But I really felt a need to serve my country, and in fact, if I didn't come here, I had almost enlisted in the Army to become a medic, but the reason I didn't was because my birthday fell two days later than the cutoff point for how their schools work, so I wouldn't be able to enlist until two days before my birthday.

Sue Sweeney: So what was your plan if the academies had not opened to women? What other colleges did you have in mind?

Lieutenant Svendsen: I had also applied to the University of Illinois, that was at Champaign. Gosh, this is so bad, it's only eight years ago. I can hardly remember. The

University of Illinois and—I think it was another branch of the University of Illinois, but in the Chicago area.

Sue Sweeney: What did you plan to study?

Lieutenant Svendsen: Pre-med. It would have been pre-med.

Sue Sweeney: And did you do that at the Naval Academy?

Lieutenant Svendsen: I didn't do that here. I was a political science major here.

Sue Sweeney: What was your family's reaction? Were they thrilled when you finally got your appointment?

Lieutenant Svendsen: I remember I called up my father at work, because my congressman called me, and I guess they said if you didn't hear anything by the first of May, you could assume that you weren't accepted. So the first of May came and went and I said, "Well, University of Illinois, here I come." And around the middle of the month, he called me up and he said, "Pamela, you're going to Annapolis."

And I said, "Wonderful!" I was so stunned. I couldn't, you know—here I had put myself in a mindset, "This isn't going to happen, and that's that." And he in fact called me up and told me I was coming.

I called up my father at work and he didn't believe me. And I said, "Dad, when the fifth of July comes and I'm not in your house anymore, then you'll have to believe me." You know, he was wonderfully surprised, and my mother was also very happy. They were both very supportive. As a matter of fact, when I had my doubts about completing the course the second year I was here—I did some serious thinking about not going through with it—they really encouraged me to stay and stick it out. And so I did, obviously.

Sue Sweeney: What made you contemplate leaving?

Lieutenant Svendsen: Well, the first year, you know, plebe year is such a strong test that I got to a point where I had to finish no matter what, no matter what happened or how terrible it was. I was going to finish. So I did. And the second year, the pressure was off, my grades went up, and things were going a lot better, but I think my perception was that the women were a lot easier to harass that second year, and that really got to me. My feelings of self-esteem were going down the tubes, because the men were very hard on us at that particular point.

I think the first year everyone was a little touchy about the women, they couldn't really say, "I don't want you here, get out of my sight," and all that stuff. But the second year, it was open season and there was nothing to stop them, and they went ahead and did that, and that really got to me after a while. I guess towards the end of youngster year I started saying, "Well, you know, I've done this for two years. I think I'll just go ahead and finish it out." And second-class summer really changed my mind, and I got to go around and do all the things. It was really fun, and I saw there was something beyond this. Before that time I didn't know that. I didn't see there was something beyond that, but now looking back, I think that that's what happened. So that's one of the reasons, or that's the reason why I did consider leaving at that point, and that's really the only time.

One time plebe summer, I guess, I called my dad and said, "I'm coming home. I've had it." And that was the only time that I really called home and said, "I'm not doing this anymore."

And he said, "Yeah, yeah, yeah."

Of course, the next day I woke up and everything was fine. So I think we all reach that point.

Sue Sweeney: Thinking back to July of 1976—how prepared were you? Did you think the Academy would just be a tough college with a nautical flavor?

Lieutenant Svendsen: Like I said, I did lots of reading. I could almost recite the catalog. That's how much—it was worn by the time I left to come here. I knew that it would be tough academically, and I knew that emotionally and physically it would be much more demanding than I had ever experienced.

Sue Sweeney: Had you seen the campus?

Lieutenant Svendsen: I did, yes. The month before induction, as a matter of fact, my mom and I took a trip out here. But everyone had gone for the summer, and it was really quiet. There were just a few guys going to summer school or doing whatever. We said, "Oh, it's beautiful," you know. And it really was. But there wasn't a whole lot going on. I guess I didn't really understand what was going to happen or what the environment was going to be like. I knew it would be difficult. I got there and found that yes, it was difficult, but there were 1,200 other people in there with me going through the same thing, so that made it seem a little bit better.

Sue Sweeney: Start with I Day. What was it like?

Lieutenant Svendsen: I remember seeing my squadron. Maureen Foley was my roommate, as a matter of fact, and the three of us, we were all so terribly nervous. We saw the most beautiful man I had ever seen in my life walk up, and we all went, "Ahhh."

And he said something to the effect of, "I don't want you to be here, but that's the law and I have to put up with it." The most beautiful man in the world had shattered my hopes and dreams.

Sue Sweeney: This is your squad leader?

Lieutenant Svendsen: That was my squad leader. It's funny because now I see him every now and then, and I ran into him at the Indian Ocean, of all places, and just in all different places, and he's not like that at all. But at the time that's what he said to us. And that was in the morning. I Day was just so hectic. I remember they just piled these bags of stuff on us, and I couldn't—I was just thinking, "This is ridiculous. I am not a pack mule." We just carried this stuff, it seemed, all over. My orientation was just totally gone. I had no orientation of where anything was, and it just seemed that we walked and walked and walked miles and miles with bags and boxes on us.

And I remember eating lunch and them telling us different things like, "Enjoy this, this is your last meal before you're inducted," and *da-da-da-da-da*. And I was sort of getting the picture that it wasn't going to be a lot of fun.

Sue Sweeney: Some of the women must have been overwhelmed by the big bag of items issued on I Day. Did anybody offer to help—or did you feel they were holding back?

Lieutenant Svendsen: They really stayed back. Really stayed back. I don't remember anybody offering assistance.

Sue Sweeney: How soon before you were aware you were in a fishbowl?

Lieutenant Svendsen: That first day I don't even remember any— it was such a long time ago—any media. I don't really recall any media. There had to be because there's pictures and different things that are in existence now, but at the time, I think I was just so wrapped up in what was going on, I didn't really pay any attention to who else was there on the outside.

Sue Sweeney: Did they become intrusive?

Lieutenant Svendsen: The first year, plebe year, I had a very bad experience. I went home on Christmas leave and talked to a woman. I had given an interview to our local town paper. They thought, you know, little small-town girl hits it rich, sort of thing. And maybe I didn't give interviews, but I was just tired of it and didn't want to talk to anybody about it. My mother wanted me to do her a favor and talk to this one woman who had given her garden club a lot of publicity. I said, "No, Mom, I don't want to talk to anybody."

"Oh, please?"

So finally I said, "Okay, I'll talk to the lady, and that's it. I'm not talking to anybody else."

So this woman was supposedly for another local paper, and we just started talking, and she asked me what I thought were rather benign questions, like what sort of things do we do. I said, "We get asked questions at the table." It's hard to describe what's going on.

She said, "What sort of things? Do you ever get asked what you think and your opinions?"

I said, "Sure."

She said, "Well, what do you mostly talk about?"

"Well, professional things, naturally."

And she said, "Well, what sort of things?" She kept pressing and pressing.

And I said, "Well, for example, we'll talk about things like people asked me if I had to push the button, could I do it. Things like that. Or if I saw somebody, could I shoot them. You know, if somebody looked me in the eye, could I shoot them. We would talk about that. The guy would say, 'Do you think you could do it?' And stuff like that. So that's the sort of stuff we talk about. We talk about what's on ships and what's on planes, what they're called, just all sorts of different stuff."

And she just twisted that all around and came out with some sort of statement like, "All midshipmen are warmongers," or something like that. The article wound up in the *Chicago Tribune*, and this was an interview given to the local lady. It wound up in the

Chicago Tribune. Someone's mother sent it to them here. The article was plastered all over all the bulletin boards in the Hall, and I got hate mail.

Sue Sweeney: Not from mids.

Lieutenant Svendsen: Yes, from mids. Just really bad. And I didn't even see the article, you know, and people came up to me and were saying stuff, and I had no idea what they were talking about. So finally my squad leader came into my room and he said, "What is this?"

I said, "I don't know. I've never seen it before."

He said, "Did you say these things?"

And I read the article and I said, "No." I said, "I don't know where this came from." So by this time I was pretty upset about the whole thing.

My mother called the woman up and said, "You really did a number on my daughter." She apologized and I think she wrote me a letter of apology.

Sue Sweeney: You should have plastered that up.

Lieutenant Svendsen: Yes, exactly. But when you're 18 years old, you don't think of those things. But anyway, that was a bad experience for me with the press, and I really stayed away from them the rest of the four years. I would not give an interview at graduation time. I wouldn't talk to anybody.

I think we almost had to speak to some member of the press as graduation time approached, and so I spoke with someone right before I graduated, and then they wanted to take pictures. I had the first wedding in the chapel and they wanted to take pictures of that, and I did not want them there. I mean, that's how—I didn't want the press to have any part of my life any more because of that bad experience.

So finally I relented and let them take pictures in the chapel. I said, "I don't want you inside the chapel. I want you outside the chapel." And so that was really my only media—and of course, before I came here I had several interviews with the hometown papers. Those were very nice interviews and very positive things were said.

Sue Sweeney: Were there female officers at the Academy you viewed as role models?

Lieutenant Svendsen: There was one that I remember, and that was Lieutenant Sue Stevens. I think she might be out of the Navy now, but anyway, she was the only one I remember. I know there weren't very many women officers here at the time, maybe a few instructors. I personally didn't think Sue Stevens was the first role model for it. She's just like—my biggest thing about coming to the Naval Academy, one of my concerns was that I would lose my femininity. I felt like they could have had better role models for us.

I made a trip to the Air Force Academy plebe year, and I didn't like a lot of the things that they did. They isolated their women, whereas we were integrated, and things like that, but they really made sure that their women were treated like women and had the special things. Not necessarily special treatment, but, like for example, when Navy played Air Force, all the women got bikini undies that said, "Beat Navy" on the bottom. And I thought that was just wonderful, you know. It was like they still had this school spirit. It was just something that they had done, and we would never have thought to do anything like that.

I think in some respects, having the women spread out all over the place, I believe it isolated us from one another, and really, really strange things. I have just a few, a handful of close friends, and people that I didn't see very much when I was here that I have gotten together with subsequent to graduation, we've had a wonderful time, but I never would have thought we'd socialize while we were here. I've spoken to other women in my class and they have said the same thing. We've gotten together and talked a little and said, "Why didn't we do this two years ago or three years ago?"

Sue Sweeney: What do you recall about your civilian professors?

Lieutenant Svendsen: I had Professor [E. B. "Ned"] Potter as a history professor. I was the only woman in that particular section, and he really thought that was different, and let me know so.

Sue Sweeney: In a negative way?

Lieutenant Svendsen: Yes. I sat right in front of him. I don't remember specific things, but I know that there were times he said things that were probably out of line but that I didn't realize were out of line at the time. I had an English professor—we had the tables and they were open underneath. I was a cheerleader while I was here, and a couple of times we would wear our outfits on Friday afternoons to class after pep rallies or whatever. And I remember sitting in the front row, I again sat in the front row, and he would say, "I love it when you wear that outfit."

And, of course, being 18 years old and scared to death of everything, I just said, "Um-hum."

Sue Sweeney: Do you recall other professors—military or civilian—letting you know they were glad the women were at the Academy?

Lieutenant Svendsen: I don't remember anything like that. If anything it was indifference, almost. I think they tried so hard to be indifferent or to act indifferent, that they pulled it off. I think that it worked. All of those little preps that they had, because I know that before we got here, everyone went through hours of training about what to do when the women get here. I think that everybody sort of went through that thing.

Sue Sweeney: Was there a sense of them being afraid to deal with you too closely?

Lieutenant Svendsen: It depended upon the person. Some people were like that, and some people could just go ahead and be themselves. But I thought that a lot of them almost went out of their way to treat us equally, whatever equally is, and I don't think we ever achieved equalness in the four years that I was here. I don't think that ever happened.

Sue Sweeney: Do you have a sense that it's better now?

Lieutenant Svendsen: Equal? I would hope so. I don't really know. The things that I've read and heard have led me to believe that that still hasn't happened. Of course, you are only supposed to believe the minimum of what you read and half of what you see. I don't know if that's changed, but I don't know if that will ever change to a certain degree here. I think this place, the whole institution makes it a lot difficult for women to be integrated into the society at large.

Even now, I can't defend the fact that I went here and graduated from here. The mission of the Naval Academy is to train men—to train people for combat. I can't do that, and I don't think that I'll be able to do that any time in the near, immediate, or far future. So when people bring up that argument, I don't have a counter argument. I can just say, "You're right."

Sue Sweeney: What was your reaction to James Webb's article in the *Washingtonian*?

Lieutenant Svendsen: I was just furious. I don't even remember exactly what it said, but I know that he didn't have a favorable opinion about women at the Naval Academy and made that quite clear in the article, and questioned our abilities and things like that. As far as I'm concerned, I have physical limitations. I can't run, jump, hang or pull or whatever as well as a man, but mentally and emotionally I am just as, if not more, capable as men are.

Sue Sweeney: One of his points was that the Naval Academy was being refined to accommodate women. He wondered how well he would have survived the rigors of Vietnam without the pressures he'd encountered as a midshipman.

Lieutenant Svendsen: He may have a point there. My philosophy about the men and women's stress throughout the four years and how men and women will do under stressful situations is, my philosophy is that I had four plebe years while I was here, emotionally.

Sue Sweeney: And the men in your class?

Lieutenant Svendsen: Had one. There was a lot of mental stress, so to speak. But until the day I graduated, you know, I mean, the last great act, the big number was that when they did the, "Hip, hip, hurray! Hip, hip, hurray!" and tossed the hats up in the air, the men were going to wait for three seconds because they didn't want their hats going into the air at the same time the women's were. And my words to my mother when they came down out of the stands was, "It's over." And I said, "Get me out of here. I don't want to be around these people. I don't want to have anything to do with them. Just get me out of here." Because I had just had it, you know. All through June Week just little stuff was going on.

Sue Sweeney: "No Girls on Herndon."

Lieutenant Svendsen: Uh-huh. You know, when we jumped in the reflection pool, guys were splashing us and like holding us under the water. Not joking around kind of stuff. Like you could tell that they were being serious, and just stuff like that was going on. I did this four years ago. I don't need to do it again. But that stuff just went on the whole time I was here. So stress-wise, I think that I endured, and the women in my class endured a lot more stress than the men endured, and came out of it pretty well, considering.

Sue Sweeney: At any point, did you feel you had changed male minds?

Lieutenant Svendsen: Just the guys in my company, and not even all of them, but there were maybe half of them that I felt like were brothers and that I could go out with them and have a good time with them. But with the group as a whole, I would say no, I never felt that way.

Sue Sweeney: Were the women better accepted by their classmates—having gone through plebe summer together—than by the upperclassmen?

Lieutenant Svendsen: Yes and no. It depended, again, on the person, but the general attitude I found was they were very resentful because of the attention that we got. They felt as if—and rightfully so, I guess—that they had done the same thing that we had done, but we were getting the glory and they were not. And I can understand their feelings. Not all of them. Some of them didn't care. They weren't quiet about it; they would tell me about it. They'd come up and say, "You guys are getting all the attention, and I'm doing the same thing you are. Why is it such a big deal?"

And I'd say, "Well, I'm not really making it a big deal."

Sue Sweeney: By the time you graduated, did you feel a real sense of camaraderie with your class?

Lieutenant Svendsen: I don't believe there was any camaraderie between the women in my class. That's what I was trying to get at before. That was missing. I see it in subsequent classes between the women. I see that they are very close to one another, much more close than we ever were.

Sue Sweeney: As a group, did you ever get to just relax and take comfort from the shared experience?

Lieutenant Svendsen: It was so competitive and we made such an effort to be accepted that I think there was a lot of jealousy between the women. It was almost like if you could get an in, in whatever way you could, whether that be socially or academically or physically, whatever, if you could get an in with the guys, you wanted to keep that to yourself and you didn't want anyone else to have a part of that, any other women to have a part of that. It kept us apart. It kept us away from each other. I don't know why that happened, but that's the feeling I got, and that's the feeling I get in talking to people now, like I told you about, well, we feel, why weren't we closer than we were at the Naval Academy. I don't know. We were just feeling isolated.

As far as how we fit in with the men, I don't know if we ever really fully achieved that. I don't think we did. As an example, I went to my class homecoming tailgate and there were guys there that wouldn't even say hello. My husband couldn't believe it. He said, "I do not believe that these guys will not even say hello to you, will not even talk to you." It's so sad.

Sue Sweeney: That would make it tough to take pride in being part of the Class of 1980.

Lieutenant Svendsen: Rationally, I know I belong—emotionally, no. I know that I graduated with the class of '80, and I know I completed all the things that I needed to do and I was successful academically. I was successful with all the PT tests and everything. But emotionally I never really felt a part of the group, so to speak. In a lot of ways, I don't think I wanted to be part of the group. I really didn't like them. I didn't like the way they treated me. I almost didn't want to be a part of the group.

Sue Sweeney: On any level, do you understand—if not sympathize with—the male perspective that the women broke traditions?

Lieutenant Svendsen: I guess I have an understanding to a certain degree, but I'm still hurt by it. It still bothers me that my accomplishments are not viewed on the same level as their accomplishments are, even though it's the same. They always felt that we had it easier, for some reason, that the girls had it easier. I always felt like we had it harder. So that was the basic philosophical difference there.

Sue Sweeney: Was favoritism shown to certain women—and was this ever abused?

Lieutenant Svendsen: Some women really took advantage of that sort of thing, and that really made me angry when I saw that stuff happening, because I just have a basic problem with that.

Sue Sweeney: Was it widespread?

Lieutenant Svendsen: It was not widespread. I can think of individuals that that sort of thing would apply to. As a whole, I don't think the women in my class did that sort of stuff, but I can think of individuals who did in fact employ those measures to get, like I was saying, whatever it took to get in, they did it. Even I did it, whatever I felt was good to get in with the group.

Sue Sweeney: Did the Academy frequently seek feedback—and were they responsive to what you said?

Lieutenant Svendsen: I guess they were. I don't really recall them, you know, giving us questionnaires or anything like that from the administration itself. But they were pretty well versed as to what was happening. I was real surprised by that. I didn't realize that people understood what was going on between the men and the women until second-class summer, and we had a brief—I guess one of the chaplains gave a little seminar about prejudice and started talking about that and said something like, "You know, it's just like when you guys walk in the yard and see a woman and you say things to her like, 'Get out of my way.'" And I almost fell on the floor, because I didn't think anybody knew that except us. Here was this captain who was saying, "I know what's going on. And not only do I know it's going on, but I don't approve of it, and I think you guys are real jerks for doing it."

I mean, I was very uncomfortable with him saying that because I thought, oh, gosh, we're going to hear it now. After this is over, they're really going to come down and say stuff. But it didn't happen. I think when they're actually confronted with it and realized that people were aware of how they were acting towards the women, they were embarrassed about it. I guess they were aware about problems, but I didn't realize it until two years had gone by.

Sue Sweeney: Did your company officers pay special attention to your welfare?

Lieutenant Svendsen: No. Aside from just the counseling that everybody got, not specifically singled out. I don't remember ever talking about anything except academics and stuff like that. I don't remember talking about anything beyond that, how we were fitting in or anything like that.

Sue Sweeney: What were your summer programs like?

Lieutenant Svendsen: Well, the first year we went on the YPs for five weeks, which I just dreaded. I thought, this is not fair. The guys get to go on real ships and we go on these stupid YPs. The crews were half women, half men. The guys that had to go on YP cruises were saying, "Yep, it's all because of the women, I've got to go on these stupid YPs." Anyway, we went and had a great time. It was a lot of fun. And I think the guys who went on those cruises really got an appreciation for the women and understood that the women were just as capable as they were professionally at that level. It really turned out to be a good experience.

Sue Sweeney: What were your duties?

Lieutenant Svendsen: We all stood watches, either engineering watches or bridge watches, navigation watches, those kinds of things. We were all assigned duties and we rotated the duties, all of us were navigator. We all sort of did different things. We went from here down to Norfolk and spent about a week and a half there, and then went up the eastern seaboard and stopped in Newport and New York City and Cape May, New Jersey. We stopped all over the place. It was really fun.

That first summer, two women, they both went to Bermuda at different times but they both went to Bermuda. There were just two of them. They stayed at like a naval station in Bermuda, just to see how it was on shore duty. And then the second summer, we went to the same places, that is, Pensacola, we got to fly, we went to Norfolk on the ships and all the trainers and everything that everyone did, and we went to Quantico. We couldn't go up to Groton and do what they did on the submarines because they wouldn't allow women on the subs, but instead, the women went to various shore billets around the East Coast, and just saw how the traditional women's role in the service was. I went to Camp Lejeune, a Marine base, because I had a leaning toward the Marine Corps.

Sue Sweeney: What kind of billets were they showing the women?

Lieutenant Svendsen: Admin, comm, that kind of stuff. It was interesting. It was a lot of fun. And for me, when I went down to Camp Lejeune, they put on a giant dog-and-pony show. They showed me how they worked with explosives and drove the tanks and land craft and all this stuff. They really went out of their way to impress me. This was the command. They just arranged all sorts of things for me, which was really nice. It was fun.

Sue Sweeney: Did you get much exposure to female officers at Camp Lejeune?

Lieutenant Svendsen: Well, I think the Marine Corps is a little bit different about—we were assigned a running mate, and the woman officer that I was assigned in the running mate was a sort of no-nonsense kind of person. The people in her office really respected her. That's the impression I got from them, that she was well respected and well liked. She was a very nice person. So I really thought that that was pretty positive, that they really, again, that's what I said before, at that point, I saw there was life after the Naval Academy.

Sue Sweeney: Did you consider going Marines at service selection?

Lieutenant Svendsen: Let me see. The Marines selected a couple of months before the rest of the service selection. I guess up until the point where they said, that night they announced it on the radio and everything, until the point that they said, "We're not going to take any more, that's the end of Marine service selection." I sort of was going down there and all that. But I think the big reason I didn't go in the Marine Corps was that my husband-to-be is in the Navy and it would be too difficult to get orders together.

Sue Sweeney: Was he a classmate?

Lieutenant Svendsen: No. So I guess then when service selection night finally came, my friends and I were going back and forth. What are we going to do? What are we doing to do? And all of that stuff. And finally about a week before service selection night, my friend came upstairs on Saturday night and she said, "I have something to tell you."

I said, "You're going to sea."

She said, "Yeah, how did you know?"

I said, "Because I am too. I've been thinking the same thing you're thinking." And so that's what I chose to do. I went to sea on the *Samuel Gompers* out of San Diego.

Sue Sweeney: Had there been advance preparations for the women, as far as options at service selection?

Lieutenant Svendsen: We had to attend all of those awful lectures and they told you great things about ships and submarines and airplanes and all that stuff, and you know, they'd flash up these career patterns, and we would all nod our heads and say, "Right, but that doesn't apply to me."

And they had one lecture for us about traditional women's billets in the Navy, and they didn't make the men go to that one, but they made us go to that one and talk about career patterns and everything. I thought to myself at the time, you know, this is really unfair. I'm sort of relegated to an admin type job, even though I've endured all of the things that the guys have, I can only do this. And it was sort of frustrating, and I think that's the sort of thing that led me to get as close to a man's career as I could, and that was going to sea.

And unfortunately when I got there, I found that the career pattern for women officers at sea is so narrow at the top that I would have no aspirations. I mean, there was like one commander command billet available and one lieutenant commander XO billet available. It's terrible. There's nowhere to go. And so I think the Navy and the Department of Defense have gotten themselves into a position, they were under a lot of pressure to allow women in to the service academies, and they did that, and now there's nowhere for them to go.

Sue Sweeney: How long do you see staying in?

Lieutenant Svendsen: I'll stay in for another tour. I have orders to San Diego in February, and I'll be working at the Nav Fleet Combat Support Center out there. I can only speak as far as that. If I keep on having fun, if I keep on being successful, then I'll stay. If not, then I'll get out. The one thing, I have a daughter who's four months old, and the one thing that I dislike now about the Navy is that they can send me overseas on an unaccompanied tour, and if they ever did that to me, I'd get out because I wouldn't be able to leave my daughter. That would be just impossible. It would be difficult enough leaving my husband, but to leave my daughter as well, or any other subsequent children, I can't do that to them, and I can't do it to myself. But some women can, and I know women who have done it, who have left babies, infants, and that's fine for them, but I just can't see myself doing that. So I'm very traditional in that respect.

Sue Sweeney: Your husband supports your career decisions?

Lieutenant Svendsen: He wouldn't like me to do an unaccompanied tour. I don't think he would support me in that direction. He would have, I think, some serious problems with that. But we've discussed me staying in the Navy for 20 years, and he sees that as a possible outcome or possibility, anyway, and that's okay. He said if that's what I want to do, that's fine. I think if I got to the point where they said, "You've got to go overseas by yourself," he would say, "No you don't," and understandably so. It's just the way that our relationship is, and our family life is very close, and it would probably endure something like that.

Sue Sweeney: How about first-class year? Did you take part in plebe indoctrination?

Lieutenant Svendsen: I did not that summer. I was assigned it. I think they had been wanting me to do the pistol-shooting thing, and I said, "Oh great." One of the guys in my company really wanted to work with the plebes during the summer and didn't get assigned it, and so I said, "Do you want to do it? Because I don't."

And he said, "Yes, I really want to." And he thanked me and thanked me.

I said, "Great, no problem."

So I didn't work with the plebes during the summer.

Sue Sweeney: What did you do instead?

Lieutenant Svendsen: Went on leave.

Sue Sweeney: No summer program?

Lieutenant Svendsen: Well, we had a first-class cruise, and I went to the USS *Lexington* in Pensacola and was there for five weeks. I stepped off the *Lexington* and said, "That's it. I'm never stepping foot on a naval ship again."

Sue Sweeney: What were your duties?

Lieutenant Svendsen: I was assigned to the supply department for the whole time I was there. I guess it really kind of burst my bubble to go there, because everything is so spit and polish here, and I went there and did things like inspected the troops, and I wouldn't say anything when the division officer walked down the ranks, but I thought to myself, these guys don't have shiny shoes. These guys don't have pressed uniforms. I mentioned it to him later that they looked really motley, and he said, "Pam, they are dressed. That's a big thing."

I said, "You're kidding me." I really kind of realized that, again, there was life after the Naval Academy and it wasn't like it was here.

One of the things that we always joke about is while we were here, everyone discussed RME, which was realistic military environment, and it's not until you graduate and go away that you realize that this place doesn't come close. It's about 700 years behind.

Sue Sweeney: Were your duties in the *Lexington* realistic compared to what you've done since?

Lieutenant Svendsen: Yes and no. When you're a guest on a ship, you really get a lot of benefits. You don't have to do things that you don't want to do. A lot of times on the *Lexington* I got incredibly seasick, and I just went to bed. When I was at sea on the *Gompers* and I felt queasy, I stayed right where I was and kept on doing stuff that I had to do, went and threw up, came back and kept going.

Sue Sweeney: You lived in the *Lexington*?

Lieutenant Svendsen: It was in Pensacola, and I was there for four weeks and we were at sea for two of those four weeks. It wasn't very long.

Sue Sweeney: How much easier was it as subsequent classes of women entered the Academy? Was there less pressure on you?

Lieutenant Svendsen: I don't really think so. I remember thinking about the women in subsequent classes, and I felt like they were sort of trying to—this was a stupid thing to think, in my opinion now when I think of how I thought then, but I didn't want them to get buddy-buddy with us. A lot of times they felt they could get in, sort of like the big-sister role. I didn't like that. I felt like they had to earn their place in the hierarchy. And that bothered me when that happened. Some of my female classmates allowed that to happen, and that was fine for them, but I didn't like that.

Sue Sweeney: Was there a marked change in male attitudes—for better or worse—as the number of women increased?

Lieutenant Svendsen: Subsequent classes—I used to have arguments with guys in the lower classes about, "Why are you here?" They would say, "Why are you here? What are you doing here? How can you be here?" And things like that, you know.

I would tell them, "I don't have to justify my place here." But you'd get in discussions with people.

Sue Sweeney: Did you ever consider your treatment by underclassmen disrespectful?

Lieutenant Svendsen: I don't really think disrespect is the right word. Maybe snotty. But I was used to people being snotty. It didn't bother me. I sort of almost came to expect it, but I'd get in arguments with them.

Sue Sweeney: Did you have occasion to fry underclass males—and was it awkward?

Lieutenant Svendsen: I remember I wasn't one for frying very much, and I fried women as well. The thing that bothered me was I had a run-in when I was in first class, I was a squad leader, I had a run-in with one of my third classmen, and he was picking on one of my women, one of the female plebes in my squad. I didn't really like the woman very much, I didn't like her method of operating, but I didn't think she deserved everything that this guy was dishing out either.

So I talked to him about it and I said, "Knock it off. I don't like it and I don't expect you to do that anymore. If you continue to do it, there's going to be some serious consequences."

And he went and talked to one of my classmates, one of the guys, and said, "She's picking on me. She's just trying to protect this woman."

My classmate came in. I think I did finally put the guy on report, because my classmate came in and said, "You don't want to put this guy on report."

And I said, "Look, the guy is being a jerk and he doesn't need to be a jerk." And he may have been even disrespectful to me, said something really out of line. We were getting really sick of each other. I'm sure he didn't appreciate me disciplining him, and I didn't appreciate him talking the way that he did. That was the one case. Otherwise, I pretty much didn't have any run-ins with other classmates, but I do remember that one time my classmates came in and tried to talk me out [of] putting the guy on report.

Sue Sweeney: Did you get many demerits yourself?

Lieutenant Svendsen: I got, I think, five demerits plebe summer and had to march those off.

Sue Sweeney: For what?

Lieutenant Svendsen: I couldn't remember what the dessert was. That was one of the things I had to march off. I'm still upset about that.

Sue Sweeney: That's an hour of marching for five demerits?

Lieutenant Svendsen: Yes, an hour of marching for five demerits. I guess second-class year I got 10 demerits for wearing nail polish. I was going out on a Saturday night and I painted my nails on Friday night, and I shouldn't have done it, it was stupid. He came in and said, "Take that off."

Sue Sweeney: Being out of uniform. This was on a weekend?

Lieutenant Svendsen: It was a weekend, but I was in my uniform Friday night. No, I painted my nails after dinner and then Saturday morning he saw me with nail polish on. I was going out Saturday afternoon. He said, "Take that off." I had to take this off and put it on again because I wanted to leave right after lunch, and so at noon meal formation, he said, "Let me see your hands." And I showed him I had taken the nail polish off. So he came after lunch, he came in my room and said, "I'm going to put you on report for wearing nail polish."

Sue Sweeney: How many demerits was that?

Lieutenant Svendsen: Ten. I sort of had an A in conduct, but it was just the principle of the thing, and I should have listened to him, but I didn't. So those were the only times I got demerits, though.

Sue Sweeney: That's pretty benign. You weren't a big troublemaker.

Lieutenant Svendsen: No.

Sue Sweeney: Did you have much privacy in Bancroft Hall?

Lieutenant Svendsen: I nearly screamed anytime anybody came to the door. They were very cautious about knocking and looking and then making sure we were dressed after a while.

The one thing, the guys would get dressed in front of their doors and not close their doors, and the first couple of times it bothered me. The second couple of times I would just laugh at them, and they'd see me and then they'd run behind the wall or somewhere, and I would just make a joke of it. I'd say, "Well, there's nothing for me to see anyway." That was first-class year we got to that point. They would get real embarrassed and oftentimes come and apologize and things like that, but they didn't really barge in very much. I don't remember being caught undressed ever. Maybe once or twice, but it was nothing. It was a funny thing, you know, I knew that it wasn't intentional.

Sue Sweeney: What would you say was the most satisfying aspect of your Academy experience?

Lieutenant Svendsen: I think academics probably gave me the most satisfaction. My grades weren't outstanding, but that was probably the part that I enjoyed the most. I think that was because I never really felt competitive academically, but I enjoyed a lot of the things that I did. Also sort of, it was something that I could do and it was mine and no one else had a piece of it. So I think that's why I enjoyed that the most.

Sue Sweeney: What aspect was the easiest—or was anything easy?

Lieutenant Svendsen: That's a good question. I don't remember. I didn't consider anything easy.

Sue Sweeney: Does something stick out as particularly difficult?

Lieutenant Svendsen: Oh, yes, the mile run. I hated it. I hated it. I mean, I would be sick for days beforehand, like three days beforehand, and that was the only thing that I really worried about.

Sue Sweeney: Do you think you came to the Academy physically prepared for its rigors?

Lieutenant Svendsen: I'm not sure. I guess swimming was easy for me because I enjoy swimming and I was always a pretty strong swimmer, so that was an easy thing for me, too. As far as physical preparation, when I got here, I had done a little bit of running and a little bit of exercises, calisthenics and things like that, but I was not prepared. It just wiped me.

Sue Sweeney: A little PEP [Physical Education Program].

Lieutenant Svendsen: Yes. I noticed for the first time in my life I could see muscles in my legs and things like that. I had a lot of muscle definition.

Sue Sweeney: What sports did you play?

Lieutenant Svendsen: I was a cheerleader for most of plebe year and that counted. I didn't have to participate in a sport. I sort of did a little bit of everything. I sailed for a while, I was in gymnastics for a while. What else did I do? I played a lot of battalion sports, badminton and sort of like a non-physical contact form of lacrosse, a thing called stick ball. And that's basically what I did, just did a little bit of everything.

Sue Sweeney: Who was your sponsor—and was that family a source of comfort?

Lieutenant Svendsen: I didn't have a sponsor. My company officer was my sponsor, because he sponsored all the cheerleaders and was my company officer as well.

Sue Sweeney: Who was that?

Lieutenant Svendsen: That was Major Sifuentes, now lieutenant colonel. But that was plebe and youngster year, and then he transferred after youngster year, so I sort of adopted some other people's sponsors, and they were very nice people. I mean, they always made me feel like their home was my home.

Sue Sweeney: Did you get much feedback from civilians as you walked downtown?

Lieutenant Svendsen: Yes. I remember the famous line that I heard the whole four years I was here was, "There's one." I heard those words so many times. I heard those out in town and I heard them here. You know, people did both things. People called my parents. Mothers of midshipmen would call my mother and say, "Why did you ever let your daughter be a midshipman? Don't you know it's a place for men and not for women? What kind of daughter do you have?" People would call my parents.

So there were pockets of resentment as far away as Chicago. There were also pockets of approval. A lot of people really, really were impressed by the fact. As a matter of fact, my honors night they presented scholarships, and I had a large percentage of my high school class, we had five appointments to military academies.

Sue Sweeney: Out of a class of what size?

Lieutenant Svendsen: There were 800, but when I went up to receive my little blue jacket appointment thing, I got a standing ovation from my high school class. Everybody thought it was wonderful, so I thought I'd come here and everybody would think it's wonderful.

Sue Sweeney: You had a rude awakening.

Lieutenant Svendsen: It was a rude awakening. So there were pockets of support. I found that the guys I saw at home thought the whole thing was a lot better idea and were just a lot more impressed than the guys here or people here. I think I got a lot more support away from here than I got here.

Sue Sweeney: From both female and male friends at home?

Lieutenant Svendsen: Yes, very much. They said, "Gosh, it must be really hard. How do you do it?" But you know, there was never any resentment. None of the guys at home said, "Well, I could have done that. I could be there. You've taken my spot." I never heard that from the guys at home, but I heard things like that here.

Sue Sweeney: What have you done since graduation?

Lieutenant Svendsen: I was on the *Samuel Gompers* for two years and made two Indian Ocean deployments. Then I came here in December of '82.

Sue Sweeney: What were your duties on the *Gompers*?

Lieutenant Svendsen: I was legal officer and I was also operations officer and navigator.

Sue Sweeney: Did you go to SWOS [Surface Warfare Officer School]?

Lieutenant Svendsen: Yes. I transferred here in December of '82, transferred to Washington to work at the Pentagon in the readiness analysis shop. I will transfer in February to go to—I think it's called Fleet Combat Direction Support Activity in San Diego, and that job will be financial management, and hopefully I'll get a subspecialty out of it. So it's a good job for me professionally.

Sue Sweeney: You said that the Academy training wasn't particularly realistic. How prepared were you for what you're doing now?

Lieutenant Svendsen: I didn't need it. I did not need it. My husband and I have arguments about this all the time, about whether I'm a better officer than a non-Academy person, and maybe in some respects I am.

Sue Sweeney: Which is his tack—he thinks you are?

Lieutenant Svendsen: That I am. I didn't need this to do what I'm doing now, you know.

Sue Sweeney: Is he an Academy graduate?

Lieutenant Svendsen: Yes. I don't know. I might be a little bit sharper than some people who didn't go here, a little bit wiser, maybe that's the right word. But I don't necessarily think that I needed this to do what I'm doing today.

Sue Sweeney: Do you find there's a lot of curiosity among those with whom you're stationed? I notice you don't wear a ring.

Lieutenant Svendsen: Initially. I don't wear it because it's too big. I should wear it; it's part of my uniform. Initially there's curiosity, and then I'm just treated like any other Naval Academy graduate among naval officers, a mixed group of non-grads and grads. The non-grads make fun. But I really, since I have graduated, have had pretty positive responses from people about it. No one has ever challenged me on the fact that I graduated from the Naval Academy, and a lot of guys think it's wonderful.

Sue Sweeney: What do you consider the greatest success of your naval career, to date?

Lieutenant Svendsen: My greatest success. Boy, it's pretty sad that I can't think of anything. I guess the fact that I'm a Naval Academy graduate is probably my greatest success within the Navy. And not only that, but being in the first class of women, I really feel that's significant. I hope it pays off for me someday, I really do. It took me a couple of years to recover emotionally from the experience here, and I'll be real frank with you, I didn't think very highly of myself when I graduated. It took me about two years to realize that I didn't need to be treated the way I was treated here.

Sue Sweeney: You'd been beaten down to the point where you didn't feel good about yourself.

Lieutenant Svendsen: Exactly. And when people started treating me nicely, I was flabbergasted, and I did not know how to handle it, quite frankly. And I realized I was in bad relationships with men, and I just had a really low self-image. I think this is the reason why, in talking to some of my other classmates, the same sort of thing comes out. So it did take me a couple of years to heal after this experience. I feel a lot stronger for it now. I feel a lot better about myself. I didn't used to be real proud of the fact that I was a Naval Academy graduate. I thought, big deal. I almost didn't want to talk about it. I almost wanted to forget about it because it was so bad for me in so many respects. But now I think, looking back on it, I can say it was probably my greatest achievement, and like I said, I just hope it pays off.

Sue Sweeney: Did you leave the Academy with respect for the system—as you had seen it?

Lieutenant Svendsen: Well, not really. I just thought that the group of Naval Academy graduates as a whole, you know, they always say, "America's finest." And I always tell my mother or whoever would say "America's finest," I'd say, "Well, if this is the finest America has, we're in real trouble." Because my opinion of the people here, the graduates, was so low because of how I saw them. And I saw them living day to day, and I saw the sort of things that they did, and I could never say they were America's finest. I never had that impression. And yet I thought of myself as being part of, I guess, deep inside felt that I was part of America's finest for doing something.

I remember when we were first class, Midge Costanza, she was in President Carter's administration, appointed on his staff. Midge came and talked to all the women in our class, and she started out her thing with, "Well, I want to get a feel for what you've been through," and all this stuff. And she said, "You must get real sick of guys asking you to go to bed with them all the time," and stuff like that.

Women started walking out of the room. We all got to say our piece, and I said that I would give my right arm if guys were clambering to get into bed with me, because I would much rather fight them off that way than have to constantly reaffirm the fact that I'm here and that it's okay for me to be here, and stop fighting that. I said, "Lady, you don't know what's going on."

Sue Sweeney: Did she ever change her tack?

Lieutenant Svendsen: Well, you know, when people started getting up and walking out on her.

Sue Sweeney: She got the idea.

Lieutenant Svendsen: They were crying. It was terribly emotional. It was almost a little bit of a cleansing for us all, I think, in some respects, but it wasn't carried far enough. I think we all sort of needed to get together and cry, you know, in a lot of ways and sort of get rid of that bad feeling that we had, and that was like a two-hour place for us to do that, but I think we needed to do it more than what we did.

Sue Sweeney: Assuming Congress lifts the ban on women in combat before too long—do you already see military leaders emerging among your female classmates?

Lieutenant Svendsen: Without a doubt. I think that the women in my class and even some of the women, not all of them but some of the women I've seen who were not Naval Academy graduates would be just as capable of serving at sea in combat situations as men. I don't really have a hang-up about women's professional capabilities. Physical capabilities I can't argue, because it's just that men are stronger. They always will be. And you can develop your physical capabilities as best you can, and I can probably do things that some men can't do physically. I don't know.

I've had really positive experiences since I've graduated, with junior people. I've had no problem with them following me, and I've had no problem with leadership at all. I've been very successful in that respect.

Sue Sweeney: Do you credit that to what you learned at the Academy?

Lieutenant Svendsen: It's just not the same. You're dealing with such a different level of people. Enlisted people are so different than leading plebes, and the environment is so different. There's just so many other factors on the outside than there are here, it's totally different. But I'm sure the experience had something to do with it. I think that my success probably is attributable to my experiences here. I don't know to what extent. I'm not real certain about that.

Sue Sweeney: What are your long-range goals? Where do you see yourself in 20 years?

Lieutenant Svendsen: Settled down in a little town in a forest.

Sue Sweeney: Far from the sea?

Lieutenant Svendsen: Yes. Well, I want to be on the water. I don't know whether it's the ocean or a lake, but I want to be near the water, but not in a metropolitan setting. I think I'm leaning towards opening my own business. I love to do things with my hands, whether it be sewing or stitching, weaving baskets or whatever. It's funny how much of a traditional person I found out that I am, a little whiz in the kitchen and a good mother and a good wife and all of that, after all of this. I wonder if that probably wasn't triggered in rebellion to this place.

I've just really—I'm a homebody and I love to be home with my family, doing things with my family. So in that respect I'm very traditional, and I see my life going more in that direction rather than—I sort of blazed all the trails I'm going to blaze in my life, I think. I don't think I'm going to try to do anything else major like this place.

Sue Sweeney: If you resign and your husband stays in, would you be content as a Navy wife, rather than as a participant?

Lieutenant Svendsen: I guess you have to understand I'm divorced from my first husband and I remarried. My husband now is about four years from retirement. So I will be in the Navy and he will be out, most likely.

Sue Sweeney: He's content to be a Navy husband?

Lieutenant Svendsen: He doesn't mind. He says that's great, because he wants to retire, and I tell him I can't do that.

Sue Sweeney: What are his plans?

Lieutenant Svendsen: He's not really sure, but that's why I say we're thinking of opening a business. That would be a possibility, something that we could work together with and spend our time working together on, like a joint goal.

Sue Sweeney: How did you meet him?

Lieutenant Svendsen: We met in the Philippines, of all places. I was introduced by the CO of my ship. We were apart for a long, long time, but corresponded and finally were in the same place. We started seeing each other and we eventually got married.

Sue Sweeney: Do you ever feel you are put on display as a token female officer—or, specifically, as a female Naval Academy graduate?

Lieutenant Svendsen: Well, on the ship there weren't very many women. We spent about a total of six months in Diego Garcia, and my first few months in Diego Garcia, there were no women. So people were doing stuff there. Like, I remember I was in the office when I was legal officer within the island's lawyer's office, and we were talking away about something or other, and he pulled out his binoculars and went to the window, and he was looking out the window with his binoculars. Realize that Diego Garcia is a mile wide at its widest point, and that's where all the activity is, so he can't be looking real far. I said, "What on earth are you doing?"

He said, "Well, the liberty boat from the *Gompers* just pulled up to the quay wall."

I said, "So what?"

He said, "Well, the girls are going on liberty." And so this guy's got his binoculars out perusing all the women coming in shore.

Sue Sweeney: This was an officer?

Lieutenant Svendsen: Yes. I believe there were like five women officers and roughly 100 enlisted women, and that's all that there were on the island. I want to say a couple of thousand. That was another fishbowl environment. They were always interested to have the women at their parties and things like that.

Sue Sweeney: How would you feel about being stationed at the Academy?

Lieutenant Svendsen: At the Academy. Let me see. I think instructor duty might be fun—maybe in political science. Yes, I think that would be a nice job.

Sue Sweeney: Would you enjoy being a professional instructor—seamanship, navigation, something like that?

Lieutenant Svendsen: I don't like those YPs very much. But I guess I could handle doing that. I think I would like to either go to the political science department or perhaps one of the leadership and law portions of the professional instruction. I think that might be fun. I imagine it would be fun to be stationed here in Annapolis. It's a great place to live.

Sue Sweeney: How about being a company officer?

Lieutenant Svendsen: I don't think I would want to do that.

Sue Sweeney: Would you be comfortable recruiting women or men to come here?

Lieutenant Svendsen: I don't know that I would be a good salesperson for the Naval Academy. My feelings about the place are so mixed up, still, that I don't think that I could really with all my heart encourage someone to come here.

Sue Sweeney: What advice would you give a little sister who wanted to come here?

Lieutenant Svendsen: Or a daughter.

Sue Sweeney: Or a daughter. Yes.

Lieutenant Svendsen: No, I would tell her, don't. My dad always teases me and says, "Elena's going to be in the class of '06."

And I say, "No she's not." She's not going to come. I say, "She doesn't only have to get over the obstacle of me, but she has to get over the obstacle of my husband." Unless she really, really in her heart wanted to come here, I wouldn't encourage her in this direction. And you know, by that time, I would hope that things had settled down, that they will have settled down and women would be part of the team by then. I really wouldn't want to put her through the same thing that I went through here, because, like I said, it's very hard, and like I said, it took me two years to get over it.

I think she could have a lot of fun at a regular college too, and I sort of missed that. That's why I don't want to go to Postgraduate School in Monterey. I want to go to a regular school. I do want to get my master's, but I don't want to get it in a naval school. I want to go to regular school just to have that experience, because I feel like I missed something.

Sue Sweeney: If you could go back in time, would you still come here?

Lieutenant Svendsen: If I knew what it was like, honestly, Sue, I wouldn't. I wouldn't have done it. Probably, being in the same situation, I would never go through it again. If someone said to me, "You have to do this again," or, "If you want to stay in the Navy, you have to go through four years of this place again," just as it was back then, I would get out of the Navy. I wouldn't do it again. That's really sad, isn't it?

Sue Sweeney: You did it, it's behind you, and you succeeded.

Lieutenant Svendsen: Yes.

Sue Sweeney: Do you have specific recommendations of how you'd like to see the Academy change?

Lieutenant Svendsen: Nothing. I don't think I would change anything, because I think that the institution, and I think it's a beautiful place physically, a beautiful place, the institution and the purpose of the academics and the sports is wonderful. I don't think I would change anything about that. As far as the stresses and all that stuff, I wouldn't change it. I think I would leave everything the same. As I used to always say, the Naval Academy is a beautiful place if you took the people out of it. And I don't mean the people like here, but I mean the midshipmen. If you get the midshipmen out, it's a beautiful place.

The first time I came back here, I had a hard time walking around. I was nervous. My palms were sweating and my heart was pounding, because I just thought bad things happened here. I didn't have a real good time. I have a lot of good memories, but the long-term effect wasn't good.

Sue Sweeney: What was the high point and the low point?

Lieutenant Svendsen: Low point had to be that interview time. That was real hard for me. High point was probably the end of first-class year when the light at the end of the tunnel was in sight. I was having a lot of fun, there were a lot of social functions, and I had a lot of friends and we had a lot of fun together, males and females. It was sort of like a sad time too, because I knew there would be a lot of people that I wouldn't want to see again. And I was happy because I knew that there were a lot of people that I didn't ever want to see again that I wouldn't have to see again. So I think that was the best time here, those last few months to graduation.

Sue Sweeney: Thank you for giving me this time. I believe it will help people understand what you went through.

Lieutenant Svendsen: God. I don't know that anybody can really understand unless they were here and either lived it or saw it in an intimate way, not just looking at it, like the superintendent. I guess the superintendent probably had a pretty good feel. But like an instructor may have reviewed the whole thing. I think that you really need be here to understand.

I think that it's a good thing. I mean, there's no reason that women shouldn't be here, except for the fact that they can't go into combat at this time. I guess the only thing I would have to say before this story ends is that I hope then it's better. I hope then this place is a better place for women to be, and it's a positive experience for them.

Sue Sweeney: How do you see the role of women in the Navy changing?

Lieutenant Svendsen: I think that there's no reason to put which sex you are on recruitment forms or anything else. I see no reason for them to be on those forms. I feel like men and women are capable as each other, and the fact that a person is a woman or a man should not determine whether or not they are allowed to participate in whatever program it is in the Navy. I don't see any difference, and I saw that from a perspective of women on ships. Some of the best people I had working for me were women.

I had a few problems when we went to mast with men and women. They were harder workers than the men. There is no reason that women can't be in an expanded role in the Navy, as far as I'm concerned.

Sue Sweeney: Do you see this coming within your time in the Navy?

Lieutenant Svendsen: Maybe at the end of my lifetime, but I think it's going to take a while yet, because it's a big thing. It's even bigger than a big thing; that's a giant thing. It's a lot of social things that have to be overcome.

Sue Sweeney: Will the change to allow women in combat be enacted as swiftly as the coming of women to the service academies?

Lieutenant Svendsen: That's what they're going to have to do. You can't get everyone's approval of an action. I think that maybe in 10 years or 20 years, society as a whole will be more prepared to accept something like that, but it's not just a feeling among men, though. It's a feeling among women. There's a lot of women who, if they found out they were eligible for the draft, they'd be real upset about that. So I'm not sure that the whole country has to come to terms with that before they're ready to accept it without really kicking and screaming a whole lot.

I support the ERA. You know, it's not because my feeling is that women deserve it; I feel like women have an obligation just as a man does. A woman has an obligation to defend her country because she has all of the rights and privileges that men do. So in that respect I guess I'm a feminist, but it's not because I think the women have a right to things as much as that they have to pay for the rights that they have.

Sue Sweeney: I appreciate you giving me your time—thank you.

***

Launched in 1969, the U.S. Naval Institute's award-winning oral history program is among the oldest in the country. Used in combination with documentary sources, oral histories offer a richer understanding of naval history through candid recollections and explanations rarely entered into contemporary records. In addition, they help depict the atmosphere of a particular event or era in a manner not available in official documents.

The nonprofit Naval Institute accomplishes its history projects through contributed funds and gratefully accepts tax-deductible gifts of all sizes for this purpose. This support allows the Institute to preserve the life experiences of today's service men and women so they may enlighten and inspire future generations.

For information about opportunities to underwrite Naval Institute oral history projects, please contact the Naval Institute Foundation at 291 Wood Road, Annapolis, Maryland 21402; by phone at (410) 295-1054; or by e-mail at foundation@usni.org.

Index to The Oral Histories of
Lts. Sandy Daniels, Tina-Marie D'Ercole, Maureen P. Foley, Chrystal A. Lewis, Barbette Henry Lowndes, and Pamela Wacek Svendsen, U.S. Navy, U.S. Naval Academy Class of 1980

toward women pilots, 62–68; aviators as action-oriented people, 27; billets and squadrons available for women, 70–74; career path for women, 7, 25–27, 73–74, 122–23; career paths for women, 248–51; Daniels aviation and flight school aspirations, 25–27; Daniels going to Academy and opportunity to learn to fly, 47; open-mindedness of people in naval aviation, 26–27, 249, 275; Postgraduate School education for aviators, 124; women in Marine Corps aviation, prohibition of, 219–20

Aviation Officer Candidate School (AOCS), 273

experience of, 52–56; flying, going to Academy and opportunity to learn, 47; football, attitude toward, 36, 50; friendships made while sailing, 35–36; friendships with female classmates, 6–7; goal-oriented characteristic in high school and losing sight of goals at Academy, 48; graduation, feeling about and almost not going to, 29; hardest thing during years at Academy, 44; hygiene films experience of, 14–16; idealist view and first impression of Academy by, 3–4; Induction Day and swearing-in ceremony, 8–10; leadership experience on boat, 45; learning about men and their views of women, 19–21; love for sailing after *Mistral* cruise, 32; male classmates attitude toward, 10–14, 17–18, 25; media interest in, 4–6; *Mistral* cruise experience, 30–32, 46; mistrust of media by, 5–6; Navy service and assignments, iii, vii; NRL assignment, vii, 56, 75–78, 81; NRL assignment, interest in, 74–75; obligation to finish and attitude about quitting, 27–28, 81–82; obligation to Navy after graduating from Academy, 27, 37–38, 80–82; P-3 flights, 56–57, 67–68, 76; parents of, attitude toward Academy education, 7–8; Plebe Detail, 42; Postgraduate School plans, 70, 78–80; prestige of going to Academy, attitude of people towards, 47; pride in accomplishments and service, iii; props, decision to fly, 53–55; rebellious attitude of, 22–23, 44, 48; recruitment and being a Blue and Gold officer, feelings about, 89–90; relationship with roommate, 44; Reserve service and assignments, vii; respect, earning of on individual basis, 32–33, 39–40; retirement of, vii; reunions, attitude toward, 29, 50–51; roommate at flight school, 53; roommates of, 6, 10, 17, 36, 43–44; sail coach assignment, 48–50; sailing abilities of, 30, 35, 44–45; sailing during the year and learning to sail, 33–36; satisfying aspect of years at Academy, 44–45; second year, difficulty of, 28; self-confidence of, 21–22, 29, 44, 47, 48, 89; skipper assignment of, 35, 45; space interests of, 48, 70, 79–80; squad leaders, experience with, 18–19; summer programs experiences of, 29–32; swimming experience and becoming manager of swimming team, 30; training of upperclassmen on how to deal with first female class, 14–17; underclass girls relationships with, 86–87; VP squadrons, restrictions on flying, 71, 73; VP squadrons, restrictions on flying and the need to learn a new aircraft, 67–68; VXN-8 assignment of, 55–62, 76–77; Webb, resentment toward and letter-writing campaign against appointment of, 63–68; withdrawal of, 22–23, 42–43, 48; yelling as upperclassman, 42–43

dating: appearance of women, importance of to men, 20–21; attitude of men toward, learning about, 19–21; board to decide policies on, 336–37, 338; civilian boyfriends, 159, 237, 371; dances at Academy, 235–36, 337–38, 371; dating classmates, 234–35; D'Ercole experience with, 100–101; female midshipmen, attitude toward dating, 13, 159, 335; Foley experience with, 158–59; formals, 235–36; Lewis experience with, 230–37; Lowndes experiences with, 335–38, 370–76, 378–79; midshipmen dating enlisted, rules against, 373; mixers (tea fights), 236; plebes dating upperclassmen, 230–35, 374, 375–76; rules about, 119–20; secretive relationships, 21–22

Defense Advisory Committee on Women in the Services (DACOWITS): planning for billets and career opportunities for women after graduation, 38; restrictions on assignments for women, changes to, iv; training program for women compared to men, meeting about, 54–55; Webb appointment, discussion at conference for, 65–66

Defense Contract Administration Services Management Area (DCASMA), 382–83, 388–91

Delaware, 215

Delta Air Lines, vii

demerits and conduct: conduct offenses by women midshipmen and reflection on rest of

too much, 20; CO drinking at and duty driver to take him home, 60–61; D'Ercole interest in things other than, 120; Foley evening out and dinner and drinks paid for, 175–76; Lewis as sailing program instructor and beer for lunch, 263; plebe squad sneaking out for beer with first-class squad leader, 232; plebe year prohibition of, 20, 175

Druce, Robin, 365
Duff, Coach, 118–19
Duke University, 2
Durham, Liz, 237, 240
Dutton, 169–71
duty officer, 60–61

E

E-2 aircraft, 135
E-3 aircraft, 296
East Asia, Lewis deployment to, vii
East Coast: billets for women on first-class cruise along, 41; yard patrol boats cruises and port visits along, 30, 162–64, 215–17, 340, 420
EEO (equal-employment opportunity), 334
engineering education: electrical engineering studies, 123–24, 130–31, 151, 362; focus of academics at Academy on, 22; Foley quiz grade and female's use of engineering education, 151; Lewis interest in, 192; space engineering curriculum, 124
England, cruise to Queen's Jubilee in, 216
EP-3 aircraft, iv
equal-employment opportunity (EEO), 334

F

F-1 Albatross aircraft, 293
F-4 aircraft, 296
F-14 aircraft, 259, 296, 300
F-18 aircraft, 296
Federal Government Employee of the Year Award (Batchelder Award), 389–90, 389n10
Feldmann, Peggy, 138, 223, 267
female midshipmen. *See* women midshipmen
fencing team, 157, 364–66
fingernail polish, 15, 16, 320–21, 380
fleet: happiest times for Lewis, flying in as, 299; Lewis experience as jet pilot, 288–95; warfare specialties emphasis, 13; women in and attitude of officers to women midshipmen, 207–8
Fleet Composition Squadron Five (VC-5), vii, 286, 289–90, 296–97
flight school: academics at, 53; Academy graduates attitude toward women in, 273–74; attitude of women toward going to, 25–27; Beeville base, 277, 280–81, 285; billets for flying jets, 54; billets for pilots, 25; class rank and date for entrance to, 52; DACOWITS representative, meeting with, 54–55; Daniels aviation and flight school aspirations, 25–27; Daniels entrance date, 49, 52; Daniels experience at, 52–56; eyesight/vision requirement for, 272–73; fear during, 275–76; Grubbs experiences at,

54, 271, 273–74, 279–81; helo dunker experience, 275–76; jet grades, 53–54, 54n3, 279; jets, Lewis training for, 54; length of, 52; Lewis carrier qualifications experience, 276–79; Lewis experiences at, 55, 271–81; Lewis instructor role at, vii, 274, 283–84, 295–98; Lewis roommate at, 271; number of women who went to, 272; prop training, requirement for women to start with before training for jets, 53–55, 279–81; props, Daniels decision to fly, 53–55; quality of students in, 283–84, 298; service selection night and getting date for, 52; supportive attitude of men toward women in Pensacola, 26; time needed to get wings and admission to, 27; training program for women compared to men, 53–56; women in flight school, acceptance of, 273–74, 275; women in flight school, appreciation for equal treatment of, 273–74

flirting, 18, 210–11, 212

Foley Nunez, Maureen, viii–ix, 143–89; academic experience of and experience with professors, 150–52, 156; Academy education, feelings about opportunities because of, 166–67, 188–89; Academy experience of, article about, 314; Academy instructor role, viii, 183–85; acceptance to Academy, feelings about, 145; alumni, attitude of toward women midshipmen, 176–77; birth and early life of, 143; career after leaving the Navy, viii–ix, 188–89; career path and general unrestricted line decision, 167–68; class ring, feelings about wearing it, 182–83; college and career aspirations before going to Academy, 144; combat duty for women, opinion about, 172–75; company adjutant duty, 180; company assignment, 146; company officers, experiences with, 152–54; confidence of, 167; dating experience of, 158–59; decision to go to Academy, 143–44, 188–89; demerits, getting and giving of, 186; division officer and leadership, 167; easiest aspect of being midshipman, 156–57; education of, viii; father's role at Academy, 143; female officers at Academy, need for, 184–85; first-class summer cruise on oceanographic research ship, 169–71; first-class year experiences of, 179–81; friendships with female classmates, 146, 154–55, 187; graduation and leave after, 181–82; graduation from Academy, satisfaction in, 189; haircut before Induction Day, 145–46; homecoming and company mate of the deck duty, 176; Induction Day experience of, 145–49; integration of women into squads better than having all the women together, 186–87, 410; leadership positions, respect for women in, 180; male classmates attitude toward, 147, 157–59, 163–64, 179; media interest in, 145, 148–50; moral support from father, 160–61; Navy service and assignments, viii; Navy service, interest in, 144–45; oceanography major of, 156, 169; parents of, attitude toward Academy education, 143; Pensacola squadron branch officer duty, 181–84; Pensacola visit and not getting sick during acrobatics, 165; point-counterpoint article between Foley and Webb views, request for, 172–73; pride in accomplishments and service, iii, 188–89; quitting, thoughts about, 159–61; recruitment and being a Blue and Gold officer, feelings about, 161; resignation from Navy after obligation is up, 187–88; respect, earning of on individual basis, 158; role model for women midshipmen, 184–85; roommates of, 146; service selection activities, 167–68; sign-in log for male midshipmen in rooms, 152–53; sports activities of, 156, 157; summer programs, 162–66; support, unexpected pockets of, 175–76; Svendsen friendship with, 404; underclass girls relationships with, 177–78, 331–32; uniforms, sizes and fit of, 147–48; Webb and article written by, opinion about, 172–73

football: athletic ability to make the team, 69; company football teams, 368; Daniels attitude toward, 36, 50; varsity sailing team and not marching at football games, 36

Ford, Gerald, 191

formation: Lewis crew team activities and absence from, 201–2; service dress whites for
      Sunday formation, 84–85; skirts and walking in formation, 355–56

Fort Belvoir, 1

Fort Benning, 218, 222–29

Francis Marion, 216

fraternization, concerns about and avoidance of, 363–64

G

Galanti, Paul, 327, 333

Garvin, Pat, 209–12

Georgetown University, 252

Gid, 49

glee club and choir, 338, 361–62, 366–67, 368–70, 375–76

Glenn, John, 95

graduation: billets and career opportunities for women after, planning for, 37–38, 38n2, 167–
      68, 422–24; Daniels feeling about and almost not going to, 29; emotional experience of
      finishing, 259; Foley graduation and leave, 181–82; Lewis graduation and media
      experience, 258–59; throwing hats in the air, 259; throwing hats in the air, timing of for
      men and women midshipmen, 414

Greg, 100–102, 121

Groton, 421

Grubbs, Suzanne: aircraft accident of, 223, 281–82, 281n5; flight school, enjoyment of
      experience by, 274; flight school experience of, 54, 279–81; jet grades of, 279–80;
      Lewis roommate at flight school, 271; PT screening for Jump School, 223–24, 227–28;
      women in flight school, appreciation for equal treatment of, 273–74

Guam, Lewis deployment to, vii, 292–93

H

hair and haircuts: D'Ercole haircut before Induction Day, 95, 98; female beautician for, 254–
      56, 320; Foley haircut before Induction Day, 145–46; haircuts and curls, 320; Lewis
      experiences with haircuts, 254–56; Lowndes experience with haircuts, 320

halo boys, 59–60

Harrington, Melissa, 139

Harvard University, 258

Hawaii: Daniels experiences and first-class cruise on repair ship from Japan to Hawaii to San
      Diego, 37–42; Foley's father stationed in, 188; worldwide military command and
      control system in, 129–30

hazing, 257

Head of the Charles Regatta, 258

helo dunker (Dilbert Dunker), 275–76

Herndon monument, 175, 322–23, 414

Hire, Kay: friendships made while sailing, 49; skipper assignment of, 35; VXN-8 assignment
      of, 63; Webb, resentment toward and letter-writing campaign against appointment of,
      63–64

HMS Pinafore, 367

homecoming: Foley as company mate of the deck, 176; fun during, 176; Lowndes attitude toward and return for, 338, 393, 395–96; meeting of women at, 392; tailgate event, male classmates that wouldn't say hello at, 416–17; tailgate events and talk about women midshipmen, 243–44

homesickness, 321–22

honor code, 233

Hood College, 368–71

Hopper, Grace, 384–85

hygiene films, 14–16

I

Illinois Institute of Technology, 121

Indian Ocean, 291, 405, 437

Indonesia: Daniels flight to with VXN-8, 57; Lewis deployment to, vii, 250

Induction Day and swearing-in ceremony: Bancroft Hall, running down hallways and yelling, 9, 198, 306–7; big bags, offers of help to carry, 147, 148–49, 405–6; Daniels experience, 8–10; D'Ercole experience, 98; emotion about separation on, 8–9, 196; Foley experience, 145–49; Lewis experience, 194–200; Lowndes experiences of, 306–7; Svendsen experience, 404–6; Tighe experience, ii; upperclassmen yelling on, 9

Inglis, Pat, 232

intelligence career decisions, 112, 122–23

Irwin, Sandee: D'Ercole friendship with, 101–2, 138; male classmates attitude toward, 313; media interviews, difference between D'Ercole answers and answers given by, 100–102

J

Japan: attitude toward women in, 289–90; Daniels experiences and first-class cruise on repair ship from Japan to Hawaii to San Diego, 37–42; Foley first-class summer cruise from, 169–71; Lewis deployment to, vii, 250, 289–90

jet aircraft: career paths for women, 248–51; ejection of female pilot, 55; female jet pilots, 250–51; first female jet pilot, 250–51; jet grades and training to fly, 53–54, 54n3, 279; jet transition training, Lewis assignment to, vii; Lewis experience as jet pilot, 288–95; Lewis training to learn to fly, 54, 279–81, 284–85, 289; number of women allowed each year in training to fly, 279; program to learn to fly, 53–56; prop training, requirement for women to start with before training for jets, 53–55, 279–81; training program for women compared to men, 53–56, 279–81

Johns Hopkins University, viii, 188

Jorgensen, Mary Lou, 251

Jump School, 218, 222–29

June Week: attitudes toward women midshipmen during, 414; D'Ercole family visits to, 93; Herndon monument and plebe status, 175, 322–23, 414; Lewis graduation memories, 258–59; weddings during, 372, 409; yawls as backdrops, 36

K

Kanewske, Charlie, 202, 232

Karlson, Kathy, 26

Kenya, 57
kickball, 367
Kindness, Tom, 95, 97
Korea: attitude toward women in, 289–90; Korean Naval Academy, 197; letter to Lewis from, 243; Lewis deployment to, vii, 250, 289–90

L

during Jump School, 227; Navy service and assignments, vii; neighbor alumni, support from, 194; optimism of, 248; Philippines duty assignment, vii, 250, 289–90; physical abilities of women and recruitment standards, 265–70; physical standards for men and women, 224; platoon commander activities, 201–2, 203–4; platoon drill for competition, 203–4; pride in accomplishments and service, iii, 299; prop training, requirement for women to start with before training for jets, 279–81; PT screening for Jump School, 222–24; quitting, thoughts about, 214; recruitment for Academy, feelings about, 259–60, 299; reputation of and playing cards in bunkroom, 238–40; role models for, 205–7, 250–51; roommate at flight school, 271; roommates of, 195, 233–35, 269; sailing program instructor after graduation, 263–65, 271; SERE school, 285–89; shoes for, 240; sports programs, opinion about, 251–52; squad leader assignment, 202–3, 204–5; Stanford, offer to go to, 213; summer programs experiences of, 215–29; support, unexpected pockets of, 243; support for decision to go to Academy, 190–94; test pilot school, application to, 300; Thai Air Force, instructor role in teaching close air support to, 293–95; training of upperclassmen on how to deal with first female class, 199–200; VC-5 assignment and duties, vii, 286, 289–90, 296–97; visit to Academy before application to, 193; volleyball team experience of, 201, 213, 252, 253; warfare specialty and promotion in Navy, 296–97; wings, earning of, 279, 280–81, 285; woman Marine general, Lewis meeting with, 218–21; women classmates, independence, personality, and intelligence of, 227–28, 266, 269–70; women in flight school, appreciation for equal treatment of, 273–74; women in Navy, changes in role of, 248–51, 260

Lexington: Lewis carrier qualifications on, 277–79; Svendsen first-class cruise on, 426–27

Lowndes, Barbette H. "Barb," viii, 302–97; academic experience of and experience with professors, 358–64; Academy, arrival at and first impressions of, 304–5; Academy, attitude toward and feelings about going back to visit, 313, 392–96; Academy education, attitudes of people toward, 338, 339–40; Academy education, feelings about, 317, 317n7, 339–40, 385; Alumni Association role of, viii; Alumni Association speech by, 396; authority of women midshipmen, undermining of, 323–27; Batchelder Award nomination, 389–90, 389n10; battalion staff position, 326, 332–33; Bermuda assignment, 379–82, 391, 394; birth and early life of, 302; braces, 374; breakfast for plebes, experience with, 324–25; camaraderie and feeling part of the class, 415–17; change in attitude toward and environment for following classes of female midshipmen, 331–32, 352–54; choir and glee club experiences of, 338, 361–62, 366–67, 368–70, 375–76; closet, hiding in, 323; clothes-folding session, 306; college and career aspirations before going to Academy, 303–4; combat duty for women, opinion about, 383–87; competition among and relationships with female classmates, 334–36; concern about doing things right and not getting yelled at, 306; dating experiences of, 335–38, 370–76, 378–79; dating policies board, role on, 336–37, 338; DCASMA assignment, 382–83, 388–91; decision to go to Academy, 302–4; dependency on Academy and ability to make life decisions, 377–78; dinner table seating issue, 326–27; education of, viii, 391; engagement of, 371–73; family of, 302–4, 321–22; fencing team, 364–66; first-class summer cruise on cruiser out of San Diego, 342; homesickness of, 321–22; husband of, 318–19, 380, 382; husband of, return to Academy with, 394–95; Induction Day experience of, 306–7; interactions and communication among women midshipmen, 311–13, 332–33; Joint Service Command assignment, 317; leave after graduate, 376–77; makeup and acting feminine, guidance on, 353–54; male classmates attitude toward, 312–13, 323–31, 332–33; marriage of, 382, 392; married servicemembers, synchronizing careers of, 318–19; media interest in, 307–9, 324; men, advice on dealing with, 333–34; *The Messiah* and Hood College girls, 368–71; Naval Academy education of, viii; Navy service and assignments, viii; night visits and harrassment by male classmates, 328–31, 332–33; oceanography major of, 358–59; officers, experiences with, 324–25, 327–30; officers, opinion about, 316–17, 316n6; physical fitness and athletic abilities of, 345–46; plebe summer experiences of, 308, 309–10; plebe year experience of, 319–21; pregnancy of and plans for childcare, 383, 387, 396; pride in accomplishments and service, iii, 339–40, 391–92; privacy in Bancroft Hall, 310–11; quitting, thoughts about, 345–47; retirement of, viii; rooming alone by, 332–33; rooming side-by-side with male midshipmen, 310–11; roommates of, 306–7, 326, 333, 347–52, 359, 361, 366; satisfying aspect of career, 391–92; self-confidence of, 313, 321, 373–75, 378–79, 391; service selection night, 343–44; ship and going to sea, desire to be assigned to, 342–44, 345; *Shipmate* article about Academy experience, 314–16, 392, 394–95; small groups and fitting in, 338; sports activities of, 361–62, 364–66, 367–68; summer programs experiences of, 340–43; Supply Corps assignment, 318–19; Supply Corps career path, 342–45, 383, 387, 392, 396; Supply School experience and grades of, 376, 377–79, 391; survey of women graduates by, 272, 314–18, 344, 394–95; travel experience of, 305; uniforms, opinion about, 354–57; weight of, 313, 374

M

Magnet, Project, 57

makeup: film on how to apply, 15; guidance on how to apply, 353–54; Lowndes avoidance of wearing, 313, 321; time for applying and wearing, 15, 320–21

male ego and dealing with men successfully, 210–12

male midshipmen: attitude about attention given to women, 99, 149, 198–200, 414–15; attitude toward women sailing big boats, 13; authority of women midshipmen, undermining of, 323–27; Daniels classmates attitude toward, 10–14, 17–18, 25; D'Ercole classmates attitude toward, 103–8, 119; dressing in front of open doors by, 432; experiences of with women and basis for prejudices against abilities of women, 11–12, 27–28, 33, 69–70, 102, 418–19; Foley classmates attitude toward, 147, 157–59; integration of women into the brigade, meetings and feedback sessions on, 154; last male class, graduation of, 180; Lewis classmates attitude toward, 198–205, 229; Lowndes classmates attitude toward, 312–13, 323–30; Mr. Studley attitudes of some, 19–21; peer pressure and treatment of women, 14, 104, 164; physical standards for men and women, 105–6, 224; rooming side-by-side with women midshipmen, 310–11; roommates, getting along with, 351; self-importance of because of being at Academy, 20–21; sign-in log for being in women midshipmen rooms, 152–53; stigma of going into rooms of, 153; survivalist attitude of, 174; Svendsen classmates attitude toward, 402–3, 410–19; switching companies by, 117; training on how to deal with first female class, 14–17, 199–200, 411–12

manicotti, throwing of during the night, 328–31

Marine Corps, U.S.: career paths for women, 112, 122–23; duty assignments for women in, 221; female officers as role models, 353; integration of women into, 219; Lewis experience at Marine Corps Headquarters, 217–22; Lewis interest in, 191, 217; service selection activities, 343, 422; summer activities and visit to Camp Lejeune, 421–22; Svendsen interest in, 421–22; woman Marine general, Lewis meeting with, 218–21; women in aviation, prohibition of, 219–20

Morris Ives, Barbara, 136, 137

N

nail polish, 15, 16, 320–21, 380, 430–31

NAVAIR, deputy program manager of, viii

Naval Academy Alumni Association: Lowndes role in, viii; Lowndes speech to, 396;
   Shipmate article about Academy experience, 314–16, 392, 394–95

Naval Academy Prep School (NAPS), 200–201, 205

Naval Academy, U.S.: acceptance of women to, D'Ercole belief about, 94; admission of
   women to, evolutionary process of, 175; admission of women to, phased process for,
   178–79; America's finest, opinion about graduates as, 440; arrogant reputation of
   graduates from, 131–32, 261–62; attitudes toward graduates of, 47, 51, 166–67, 182–
   83, 261–62, 338, 339–40, 438–41; change in attitude toward and environment for
   following classes of female midshipmen, iii–v, 12–13, 114, 185–86, 240, 260, 331–32,
   352–54, 412, 414–15, 427–28; changes at, Svendsen opinion about, 448–49;
   competitive admission process, 97, 132; Daniels acceptance to, 1–3; dependency on
   ability to make life decisions, 377–78; D'Ercole acceptance to, 93–97; environment at,
   impact of first female midshipmen on, ii–v, 86–87, 177–78; female officers at, need for,
   184–85; Foley acceptance to, 143–44; fuss made by toward first female midshipmen,
   12; high school students achievements and competition at, 22–23, 435–36; honors
   violations and being kicked out of, 347–50; hostile environment toward first female
   midshipmen, ii, iv, 10–14, 103–8, 157–59, 402–3, 405, 410–19; idealist view and first
   impression of Daniels toward, 3–4; integration of women into squads better than having
   all the women together, 186–87, 242–43, 410; last male class, graduation of, 180; law
   to allow women to go to, 191; Lowndes education at, viii; mission of, 246–48, 412;
   obligation to Navy after graduating from, 27, 37–38, 80–82, 187–88, 342–43; physical
   abilities of women and recruitment standards, 265–70, 349–50; prestige of going to,
   attitude of people towards, 47, 97; pride in education from, 179, 439–40; questionnaires
   for feedback about, 272, 314–18, 357–58; quitting, thoughts about, 10, 27–28, 159–61,
   214, 342–43, 345–47, 402–3; recruitment for, 89–90, 161, 259–60, 299, 446–48;
   refinement of to accommodate women, 413; socializing with classmates, 36, 45–46,
   119–21; Svendsen attitude about education from, 437–38, 442; tourist visits to, 84, 308;
   training on how to deal with first female class, 14–17, 199–200, 411–12; women
   midshipmen, first class to graduate, ii; women stationed at, 13. *See also* academics at
   the Naval Academy

Naval Air Training and Operation Procedures Standardization (NATOPS), 295

Naval Command, Control and Ocean Surveillance Systems, military deputy to the director of
   the Joint Research and Development Center of, viii

naval flight officers (NFOs), 25–26, 49, 61, 77, 272

Naval Investigative Services (NIS), 330

Naval Operations for Information Dominance, senior advisor for Space to Deputy Chief of,
   iii, vii

Naval Postgraduate School, Monterey: aviators going back to flying after education at, 124;
   Daniels plans for, 70, 78–80; D'Ercole education and experience at, 124, 130–31; Lewis
   interest in, 300; obligation after finishing, 80; score for entrance to, 79; space systems
   operations and space subspecialties, 79–80; Svendsen opinion about going to, 448

Naval Research Laboratory, U.S. (NRL): Daniels assignment to, vii, 56, 75–78, 81; Daniels interest in and, 74–75; women working at, 77–78

Naval Space and Warfare Systems Command, 130, 133–34

Naval Space Surveillance Center, vii

Naval War College, 78, 129

Navy, U.S.: attitude toward women in, iv, 109–14; benefit of 100 percent of investment in D'Ercole, 124, 133; billets and career opportunities for women, planning for, 37–38, 38n2, 167–68, 422–24; billets and manpower for 600-ship Navy, 71–72; Daniels service and assignments, iii, vii; D'Ercole service and assignments, viii; flight operations and Daniels interest in, 2; Foley interest in joining, 144–45; Foley service and assignments, viii; leadership positions for women, 180–81, 249–51; Lewis service and assignments, vii; Lowndes service and assignments, viii; naval aviation, open-mindedness of people in, 26–27, 249, 275; obligation to after graduating from Academy, 27, 37–38, 80–82, 187–88, 342–43; opportunities for women in, 37–38, 38n2; role of women in, changes in, 248–51, 260, 450–51; SEALs observation of SERE school, 288; service selection activities, 52, 167–68, 343–44, 422–24; Svendsen service and assignments, ix; Tighe service and assignments, ii–v; warfare specialty and promotion in, 296–97

Navy Fleet Combat Support Center, 424, 437

Navy Reserve Space Program, vii

Navy Reserve, U.S.: Daniels service and assignments, vii; reserve VP squadrons, 67–68

Navy Space and Network Warfare Program, vii

Navy Yard, 78

nervous breakdowns, 392

New Orleans, 237–40

New York City: cruises to, 163, 215, 216, 420; Defense Contract Administration Services Management Area (DCASMA), 382–83, 388–91

New York Federal Executive Supervisor of the Year Award, 390

Newport: cruises to, 163, 215, 420; 90-day wonder program, 262

Newport-to-Bermuda race, 45

Norfolk, summer activities and visit to, 165, 166, 340, 341, 420, 421

NROTC: D'Ercole interest in, 94, 96; Illinois Institute of Technology program, 121; Lewis father at Stanford University, 190

Nunez, Maureen Foley. *See* Foley Nunez, Maureen

O

Officer Candidate School (OCS), preparedness of Academy graduates compared to, 262

officers: Academy women, dedication and leadership abilities of, 316, 316n6; attitude toward women at Academy, 25; D'Ercole experience with officers and professors, 150–52; female officers as role models, 353, 409; Foley company adjutant duty, 180; forward-looking women officers, 220; general unrestricted line officers, 121–25, 167–68, 316, 344–45; leadership positions for women, 180–81, 249–51; Lewis as sailing program instructor after graduation, 263–65, 271; Lewis experience with, 207–8; Lowndes experiences with, 324–25, 327–30; Lowndes opinion about, 316–17, 316n6; Mayer as company officer, 206–7; naval flight officers (NFOs), 25–26, 49, 61, 77, 272; non-Academy female officers, survey of experiences with, 316; physics class and professor,

24–25; restricted line officers, 344–45; staff corps, 344–45; striper positions and grooming women for stripes, 181, 185; Svendsen experience with officers and professors, 410–12; Svendsen feeling about being female officer, 445–46; woman Marine general, Lewis meeting with, 218–21; women midshipmen, attitudes toward, 328

O'Neill, Pat, 10

P

P-3 aircraft: Daniels flying of, 56–57, 67–68, 76; NRL P-3 flights, 76, 77–78; VP squadrons use of, 67–68, 71; women flying VP, attitudes toward, 67

pantyhose, 309

patrol (VP) squadrons, 67–68, 71, 73

Patrol and Reconnaissance Group/Patrol and Reconnaissance Group Pacific, vii

Patuxent River NAS: NRL P-3 flights out of, 76, 77–78; VXN-8 based at, 56

peer pressure, 14, 104, 164

Pensacola: acrobatics, not getting sick during, 165, 340–41; Foley assignment as squadron branch officer, 181–84; Foley career path and general unrestricted line to a squadron in, 168; Lewis experience at, 217; Lewis flight school at, 271; Lewis instructor role at, 274, 283–84, 295–98; Lowndes experience at, 340–41; summer activities and visit to, 37, 165, 217, 340–41, 421; supportive attitude of men toward women in flight school in, 26; Svendsen first-class cruise on *Lexington*, 426–27

Pentagon: Lewis visit to, 221; Svendsen Pentagon duty in readiness analysis shop, 437

Personnel Support Activity Department, 380

Perth, Australia, 57

Philadelphia, 215, 382, 396

Philippines: Daniels flight to with VXN-8, 57; Lewis deployment to, vii, 250, 289–90; Svendsen meeting husband in, 444. *See also* Cubi Point NAS

physical abilities of women and recruitment for Academy, 265–70, 349–50

platoon commander activities, 201–2, 203–4

platoon drill for competition, 203–4

plebe summer: attitude of plebes, 204–5; Daniels difficult time sailing during, 30; hygiene films for women, 14–16; integration of women into squads better than having all the women together, 187; Lewis as sailing program instructor after graduation, 263–65, 271; Lewis squad leader assignment, 202–3, 204–5; Lowndes experiences during, 308, 309–10; media presence during, 308; Plebe Detail, 42, 100; room doors, keeping open, 311; sanitary napkin for polishing shoes and belt buckles, 82–83; showering during, 15; survivalist attitude during, 174; Svendsen memories of, 403

plebe year/plebes: bets, requirement to make, 231–32; D'Ercole memories of, 102–5; difference between Daniels as plebe and sailing coach plebes, 49; difficulty of, expectation for, 160; Herndon monument and plebe status, 175, 322–23, 414; indoctrination by first class, 425; Lowndes experience with taking plebes to breakfast, 324–25; Lowndes experiences during, 319–21; role of, awareness of and ease of being a plebe, 28; room doors, keeping open, 153; support network role of youngsters during, 178; Svendsen memories of, 402–3

Postgraduate School. *See* Naval Postgraduate School, Monterey

Potter, E. B. "Ned," 410–11

basketball team experience, 201, 224, 252, 253; Lewis crew team activities and varsity athletes, 201–2; Lewis crew team and boathouse experiences, 215, 252–53, 258; Lewis sports activities and playing Army, 253; Lewis volleyball team experience, 201, 213, 252, 253; Lowndes activities, 361–62, 364–66, 367–68; money for sports programs, 251–52; socializing opportunities around, 36; Svendsen activities, 434; Svendsen cheerleading activities, 411, 434; track team, 118; volleyball lessons and season, 367. *See also* sailing

squad leaders: concern of squad leader about women crying, 16; Daniels experience as, 43; Daniels experience with, 18–19; Foley problem with uniform sizes and altering uniform with staples by, 147–48; plebe squad sneaking out for beer with first-class squad leader, 232; Svendsen experience with, 404–5; Svendsen interview, questions about from, 408

Sri Lanka, 57

Stanford University, 190, 213

Stapler, Sue, 139

Statue of Liberty, 216

Sternaman, Liz, 136, 137

Stevens, Sue, 206, 409

submarines: career path for men, 112, 122, 423; summer programs and women not allowed on, 113, 165–66, 217, 341, 421

summer programs/activities: billets for women on first-class cruise, 41; Daniels experiences, 29–32; Daniels experiences and first-class cruise on repair ship from Japan to Hawaii to San Diego, 37–42; Foley experiences, 162–66; Foley first-class summer cruise on oceanographic research ship, 169–71; Lewis experiences, 215–29; Lewis first-class cruise on *New Orleans*, 237–40; Lowndes experiences, 340–43; modification of for women, 165–66; Plebe Detail, 42, 100; plebe indoctrination, 425; second-class summer as make-or-break point, 342–43; shore assignments, 41–42; Svendsen experiences, 420–22, 425–27; Svendsen first-class cruise on *Lexington*, 426–27; Svendsen second-class summer memories, 403; women on cruises, attitude toward, 163–64, 420

Supply Corps: career path for women in, 342–45; career paths for men, 112; Lowndes assignment to, viii, 318–19; Lowndes summer activities in, 341

Supply School: dating experience of Lowndes at, 376, 378–79; Lowndes experience and grades at, 377–79, 391; social functions at BOQ, 378

Surface Warfare Officer School (SWOS), 39–40, 437

survival, escape, resistance, evasion (SERE) school, 285–89

Svendsen, Pamela Wacek, ix, 398–452; academic achievements of, 402, 417; academic experience of and experience with professors, 410–12, 432–33; Academy, attitude toward, 413–14, 417, 437–41, 448–50; Academy changes, opinion about for, 448–49; Academy education, attitudes of people toward, 438; Academy education, preparedness for career after, 437–38, 442; Academy graduates as America's finest, opinion about, 440; Annapolis, feelings about, 446; approval and support, pockets of, 435–36; attitude of parents toward Academy appointment, 401–2; beauty of Academy, 449; billets available for, 422–24; birth and early life of, 398; camaraderie and feeling part of the class, 415–17; career after leaving the Navy, ix; change in attitude toward and environment for following classes of female midshipmen, 412, 414–15, 427–28; cheerleading by, 411, 434; class ring of, 438; college and career aspirations before going to Academy, 400–401; combat duty for women, opinion about, 441–42, 451–52;

attitudes of some, 19–21; plebes dating upperclassmen, 230–35, 374, 375–76; second year, difficulty of, 28; training on how to deal with first female class, 14–17, 199–200, 411–12; underclass girls relationships with, 86–87, 177–78, 331–32, 427–28; underclassmen, disrespect from, 429–30; yelling by, 9, 42–43

V

Valentine Ball, 236

VAQ-34 squadron, 295–97

VC-5 squadron, vii, 286, 289–90, 296–97

Vice Admiral Robert F. Batchelder Award, 389–90, 389n10

Virginia: T. C. Williams High School, Alexandria, Virginia, 192–93. *See also* Annapolis

volleyball lessons and season, 367

volleyball team, 201, 213, 252, 253

VP squadrons, 67–68, 71, 73

VXE-6 squadron (Antarctica support squadron), 55–56

VXN-8 squadron (World Travelers/oceanographic research squadron): barhopping with guys while traveling, 58; choosing sqaudrons, 55–56; Daniels assignment to and experience in, 55–62, 76–77; female aircraft commander, abilities of, 59; hotel accommodations for when traveling, 58; last CO, negativity of toward women by, 57–62, 76–77; length of Daniels assignment to, 56; nickname of, 56; orders for women after assignment to, 73–74; Patuxent River base of, 56; places flown to be, 56–57; Project Magnet, 57; resentment toward women in, 62; sexual harassment by CO, 58–59, 60–62; women on crew, 57

W

wall, going over the, 43, 230–35

Warner Springs, 285, 288

Washington, D.C.: learning to deal with politics in, 112–13; Lewis experience at Marine Corps Headquarters, 217–22; Lewis Pentagon visit, 221; summer activities and visit to, 166, 341; Svendsen Pentagon duty in readiness analysis shop, 437

Webb, James: approval of appointment, 65–66, 127–28; article written by, 63, 66, 109–14, 127, 172–73, 174, 185–86, 245–46, 384–85, 413; article written by, discussion about in classes, 109–10; attitude of toward women, 63–69, 109–10, 384–85; charisma of, 68–69; culture created by, concerns about, 68; grooming women for stripes, 181; letter-writing campaign against appointment of, 63–68, 127; opinions about appointment of, 63–68, 125–29; power of, 67; refinement of Academy to accommodate women, 413; speech at Academy by, 185–86; speech to WOPA by, 66–68

Wellness Center, Navarre, Florida, ix

West Point: integration of women into squads at, 242; Jump School experience with women from, 225–28; Lewis sports activities and playing Army, 253; Svendsen interest in, 398, 399–400; type of woman who went to, 227–28; woop nickname for women from, 225

Whiting Field, 271

Winnefeld, Rear Admiral, 362, 365–66

women: abilities of, judging on individual basis, 69–70; billets available for, 71–74, 167–68, 344–45, 422–24; children, leaving of when sent on unaccompanied tour, 424;

dependency on Academy and ability to make life decisions, 377–78; earning respect on individual basis, 32–33, 39–40; leadership positions for women in Navy, 180–81, 249–51; leaving Navy before obligation is up, 81–82; Lewis experience as jet pilot, 288–95; limited previous experience of some men with, 11–12, 102; mentors and reaching back down to help other women, 87; obligation of women to defend her country, 451–52; prejudices against abilities of, basis for, 27–28, 33, 69–70, 102, 418–19; professionalism and dealing with men successfully, 210–12; survey of women graduates by Lowndes, 272, 314–18, 344, 394–95

CPSIA information can be obtained at www.ICGtesting.com
Printed in the USA
LVOW09*0956310816

502086LV00013BA/61/P

9 781682 690062